Chasing My Father

a memoir by

Agatha Nolen

Copyright Page

This is a memoir of true stories as remembered by the author or retold by family members. A few names and identifying details have been changed to protect the privacy of the people involved.

HOLY DESIRES PRESS.

Cover design by *Jessi Hammond*
Content editing by *Kimberly Messer*
Line editing by *Dana Micheli*
Author photo by *Matthew DeBardelaben*

Contents

"Agatha Nolen knows that it's life's hard things that often open our eyes to the crucial things. As she recounts here her pursuit of meaning and faith, she shares without flinching the detours and discoveries of her compelling story. We see how even amid setbacks a divine Presence does not give up on bringing us into new possibilities."

-The Very Reverend Timothy Jones
Dean of Trinity Episcopal Cathedral
Columbia, South Carolina, and author
of *The Art of Prayer: A Simple Guide to Conversation with God.*

"Chasing my Father is a compellingly honest insight into Agatha Nolen's personal journey of transformation through multiple challenging situations. Her story reminds us that the places we go in order to help others transform all too often become the places of our own transformation, if we are open to that possibility. Agatha is clearly open to it and this makes her story worth reading."

-Craig Stewart, Director
The Warehouse
Cape Town, South Africa

CHASING MY FATHER

1

Transitions

There's a time for daring and there's a time for caution, and a wise man understands which is called for.

– Dead Poet's Society

My plane was late, but I'd still made it to the cemetery before the caretaker pulled the gate shut for the night. I'd already filled in Mom about the drama in my life over the past five years, but now I reverently knelt down to say a prayer before I began the discussion with Dad. Mom had been gone 17 years and Dad 27, but I faithfully came to visit them when I traveled to Geneseo, New York for my every-five-year high school reunions. This was my 30th and a whole lot had happened, good and bad, since my 25th.

"Dad, I know you heard me telling Mom all about the divorce. You never met Dave but Mom had reservations even when we were dating. He'd called me out of the blue, trying to sell me stock after finding my telephone number in a zip code directory. I thought it was a sign from God because he was so different from any guy I'd ever dated. He was funny and the life of the party. I'd never dated a salesman either, and Dave had a good job with Dean Witter. I guess I should have given our courtship more time, but it seemed so right; we were married six months after we'd met. Looking back, I was still on the rebound from a three-year, long distance romance with a doctor, but love doesn't always make sense. Plus, I was 30 and felt like I needed to get married before time ran out for me to start a family."

I debated if this was too much information to share with Dad, but I tend to over-explain my actions when I think I'm being misunderstood or judged.

"Dave was anxious to learn about Scripture and even agreed to a full immersion baptism before we got married in a Southern Baptist Church. By the way, I've already apologized to Mom for that. Now I realize what a demonstration of love it was for her to walk me down the aisle since you were already gone. Mom never really accepted me joining Northwest Baptist Church after being raised Roman Catholic, but it was really good for me because it was the first place I learned about the Bible. Dave was raised Methodist but was willing to join the Baptist Church so we could be together. Marrying Dave was a happy day in my life. We were settling in to married life, but Dave wanted to buy a bigger house and save some money before we got pregnant. But 'none of the above' ever happened after his business failed.

"I was heartbroken when, after five years of marriage, I learned that Dave didn't want to have children. I just can't imagine what happened because that's all we talked about when we were dating. Something changed when his dad died; he never mentioned his dad again, but on some evenings, I'd find him just sitting in the dark with the music on. Well, those dark nights got to be more and more frequent.

"He did say he was willing for us to be foster parents so 'if it doesn't work out we can give the children back', but I didn't think that was fair to the children. The last two years of our marriage we either avoided the topic of raising children completely, or argued constantly about whether I should get pregnant. I never understood why there was always one more thing we needed before we could start a family: a bigger house, a boat, or more vacations at the beach.

"When I finally announced that I was going off the pill, he forbade me, saying that he was never going to bring a child into the world. I thought he was joking, but he was firm, absolutely forbidding me from trying to get pregnant. I guess I should have stuck it out longer in the marriage, or gone to the pastor for some counseling, but I got so angry with him when he drew that line in the sand and declared that we weren't going to have children. It wasn't his decision to make alone.

"There were other things that were troubling, but the prospect of never having children was what led me to file for a divorce. Even though we weren't married in a Catholic Church, I went to St. John's Catholic Church in Edmond, Oklahoma and filed the paperwork for an official annulment. This meant that in the eyes of the Catholic Church, the marriage would be void, as if it had never happened. The priest was sympathetic when he heard that we weren't going to have any children and the annulment came through in record time. Within six months I was divorced and my first marriage had been erased.

"I'm not proud that I was the one that filed for the annulment and the divorce. It isn't a very Christian thing to do, and I'm still ashamed that I started seeing Curtis before I filed for a divorce from Dave. But I felt trapped in a marriage that wasn't going to produce children, and that is what I wanted more than anything else in the world.

"I'm sorry I disappointed both you and Mom, but the good news is that I'm married again. I know you are thrilled that this time it's to a good Catholic boy. I've made a lot of mistakes, but I'm working harder at being a great wife and mother. Curtis has twins, a boy and a girl who were thirteen when we met, and we're planning to add to the family. I know you were disappointed that you didn't have any grandchildren when you were alive, but now I have another chance. Curtis comes from a big family, with four brothers and a sister, and they all have plenty of children of their own. Of course we share custody of the twins. It's the family I've always wanted.

"Even better news is that Curtis wants to have more children and since he already has one set of twins there is no telling how fast our family will grow. I want you to be proud of me, and your grandchildren will make you proud, too. I have more news, Dad. I'm transferring to Nashville to take a new position with HCA, the hospital company that I work for. Curtis and I will get to start a new life together, in a new city, with new jobs! Plus we'll be a little closer to you and Mom than we are now. I'll miss San Antonio and my wonderfully warm Hispanic friends, but Curtis wanted a change. Dad, I know that you'd like him; he's a lot like you."

I slowly got up from my knees and whispered another short prayer.

"See you in five years, Dad. I know I'll have lots to tell you then and you'll be proud of what I've become."

I believed that telling little white lies is appropriate when you are guarding your heart or trying to spare someone's feelings. A monologue with minimal details was the best way to communicate with Dad. I couldn't tell Mom or Dad that Curtis and I had been trying to have children for eight years and were still praying for a miracle. If Dad knew, he would have used it against me, saying words that sting: "You're too old to raise a child. A child will bring you nothing but heartache. And this husband of yours--you dated this second guy for nine months and you think he's 'the one'? You cheated on your first husband with him; that's a great way to start a second relationship. I hope this marriage doesn't turn out to be the disaster your first one was. Just because you've been married for eight years doesn't mean he's the right guy. You always were stubborn."

Dad didn't have to be alive for his words to hurt, but I was determined to prove him wrong. At the age of forty-seven, I knew that I was mature enough to be the best wife and mother ever, hands down. Even though Curtis was six years older, we both still had a youthful appearance and had kept up the physical closeness from early in our marriage. I vowed to keep in shape and have the marriage that everyone dreams of. We knew that marriage was

4

hard work, especially with two twenty-year-olds, but we'd often joke that as long as we were communicating in the bedroom, everything else would work out. I felt blessed to finally be part of a big family and was eager to take pleasure in raising children to know the Lord.

As I started to walk away from the gravesite, I thought I heard Mom's voice say, "I love you". But it was early summer and the leaves were rustling in the breeze blowing in from the lake.

"I love you too, Mom," I said, just in case.

2

A New Life

"Although no one can go back and make a brand new start, anyone can start from now and make a brand new ending."

– Carl Bard

It was January 2003, and Curtis had already given notice at work. We were both moving to Nashville, even though the house hadn't sold and he didn't have a job. It was time to bury the statue of St. Joseph upside down in the yard. I wasn't superstitious, but I'd made time to pray since I was a little girl and I'd been praying in earnest that the house would sell. But after four months and no showings, it looked like help from a Patron Saint like St. Joseph might be needed. Since we'd married, Curtis and I had been faithful attendees at Catholic churches all over San Antonio. I knew I needed to trust, but this move to Nashville had me anxious. It wasn't just the house not selling, either; Curtis didn't get the one job he'd interviewed for in Nashville and didn't have any more leads. I was starting to worry that one paycheck wouldn't be enough to cover the child support, college tuition payments, and two households.

I've never been good at memorizing Scripture verses, but there was one that always seemed to help when I was overwhelmed, 1 Peter 5:7: "Cast all your care upon Him for He cares for you." I knew the words well enough, but it was hard not to be anxious when worries are about money. Mom and Dad always argued about finances, and I'd lost a lot of money when I sold the house after my divorce. I'd always had a good-paying job as a pharmacist, but sometimes your wants and needs, or those of your family, exceed your income. Now that we had two college students to care for, the expenses had gone way up.

My transfer to Nashville wasn't much of a promotion, but I hoped that it would be enough money to start our new life on a clean slate. I kept praying that Curtis would find a job right away once we got to Nashville.

The time for our move was growing closer and the house still hadn't sold; yet I was excited when we flew to Nashville one weekend to look at rental homes. I really wanted to buy a house, but on the other hand, renting would give us a better idea of what part of town we wanted to live in. When I went to Nashville to interview for the job, a realtor had spent the afternoon driving me all around Middle Tennessee. She liked the Belle Meade area, and Franklin, but Curtis and I couldn't commit to buying anything until the house in San Antonio sold. We agreed the best plan was to rent a house fairly close to Centennial Park, where I'd be working at Centennial Medical Center. The airplane tickets were booked for our house-hunting trip and I found a Marriott on West End with a reasonably priced room. As a surprise, I'd also purchased two tickets to the Nashville Predators-Minnesota Wild game for that Saturday night. Curtis loved hockey and had never lived in a city with an NHL team.

♱ ♱ ♱

I glanced, smiling, at the large vase of beautiful flowers sitting next to me on the car seat. I've always loved flowers, and these especially so, for they were a reminder of the fun going-away party my coworkers from Metropolitan Methodist Hospital had thrown for me. I'd worked there for six years, and I sure was going to miss everyone.

As I started down the driveway, I called Curtis to let him know that my hands were full of flowers and stuff from my desk, and that I needed help getting everything into the house. I was on the top step of the porch when the door flung open and my youngest puppy made a dash out the front door, almost knocking me over! As I teetered to keep my balance, she escaped, making a beeline down the stairs and heading off to a distant spot on the neighbor's property.

I took one glance at Curtis and felt the flame rise in my cheeks. "What's going on? Now Rachel's loose and I have to go look for her. Have you been drinking this afternoon?"

"Not me. You know how that dog is—she's always trying to escape. She'll be back when she gets hungry."

I set the flowers down inside the front door and ran off, calling for Rachel to come home. After two hours of searching, I finally spied her playing with the neighbor's dog in the community pond. I walked into the house, elated that I'd found her, but I was greeted with an icy stare.

"It's nice of everyone to give you a going-away party. It's too bad they didn't appreciate you more when you were working there. I won't expect a party at my work next week. Nobody likes each other."

"The past doesn't matter; I'm happy that we're going to start a new life in Nashville. Let's just order in some pizza and finish packing for our trip tomorrow."

I went to bed with dreams of a small, white cottage nestled among some tall trees. We'd driven through Knoxville a little over a year before and I could still remember the tallest trees I'd ever seen. My little cottage wouldn't be very big, just large enough for Curtis, me, the twins and a baby or two. As I was dozing off to sleep, I had a vision again of rounding out our family with twin girls and a baby boy. I knew with the house not sold and Curtis without a job that we would have to wait for a while to own a home and start a family, but that would give us time to get settled into our new life. Curtis' twins were already planning to come visit for Spring Break and I was looking forward to exploring Nashville with them.

I'm a light sleeper, and at 1 a.m. I was startled awake by a loud thump in the living room. I got out of bed and went to investigate. I found Curtis lying on the sofa with a gash in his forehead.

"What happened? Did you fall? How long have you been up?"

"I got up to get a glass of water and fell."

I rushed to the kitchen to get a rag and some cold water and noticed two beer cans in the trash that hadn't been there when we finished our pizza the night before.

"How long have you been up? Have you been drinking?"

"No, I haven't been drinking. I fell. But I'm not going to Nashville with you tomorrow to look for a house. In fact, I'm not going to Nashville at all. This move is all about your job and your success, not about me. Why should I go with you? You'll just work long hours and I'll never see you anyway. I might as well stay here and be alone."

"What? You were going to stay here and keep working until the house sold, but then you said you'd miss me too much, so you quit your job—without even telling me first— and announced you were moving with me." I was trying not to be confrontational, but my words sounded harsh: "So what is it going to be? You don't have a job here anymore, so there is nothing to keep you. We might as well start a new life in Nashville."

"I said, 'I'm not going with you.' This is all about you and your career success. It's never been about me and what I want."

With that, I started to cry. "But you said you wanted to move and start our life together in a new place. We could have stayed here in San Antonio, at the jobs we had. You were the one that didn't like your new boss and wanted to leave. We agreed that we'd consider moving, wherever one of us got a job first. What's changed now?" I said through the tears.

"I just don't want to go."

"But I have to go. I signed a one-year contract and there are penalties if I don't take the transfer. I don't even know if I could have my old job back here in San Antonio. If I turn this move down, I'll never be able to get a promotion and it will cost us even more money to back out, like the $10,000 sign-on bonus. You don't have a job here anymore, and the one that I have is in Nashville. I'm going to bed. You can decide whether or not you want to be on that plane with me tomorrow."

I went to bed at 3 a.m., not knowing if Curtis was going with me or if I was going alone. Grudgingly, we both got on the plane at 9 a.m. the next morning, neither of us having slept much the night before. I hoped for an apology, but one never came.

ॐ ॐ ॐ

We found a rental house in Green Hills, just ten minutes from Centennial Park, and moved the next month. I worked and Curtis continued to look for a job. Our bills continued to mount; the San Antonio house was still on the market, with plenty of lookers but no offers. If only we had put in a separate bathtub in the master bathroom. It seemed like the common complaint from every potential buyer. Six months after we moved to Nashville, one credit card was maxed out and we'd still had no offers on the house or job offers for Curtis. With child support, college tuition and two house payments, I was growing increasingly anxious. Curtis was depressed about not having a job and stopped sending out resumes all together. I pleaded with him not to drink and suggested instead that he hit golf balls at the driving range or volunteer at church or a non-profit in town.

"Just do something," I'd say. "Be useful. You'll feel better about yourself."

"Easy for you to say; you have a job."

It became easier for me to work long hours, just to prolong going home. One night, after we'd been living in Nashville for seven months, I got home late from work.

"I'm sorry I'm so late; I had to work on a new project proposal to present first thing tomorrow. I called but you didn't answer. Did you get my message?"

"Yes. I got your message; it's the third time you've worked late this week."

"I'm sorry. It's still a pretty new job and there is a lot to do. We have a Joint Commission inspection next week and everyone is staying late to make sure everything's in order. All the department heads are working extra."

"Well, I've decided we're moving back to Texas. I've never liked Nashville; there's nothing to do here and everyone seems pretty backward and not very friendly. I could get a job in San Antonio, just like that," he said, as he snapped his fingers, "but here everyone wants a Registered Nurse as the hospital Risk Manager. I'm sure you can get a pharmacist job somewhere at Wal-Mart or Walgreens. There's always an opening for a pharmacist if you want to work hard enough."

I knew it was pointless trying to argue with him so I went into the kitchen to start dinner. When I opened the pantry door I saw the empty beer cans in the trash. I knew it had been hard for him, not having a job for so long, but drinking wasn't going to make it any better. I counted to ten before I walked back into the living room, but instead of being calm, I started to sob. "I like my job here. The people are nice and it's a busy hospital. Texas was too hot; there are real seasons here. With the fall leaves turning brilliant colors, it's just beautiful here."

"I don't care, we're moving back to Texas."

"Well, there's just one problem. I signed a one-year contract and we'll have to pay back my $10,000 sign-on bonus if I don't stay the full year, not to mention that we'll have to repay the

$11,000 in moving costs the hospital paid for us. We're $40,000 in debt and we can't take on any more. We still have to pay next semester's college tuition for the twins. Where are we going to find $10,000 by December 1? I guess if you want to move back to Texas, you can go tomorrow. But I won't be able to join you for another five months. Maybe the time apart will do us good. In five months, we can decide if we're going to move back to Texas, stay in Nashville, or get a divorce. Is that what you want?"

"I didn't say anything about a divorce. I said we're moving back to Texas."

"It sounds like you've been drinking this afternoon and I'm not talking with you anymore. You can move back to Texas now, but you're going alone."

The next morning, Nashville must have looked a little more welcoming, because Curtis decided to stay. By the time we reached the one-year mark in Nashville, we had a six-month lease-purchase agreement on the house in San Antonio, which eased the financial pressure.

ço ço ço

A week after my one-year anniversary at the hospital, I was working late when I got a call from Jackie, the new Director of Nursing.

"I'm working late too," she said. "Do you want to head over to Maggiano's and get a drink? I'd like to talk about the Code Blue Committee policy a little more. No one would ever believe a Nurse and Pharmacist going out for a drink together!"

"Sure, let's head there now." I quickly called Curtis and left a message that I had to work late and that I'd eat at the hospital.

When I got to Maggiano's, there were three people waiting at a table in the bar: Jackie, Kim, the Director of Medical Records, and Carol, the Director of Cardiovascular Services.

Jackie said, "Hope you don't mind. I found Kim and Carol working late too and asked them to come along. We're all pretty new at the hospital and I thought it would be a good way to get to know each other."

We didn't talk much about the Code Blue Committee that evening, but we did share some personal information. I told my story of transferring from San Antonio; Jackie had come from another health system in Indiana; Kim had been recruited from Florida, and Carol from Wisconsin. We had all been at the hospital about a year. Kim had moved to Nashville with her husband and two children, but her home in Jacksonville hadn't sold yet. Carol didn't have any children, but she and her husband were renting an apartment close to the hospital. Jackie's husband would stay in Indiana until he could sell their house and find a job in Nashville. Jackie visited him on weekends. I didn't tell my new friends everything going on in my personal life, but I did reveal that I was worried about our bills, and about the fact that Curtis still hadn't found a job.

Six weeks after our first meeting at Maggiano's we found out that the hospital had passed its inspection with flying colors. Carol sent an email: "It's time for the PORCH CLUB to have another meeting to celebrate our good news! Maggiano's at 6 p.m."

PORCH CLUB? I had no idea what she was talking about, but I asked as soon as I joined Jackie, Kim and Carol at the same table we'd been at six weeks before.

Carol explained, "Well, it's the four of us, sitting around on our front porch, drinking some wine, watching the trees start to bloom and shooting the breeze. *WE ARE THE PORCH CLUB!*"

With a toast of our glasses and two more lemon drop martinis, we became four fast friends that night.

෯ ෯ ෯

It was a huge blessing when Curtis started his job with the State of Tennessee. We had been in Nashville for eighteen months, and had struggled since the move with a house payment, rent payment, and two college tuitions. We were $80,000 in debt and had maxed out every credit card. I'd find myself in daily prayer, trying to control the world that was spinning around me. But now there was a light at the end of the tunnel; finally, we had two paychecks again! I liked Nashville and since Curtis was working full-time, it seemed like we would be staying. Even more prayers were answered when the house in San Antonio closed three months later, exactly two years since we'd put it on the market. We had just enough money to buy a house in a new subdivision in Bellevue, just west of Nashville. It was smaller than the one in San Antonio, but we didn't need as much room now that the kids were grown. It was great to have our own place, where we could finally begin again and hopefully start a family. With two jobs, a house, and our credit card debt starting to dwindle, it felt like things were running headlong in the right direction.

There were some fun times in those early days in Nashville, especially when the twins or some of Curtis' family came to visit. I had been raised as an only child, ever since my brother died when I was eight. I'd lost my father at twenty-five and Mom at thirty-six. I had finally married at thirty-one, when I faced the reality that my mother wouldn't be around very much longer and I felt it was time to start a family. I wasn't proud of the affair I'd had with Curtis when I was still married to Dave, but I'd rationalized that my marriage wasn't a happy one and it was better to finally find true love.

We all have things that we aren't exceptionally proud of, and my marriage wasn't unique. Seemed like a lot of marriages end up in divorce these days. My freshman year of college I'd dated a married man whose marriage had started to fail, so I knew firsthand that it wasn't at all unusual to hear of a new romance starting before the old one had died. I'd filed for a divorce from my first husband a few months after the affair started with Curtis. After a short romance, Curtis and I were engaged. I resolved that this marriage would be different, and I'd be a faithful wife.

Curtis seemed to like his new job at first, but then he started complaining about his boss and that he should be making more money. I was just thrilled that he was working and we had money coming in, but he didn't seem to be happy. We'd have a good time on Saturday evenings after a long workweek, but then we fell into a pattern of conversations that were too lively after early church on Sunday mornings. We always seemed to end up talking about me having to work late and not cooking as much anymore.

෴ ෴ ෴

I don't know exactly when I started sharing my previous infidelities and current roller coaster marriage with the PORCH CLUB, but they all agreed that everything that was said was in the strictest of confidence. We'd talk about work, but even more about our families. It's always comforting to hear that others are making it through the inevitable bumps in their relationships.

I asked their opinion about how to make Curtis happier. I still thought that if he volunteered at a non-profit or our church he'd have more to look forward to each day. But Curtis seemed to be focused on only two things: going to work and the next time his children were coming to visit. With the twins finishing college in two different states, it was harder for us to coordinate schedules to be together. The more missed holidays with the kids, the more depressed Curtis got about the way the kids were growing up and his inability to influence them. We'd faithfully made the child support and college tuition payments, but it never seemed like there was enough money or time. The PORCH CLUB sympathized that there are never easy answers when it comes to marriage and children.

❧ ❧ ❧

Two years after we'd moved to Nashville, I confided in the PORCH CLUB that I'd been dreaming of a guy who went to the same Catholic Church as me and Curtis. I had met him at the annual chili cook-off when we happened to end up at the same tasting station. Curtis was over in the beer tent, drinking with the men from the Knights of Columbus and hardly noticed that I had wandered off. I only talked to Jimmy briefly that night, but I couldn't get him out of my mind. I told the PORCH CLUB that I didn't know what to do. Curtis was drinking more often and verbally taking all his frustrations about the kids and money out on me.

Jackie suggested that I be open with Curtis, tell him what I was thinking, and then ask if he would go with me to see a priest for counseling. Carol suggested that we should go to a Christian counselor not affiliated with a church. She thought it might be easier for Curtis if he didn't have to admit to a priest that his marriage was rocky. But I was pretty sure that Curtis wouldn't go to counseling, and I certainly couldn't tell him that I was attracted to another man. I'd tried to talk with him a few times, but he didn't see anything wrong with his behavior or his drinking.

Kim had been quiet, but finally offered, "It sounds like he is the STRICT FATHER type. He's insecure and barks orders all the time. He gets angry if you even question him. He doesn't know how to love anyone because he doesn't feel loved. But you married him. The right thing to do is NOT to have an affair, and work through your marriage. Why would you risk your whole family life to have an affair?"

"I'm tired."

"What do you mean? Tired of what?" Kim asked.

"I'm tired of everything. When I was a little girl, I was always trying to distract Dad from yelling or threatening Mom; he'd take a butcher knife and threaten her after he'd been drinking. I grew up pretty fast. I was on my own right after

16

college and fell into the role of trying to please everyone. Even at church, I was the first person to plan ski trips and group events. I thought if I was organized, efficient, and cheerful all the time, everyone would like me and eventually a Christian guy would fall in love with me and we'd get married, have three children and live happily ever after. Instead, I just dated a lot until I turned thirty, and then I decided it was time to get married. When I met Dave, I thought he was a sign from God. He never had a chance. When that didn't work out like I had planned, I just dusted myself off, started an affair and then married Curtis when the divorce was final: same chapter, second verse.

"Curtis had been divorced for six years and had two beautiful children when we started dating. It was a ready-made family; I knew he was the right one. I went after him, too, cooking dinner for him, planning vacations and always stepping aside when he was with the kids. I never wanted any controversy in our relationship, only 'fun times', and it worked; he moved in with me within nine months."

"So, what are you tired about?"

"I realized that I was creating all my busyness, trying to be 'super woman' and take care of everything in my marriage. With Dave, I worked full-time but still did the cooking and paid all the bills. He never had to do much. When something tough came along, like putting his mother in a nursing home, he just stepped aside and let me take care of it. 'After all, you're the one in healthcare,' was all he offered. I made the hard decision when his grandfather was taken off the ventilator in ICU; no one else in the family was willing to tell the doctor to let him go, even though it was Grandpa's wishes in his living will.

"With Curtis, I've been the only breadwinner for two extended periods in our marriage. Every time it seems like we are getting out of debt and can start a family of our own, some crisis happens with the kids or his family, and everything falls apart again. I'm just tired of always being the go-to person, the one who takes care of everything, who works and pays all the bills. I want someone to take care of me for a change, to delight in being with me, someone I look forward to being with because he wants to treat me and take care of me, not waiting for me to do everything. I'm just worn out after all these years."

I knew that Kim was right– that I shouldn't have an affair– but it was hard. The marriage hadn't been anything like I'd expected. When we were dating, Curtis was enthralled with me, and I couldn't do anything wrong. Now I felt like I couldn't do anything right. The harder I tried to please him the more inadequate I felt. It was a moving target. Just when I thought I'd earned his affection, he'd blow up about some other little thing. But I knew that the answer wasn't to move on to another man. I needed to figure out what was wrong with me, and change. Hopefully I could figure it out before it was too late to save my marriage.

I didn't dare bring up counseling with Curtis and resolved to be a better, loving, Christian wife and to keep praying for a better marriage. But no matter what I did, I was still haunted by the dream of a possible life with Jimmy. It was craziness!

I hardly knew Jimmy, except that he was a reader at Sunday mass. But I imagined what life would be like married to Jimmy, or someone like him, who knew God and had such a disarming smile. I longed for someone who studied Scripture, was willing to teach me and to share with me what he knew about God's kingdom. Each week, I suggested that we go to the early service because that was the one Jimmy attended with his two boys. I felt like I was cheating on Curtis just by saying hello, but I couldn't help myself.

After a few months, I noticed that my "lively discussions" with Curtis after mass each Sunday had accelerated into verbal warfare. We'd come home after church, have sex, and then I'd start cooking. Over brunch, I'd want to talk about the Scripture reading or sermon and we'd always end up in a huge argument. My God is a God of love and Curtis' God is a God of punishment. Curtis could never see my side of God's story, and I could never see his.

We seemed to be moving further and further apart and I had no idea why. Every time we argued, I gave in just to keep peace. I thought we had a lot to be thankful for: we both had good jobs, went to church every Sunday, enjoyed fine restaurants and our sex life hadn't cooled after ten years of marriage. But whenever we fought about how God treats His children, I found myself wondering, *How does Jimmy view God? Is He a God of love in Jimmy's eyes, too?*

It didn't make sense that I was unhappy in my marriage. I had the large family I'd always wanted and our financial crises were over. Mother had always told me that I should marry a Catholic, that a "mixed marriage" would be a curse, and I'd rejoined the Catholic Church when I'd married Curtis. But I was starting to realize that just because we were both Catholic didn't mean we had a marriage blessed by God. Just like my father, Curtis was spending more and more time with the bottle and less and less time working on being a good husband and dad.

I thought things would be rosier when our money woes eased. Everything looks worse when you are $80,000 in debt and sinking fast! But as they say, money can't make you happy, so even though we did have some money in the bank and a roof over our heads, I was far from happy. As the twins got older, I felt like I was taking a backseat in my relationship with Curtis. I tried to convince myself that the kids were important too, but it seemed more like a competition than a family. Jimmy was divorced with two teenage boys; they seemed like wonderful, devoted children who loved to spend time with their dad and enjoyed going to church with him.

The PORCH CLUB kept warning me that I needed to get Jimmy out of my mind; a good Christian woman doesn't dream about having an affair. But the dreams continued. Every time Curtis drank and fell asleep in his chair by 7 p.m., my heart wondered what it would be like to be kissing Jimmy. Jimmy and I had never done anything except say hello, but I still felt guilty. It was all in my imagination, but some days the tape would play over and over in my head. All I could think of was how sweet Jimmy's slow kiss would be, a kiss that I'd never had.

The dreams were becoming more real. I was wondering what it would be like to be married to Jimmy and have his two boys living with us.

My life was about to change, but not in the way that I imagined.

3

Angry at God

"My God, my God, why have you forsaken me?

Why are you so far from saving me, from the words of my groaning?

O my God, I cry by day, but you do not answer,

and by night, but I find no rest.

- Psalm 22:1-2

The PORCH CLUB had only gathered a few times when bad news reached us. David, one of the other department directors at the hospital, had missed a management meeting and we soon learned why: his son Jason was at Vanderbilt Medical Center and it didn't look good.

   I traded emails with David, asking how Jason was doing and offering help, but only received a short response: "We're still waiting on tests; I'll let you know when we hear." David was a great guy; he attended a Southern Baptist Church in Nashville and was married to a lovely, gracious woman who home-schooled their four children. Hundreds of people were praying for David and his family, including me.

I'd prayed all my life, but it was always more of a private thing, not like the spontaneous, out loud prayers that I remembered from the Southern Baptist Churches I'd attended. As I was deep in prayer for David's son, I realized that I usually prayed when I wanted something. It wasn't always selfish; many times the prayers were for others, not just me. There couldn't be anything wrong with that.

Three weeks later, the news came. David's son, Jason had rhabdomyosarcoma, a rare and highly aggressive form of cancer. My Mom had died of cancer so I knew how awful it is when a loved one is diagnosed. I immediately called David: "I am so sorry. I'm praying for you and your family. Please let me know what else I can do."

As the weeks went on, there would be good news followed by bad news. Jason's tumor would respond to the chemotherapy, then start to grow again. Jason was incredibly strong through it all, inspiring others with his wit and his smile. Even on days when he felt awful, Jason was still more concerned about his family and friends and what they were going through. I kept praying and sending notes to David on behalf of the PORCH CLUB so he would know that we were all praying for Jason and the family. Finally after one year, good news! The tumor had shrunk; in fact, it had disappeared on CT scan! They were going to start radiation therapy in three weeks.

I called David the moment I heard and suggested that we meet for a beer to celebrate. David shared how his whole church had been praying for healing and that others were too; people they didn't even know in churches across the United States had prayed for his son's recovery. Jason's doctors were sure it was a miracle because they had said initially there was no cure. They were amazed that the tumor had disappeared completely! It was good to relax and enjoy a beer with David. I was especially interested when he told me how important certain Scripture passages were during Jason's illness.

I asked David if we could meet every three or four weeks so that I could learn more about his faith and the role Scripture had played in his life. I told him I'd been raised Catholic and felt very inadequate in my knowledge of Scripture. I'd heard the phrase "Bible illiterate" and was sure it described me.

We met four times over the next six months and I enjoyed the sessions immensely. David was a wonderful teacher of Scripture and made the verses seem real, like they were relevant to my life. I had always thought the Bible was another thing to memorize, like algebraic equations in math class, but somehow it was starting to seem like a living, breathing thing. It was also a mystery; sometimes I'd read a passage that was totally confusing and made no sense. It was good to have someone to discuss it with, someone who didn't judge or make fun of me when I asked simple questions. Over those six months, I began to appreciate David as a man of such a strong Christian faith that even when his son was so sick, he still believed in Jesus and His message.

When I was ready to meet David for our fifth session, I got an ominous email: "Can't meet today; I'll explain tomorrow." And the news was grim. The CT scan from the previous day showed that the tumor had returned, not only in the same spot but in two other areas as well. Now the doctors were considering amputating Jason's right leg.

I really didn't know what to say, but I quickly sent a message. "I'm still praying for Jason and your family. Keep your spirits focused on the Lord." But as the days wore on, the news became worse. David was at the hospital around-the-clock. I kept praying in private, every morning and evening; I mentioned Jason's illness to Curtis only in passing.

I'd also reverted to my religious upbringing, finding some novenas on the Internet for when people were really sick. Novenas are a tradition in the Roman Catholic Church; it's when you say the same prayer for nine consecutive days. I remember my mother praying novenas for all sorts of things: to lose weight, for my father to get a job, for me to get into a good college. I remembered the rosaries, too, particularly those said as a group. I was overcome with a childlike fervor to "pray unceasingly" (a Scripture verse that David had shared with me). I just knew that if I were sincere, God would answer my prayers and spare Jason.

I thought back to my childhood, when I had lost my brother and grandmother in the same year. There were funerals with lots of praying for the "repose of the souls". But my brother had had health problems when he was born, and my grandmother was old; neither death was unexpected. People at the funeral home said they were better off in the next life and that we shouldn't be too sad. But death is hard to explain to an eight-year-old. I shook my head gently to clear the memories.

The news came from a mutual friend three months later: David's eldest son Jason had passed away in his father's arms at the age of nineteen.

A friend called and asked if I was attending the funeral service. "Yes, but I don't want to go alone." Good friends say, "I'll go with you," and that's what we did. But we both dissolved into tears when the soloist started the first verse of MercyMe's *I Can Only Imagine.* One of my favorite Christian songs, it's about what we will do when we finally meet Jesus. But instead of thinking about a glorious moment in the future, my tears reminded me of my present sorrow. I had only one thought: "God, how could you be so cruel as to take Jason's life away? His whole family is so devoted to You, and You had no right to take him away. I don't care if there is a lesson here or if it is Your will. You've answered my prayers before for lots of other things, even when I was praying half-heartedly. Why couldn't You answer them this time, when all I've asked You over the past twenty months was to spare Jason's life?"

In my grief, I became angrier and angrier with God for taking Jason's life. In the past I'd prayed for small things and they'd usually happened. I'd been afraid to pray for something really important like finding the perfect mate, having children or making a lot of money. I guess I was afraid that if I prayed for it and it didn't happen, it would be a clear sign from God that I wasn't in His favor. If I didn't ask Him, at least I wouldn't be disappointed.

I'd prayed when I wanted to get pregnant and have a child of my own, but when I married Curtis I was already a few weeks short of forty and it seemed a long shot at best. When my mom was suffering with cancer, I prayed that she would be spared any more pain. But this time with Jason was different. It was the first time I'd prayed in earnest *and* told the people I was praying for them. Not only did I feel like a failure, but a fool, too. I'd always heard how God answers prayer, but obviously not mine.

After the funeral, I didn't see David for a while; then a few months later, I bumped into him in the hospital cafeteria. "How about a beer after work?" I asked. "I've missed our conversations about Scripture." It was good to talk to him again. I learned that Jason had been buried in the family plot in North Carolina. David shared how each family member was working through their grief in their own way.

I told David how angry I was at God for not saving Jason, but he said, "You need to realize that as hard as it is, Jason's death is part of God's plan. We as humans can't imagine everything that God knows, but we have to trust Him. God didn't take Jason away from us. He was born of God and always belonged to Him. We are grateful that we got to know him for nineteen years, and are looking forward to seeing Jason again in heaven."

David's unwavering faith, even in the wake of losing his son, didn't make any sense to me. I felt like I was asking questions for which there were no answers, and it was taking me back in time. I told David more about my childhood than I'd ever shared with anyone, even Curtis.

"I had a brother who was nineteen when I was born. My mother had German measles when she was pregnant, so my brother was born with an enlarged heart and he could barely see. He spent most of his time in the Batavia School for the Blind, so I didn't really know him. He died at home when I was eight years old. I had no idea what was going on at that young age, but Mom said that my brother's death almost killed my father; in fact, that was when he stopped going to church completely."

"How did you find all this out?"

"Mom would talk about it in kind of dreamy terms over the years, like she wasn't sure whether it had really happened. Mom was the one who took me to church every Sunday. I never remember my Dad going. I didn't understand growing up, but now I can see how devastating it must be to lose a child. I can't imagine your loss, David."

ဪ ဪ ဪ

Over the next few months, I saw David a few times for a beer but we didn't talk much about faith. I was struggling with the whole concept of a God who didn't care for His children and remained perplexed by the strength of David's conviction. I looked to him for answers to my unresolved questions, but at the end of the night, after I had closed my Bible and there was only stillness in the room, my mind would wander back to the same nagging question, "How could a loving God be so mean?"

I had no emotion for God except anger, and nothing David said could change my mind. I dutifully went to early Mass with Curtis each Sunday, but we'd arrive, sit in the pew, and leave when the last hymn was over. We didn't talk with anyone or know anyone from church. My prayers seemed to be useless to everyone.

My mind often wandered during the sermons, which was unusual for me. I'd be thinking about work, the next novel I wanted to read and what I'd buy at the store to fix for dinner. Even a vacation scheduled six months in the future would distract me from listening to the Scripture and the sermon. I wanted to shout out, "*Hypocrites! If you only knew what God was really like, you wouldn't be as fond of Him and want to be like Him. After all, who would let their Son die if they really loved him?*" The voices in my head immediately made the connection: If God didn't love Jason enough to let him live, He probably didn't love me enough either.

I was constantly conflicted. I would see a vivid image of a violent God, angry with His children, but then it would fade to a scene of a snowfall when I was six years old. I was in my bedroom, listening to my parents arguing downstairs. Outside, the backyard glistened from the moonlight on the newly fallen snow. When I looked at the snowfall through my six-year-old eyes, I was convinced that no human could create anything so beautiful!

These two images would alternate in my child's mind. I could see God's beautiful creation all around me in snowfalls, waterfalls, butterflies, and the first robin of spring. I recognized God's handiwork, but I wasn't living it. My life didn't seem to be like heaven at all. Dad was distant and yelling at Mom constantly. Mother could never do anything right, from the way she paid the bills to the way she folded the clothes. During their arguments mother would bring up someone named "Caroline"; she sounded like a bad person who had interfered early in their marriage, when Mom was pregnant with my brother, Jerome. I never learned more information but I suspected that it was an affair that had left Mom bitter.

As a six-year-old I had been conflicted and now, forty-five years later, I still didn't understand God.

"So, God loves His people, right? He lets women take husbands away from their wives and then lets wonderful nineteen-year-old boys die. Some God of the universe! Why would I want to pray to Him or even believe that He exists? I'm better off without Him in my life."

It was a cold winter night in December 2005, and one week after my birthday when I pleaded with God to leave me alone. He'd disappointed me and I didn't want to be His friend anymore. At fifty-one, I'd made a pretty successful life for myself, and I hadn't really needed God so far. It was easier not to care if He loved me than to try to figure Him out.

I was convinced that I was done with the "God of the universe," but He had other plans.

27

4

Cancer

Picture yourself in a hospital bed. The fog of anesthesia has begun to wear away.
A doctor stands at your feet, a loved one holds your hand at the side.

'It's cancer,' the healer announces.
The natural reaction is to turn to God and ask Him to serve as a cosmic Santa. 'Dear God, make it all go away.
Make everything simpler.'

But another voice whispers: 'You Have Been Called.' Your quandary has drawn you closer to God, closer to those you love, closer to the issues that matter, – and has dragged into insignificance the banal concerns that occupy our 'normal time.'

– Tony Snow

A few months after Jason died, I transferred to a position with the HCA Corporate Office across the street from Centennial Medical Center. It was a great job with weekends and holidays off. Although I missed the people I'd worked with, and the excitement of taking care of patients in a hospital setting, Curtis had been complaining about my long work hours. It had been like that most of my career. A nationwide shortage of pharmacists made it difficult to staff hospital pharmacies, so I often found myself working on nights and weekends. Although I'd gone into pharmacy to help patients, I had to make a choice, and I thought that having a predictable schedule would help my marriage and allow me to volunteer at our church.

The Fourth of July was approaching and I was excited to have the long weekend off. Curtis' younger brother, J.P., and his girlfriend Connie were coming from Oklahoma for a visit. It was their first time in Nashville, and I was delighted to plan all the activities, particularly the Fourth of July Nashville Symphony Concert at the River. I was always glad to see Curtis' family and wished we lived closer to them. But Curtis had made the final decision for us to relocate to Nashville, rather than Oklahoma City or Houston, where his relatives lived.

J.P. and Connie arrived on the afternoon of the third, and we headed downtown to Broadway, where all the honky-tonks are. We had a wonderful dinner at our favorite barbecue restaurant, Jack's on Broadway; then we slept in the next morning before heading out to brunch at the Loveless Café. Connie and I couldn't miss the Fourth of July sales in Franklin, even though it was a miserably hot day. The weatherman predicted 100-plus degrees, but we were determined to join the crowd of 100,000 on the banks of the Cumberland River that evening, listening to the Symphony and watching the fireworks.

Curtis and I were both in graduate school, and although I was a bit anxious about a paper I had due the next evening, I was grateful for the diversion. We packed a cooler of water and beer and got to the riverfront around the same time thousands of other people were staking out their spots. Even at dusk, the temperature was in the high 90s. The concert had barely gotten underway when Curtis suggested we leave, that it was "too hot". I was hot too, but I couldn't tell outside temperatures from my "hot flashes", and besides, I didn't want to disappoint J.P. and Connie. I pleaded to stay a little longer, but it fell on deaf ears. As we were leaving, I started feeling faint; it was a good thing that we reached the car and cool air conditioning when we did.

"Are you pregnant?" asked Connie.

"Oh, I can't be! I'm fifty-one—this isn't pregnancy; it's just too much heat!" It did bring back memories of how we'd tried to have a baby when we first got married, but when it didn't happen, I'd accepted that I was called to raise two stepchildren. *"How funny! I read in the Bible about people like Abraham and Sarah having kids when they were eighty, but miracles like that don't really happen anymore."*

After my funny quip, a more serious thought popped into my head. Over the past few months, I'd notice an occasional spot on my nightgown, a light brown spot over my left breast. It wasn't there every morning; in fact, I usually saw it after a night of bad hot flashes and had decided it was probably "hormonal". Drifting back to the thought of being pregnant, I laughed again. My periods had been spotty for the past six months. I guess it could be true that I was pregnant, but my thoughts turned back to entertaining our houseguests.

The rest of the week was uneventful and J.P. and Connie left on Friday to return to Oklahoma City. I had a restful weekend until I woke up on Monday morning with another small brown spot on my nightgown. With the holiday over and company gone, I decided it was time to find out what was going on. I called my OB/GYN, Dr. Maikis, as soon as I got to the office.

"I'm sure it's nothing," I told the girl who answered the phone. "There is never any pain or discomfort and I've been having hot flashes lately. It seems like the spot appears after a bad night with them. I can't express anything. Do I need to see Dr. Maikis or just watch it for awhile longer?"

Dr. Maikis was a friend from the Nashville EWGA golf league and one of my favorite doctors. I didn't mind my annual trip to see her since she was a personal friend, as well as a respected and competent doctor.

"No, we need to get you in to see Dr. Maikis right away. How about this afternoon at 3 p.m.?"

I was surprised by the urgency of the appointment. Usually doctors' appointments are booked months in advance, but I thought that maybe they'd had an early morning cancellation they were trying to fill.

When Dr. Maikis arrived in the exam room, we exchanged pleasantries, and then I explained about the intermittent nipple discharge. As usual, Dr. Maikis was thorough in taking a history of how long it had been going on, what, if anything seemed to trigger it, and if there was any pain. She couldn't express anything either and didn't feel any lumps or swollen areas. It was a normal breast exam.

"I don't think it's anything to be concerned about, considering the symptoms and what you've told me of your history. It's probably just a wart-like papilloma that is plugging up the milk duct and needs to be removed. I need you to go see Dr. Cooper. He's a general surgeon and a close friend of mine. I wouldn't worry about it; there's less than a ten percent chance that it's anything more serious. I wouldn't rush to see him, but sometime in the next couple of weeks would be good."

"Dr. Cooper; is that Dr. Mark Cooper?"

"That's the one. He specializes in breast surgery and will take good care of you."

It was good news. Mark Cooper was my friend too. We'd served on a number of committees together at Centennial and Mark was a very thoughtful and compassionate doctor. He was also considered one of the top breast surgeons in Nashville. I was surprised when I was checking out at Dr. Maikis' office that they had already made an appointment for me to see Dr. Cooper the next week. I checked my calendar and realized that I had some meetings at work that conflicted with the appointment.

"That's okay. I'll call Dr. Cooper's office and get it changed to another time."

I got busy at work the next day and forgot to call, but first thing the following day, I called Dr. Cooper's office and explained that I would need to change the date of the appointment.

"Yes, Dr. Maikis has already called and instructed us to work you in as soon as possible, but no later than next week."

"How about the following week? That is a better time for me with my work schedule."

"Dr. Cooper said to work you in this week or next. How about next Tuesday afternoon?"

It was going to be tough with my work schedule, but I decided that I'd just have to explain to my boss that I needed to have the afternoon off. I was debating how much information to share. Since I didn't know exactly what was going on, there really wasn't much I could say. It sounded like a simple office procedure and I'd be back at work the next day.

The following week was hectic, but I managed to keep the appointment with Dr. Cooper on Tuesday afternoon. He said the same thing after another normal breast exam. After reviewing the negative mammogram that I'd had only three months before, he said, "It's probably a papilloma; about ninety percent chance that it's nothing to worry about. We just need to remove it. I'll schedule you for a ductectomy at the end of the week at the Ambulatory Surgery Center and that should be the end of it."

"Gee. I thought this was going to be a simple office procedure; hadn't planned on 'surgery'. Do I need to have anesthesia?"

"We'll give you something to sedate you, probably Versed. You won't feel a thing; it's not really anesthesia, more like conscious sedation."

Curtis wasn't too pleased with the news that I was going to have surgery. He wanted to know everything involved in a ductectomy and how much tissue was going to be removed.

"I really don't know about that; in fact, I didn't even think to ask. I trust Mark completely. I'm more worried about this 'papilloma.' What if it turns out to be something else? But Dr. Cooper was very reassuring and said that the ductectomy was the way to go."

It was the first time I'd ever had surgery. I couldn't sleep at all the night before, but Friday came and the surgery went smoothly, with only mild discomfort controlled by oral pain medications. Dr. Cooper said I was a great patient and that he'd call with the pathology results on Tuesday or Wednesday when they were back from the lab. He told me I should rest for a few days, but that I could return to work on Monday if I felt like it. I called my boss and she was very understanding, even suggesting that I take Monday off even if I felt better.

By Tuesday morning, I was feeling pretty good, so I took two Aleve and headed out to work. I didn't explain my absence to anyone but my boss; it was a private matter. Besides, I wasn't that worried. I'd had a negative mammogram ninety days before, and Dr. Cooper had said it wasn't unusual for a papilloma to not show up on a mammogram.

At 1 p.m. that afternoon, I was sitting at my computer doing some Internet research when the phone rang. The Caller ID showed that it was Dr. Cooper's office. I picked up the phone cheerily, expecting to hear Dr. Cooper's nurse deliver the news of a negative pathology report.

"Please hold for Dr. Cooper."

"Agatha, it wasn't what I expected, but it's not cancer. That is the good news. It is not cancer. But the pathology report shows some pre-cancerous cells and I need to do a second operation to make sure that we've gotten them all. When can we operate again?"

"What? Pre-cancerous cells?" I was in shock. I listened intently as Mark explained that the cells were DCIS or Ductal Carcinoma In-Situ– a forerunner for cancer. I didn't like the sound of the words, especially the "pre-cancerous" part. I also was dismayed at the idea of another surgery. I felt overwhelmed and wanted to cry but dutifully looked at my work calendar and said that I could schedule another surgery for the following week.

"I'm glad you're in a hurry to get this done, but we need about two weeks in between surgeries so you'll have time to heal. This one is a lumpectomy and you'll need general anesthesia. My office staff will call to get you on the schedule at the Atrium at

Centennial and they'll let you know what day and time to be there. I promise I'll take good care of you."

I swallowed hard, choking back the tears. I'd never had surgery before last week and never had general anesthesia. I'd seen sick patients die in surgery when I was an operating room pharmacist at St. Anthony's Hospital in Oklahoma City. My thoughts were traveling a mile a minute. *What was I going to tell my boss about needing more time off and more importantly, what was I going to tell Curtis about needing more surgery?* His mother was doing poorly after being diagnosed with liver cancer the year before; I didn't want to add to his worry.

I could not get my mind to focus. It was drifting into all different areas of my life, ranging from what to tell the kids, to wishing my mother were still alive to comfort me. Normally I was good at making decisions, but now I was lost. This sounded much more serious than just a "papilloma", but I hadn't had time to do any research, my typical way of handling things when I was uncomfortable. If I just had enough time, I could investigate this diagnosis and come up with the right plan. My scientific mind and all my training had taught me that there is always an answer for everything.

φ φ φ

I was shocked when I looked through misty eyes and realized that I had been staring into space for over an hour. It was an hour of my life that I would never get back. I started to cry, knowing that unlike past times when I was distraught or angry, this time I hadn't turned to prayer. God had been so distant during the eleven months since Jason's death; I just couldn't deal with Him now. But then I thought, *"What if this is my payback for being so rude and demanding of God? It seems like God always has the upper hand."*

I just kept hanging on to Dr. Cooper's words–"It is not cancer"–and after a few minutes, the crying jag was over. It is not cancer. I kept repeating it over and over in my mind, like a mantra. Dr. Cooper had said one more surgery and I'd be as good as new. As hard as I tried, I couldn't think positively. All I could think of was dreading another surgery, this time with general anesthesia.

I was fighting back more tears when I remembered that the Chief of Anesthesiology at Centennial had given me his mobile phone number before I'd transferred to my new job. *Did I still have it?* I'd never had a talk with him about God, faith, or religion, but Jackie had mentioned once that he attended an Episcopal Church in Nashville. He was definitely one of the best anesthesiologists on staff. I checked my phone contact book and there it was, his mobile number. Shaking, I dialed it and was dismayed when his voicemail picked up. I didn't know what message to leave, so I just hung up. A few minutes later, my phone rang.

"This is Dr. Rodes," he said hesitantly, "I just got a call from this number."

"Yes, this is Agatha Nolen. I was the Director of Pharmacy at Centennial and transferred three months ago to the Corporate Office. Do you remember me?"

"Of course I remember you; how are you doing? And please, call me Dyer."

"Good. Well, actually, I'm not doing very well at all. I need to have surgery." As the story tumbled out, I could hardly talk through the tears. "Would you be my anesthesiologist? My surgery is being scheduled in two weeks."

"Of course, I'd be honored to. I will care for you."

The words, "I will care for you" washed over me like an artesian well! I was so grateful that he was available and willing to take care of me during surgery. For just a moment, I thought about asking him to pray for me, but considering my current relationship with God I didn't think it was appropriate.

৯৹ ৯৹ ৯৹

This surgery was rougher than the first one. Dr. Cooper came by to see me in the recovery room and said the procedure had been a success. He said to take the rest of the week off since the surgeries were so close together and I was going to feel more pain this time. "It's good news that the sentinel node was negative when the pathologist looked at it during surgery. I promise to call you as soon as the final pathology report hits my desk."

Mark and Dyer were very reassuring before and after surgery, but I did have a lot of pain as soon as the anesthesia wore off. However, the physical discomfort was nothing compared to the shock. The day after the surgery, I took off the bandage to find that my nipple had been removed. I knew Mark had probably told me that it was part of the surgery, but there was a lot going on in my head during that office visit and I didn't remember everything he said.

I stayed in bed the rest of the day Tuesday and all day on Wednesday, taking around-the-clock pain medication for a huge, painful hematoma. I called Dr. Cooper's office to ask about it, and the nurse told me that he would look at it when I had my office visit the following Tuesday. *Ouch!* I didn't know if I would make it until Tuesday. I'd have to get at least one refill on my Vicodin before my office visit. It was a blessing that I was on pain medication and sleeping a lot. Curtis wasn't very happy after the bandage came off.

"Did you know that Dr. Cooper was going to remove your nipple? How come you didn't tell me that?"

"I think he mentioned it, but I forgot myself. It didn't seem like it was negotiable and I trust him. He wouldn't have removed it unless it was necessary."

I awoke on Thursday with tremendous pain in my left breast. It felt like the hematoma was about to burst. I called Dr. Cooper's office again and left a message that I wanted to talk to the nurse or come in to have Dr. Cooper take a look at it. It definitely hurt worse than it did on Tuesday or Wednesday. I sat up in bed most of the afternoon, well medicated and hoping that Dr. Cooper would be able to see me later that day, but no call came until after 5:30 p.m. Dr. Cooper had been tied up in surgery all day, and would be again for most of Friday. The nurse recommended that I just keep taking the Vicodin and keep my appointment on Tuesday of the following week.

"Will I get the pathology report results on Tuesday too? "

"Dr. Cooper will call you when he gets the final report. It may be before Tuesday, but we'll definitely have it by the time you come in for your appointment."

I slept fitfully throughout the night but resolved that I would stay comfortable with medication until my doctor's appointment. I'd never been one to advocate lots of pain medication, but I finally understood why people sometimes take large quantities. There is nothing worse than being in pain that you can't get rid of. Your whole perspective changes when even small things seem like insurmountable mountains.

I awoke on Friday and realized that Dr. Cooper hadn't called with the pathology results yet. After all, he did say he thought they'd be back Thursday or Friday, but if he was in surgery all day, I wondered if they were sitting on his desk and he had just missed them. I reminded myself that he'd said he'd call me as soon as he got them. I just had to trust him.

As I was reading the morning paper, I noticed the date: August 25. It was one year to the day that Jason had died. With everything going on in my life, I had almost forgotten. I remembered a conversation I'd had with David before my surgeries; he'd mentioned that his family would be in North Carolina this weekend for a graveside remembrance. A number of Jason's friends from high school and guys from the track team were going to make the trip too.

I started to cry, overwhelmed with sadness for David and his family. I couldn't imagine how they must be feeling on the one-year anniversary of their nineteen-year-old's death. I felt stupid that I was feeling sorry for myself over a little surgical pain; it was nothing compared to the anguish of losing a loved one, particularly a child. I was sad to think that God had deserted both of us when we needed Him the most.

The pain was returning so I decided on two more pain pills, a quick bowl of soup for lunch and a nap. I slept intermittently, but woke up every time I turned over on my left side, where the hematoma was throbbing. When I did fall back asleep, I'd dream about David and his family at Jason's graveside in North Carolina.

At 2 p.m., Curtis came into the bedroom and shook me awake. "Dr. Cooper's office is on the phone for you."

"Great, I want to talk with him about the pain I'm still having. I don't think I can make it until Tuesday." Curtis closed the bedroom door gently as he left the room.

"Hi! This is Agatha," I said into the telephone.

"Agatha, this is Karen, Dr. Cooper's nurse. Dr. Cooper wants to talk with you."

"Hi, Dr. Cooper, thanks for returning my call."

"Actually, Agatha, I'm calling because I just got your pathology report back, and I knew that you would want the results right away. I've asked the laboratory to check because I was convinced that they got your results mixed up with another patient I operated on the same day. Agatha, I'm sorry to tell you that you have cancer. There was a 1.7 centimeters, invasive tumor that we didn't see on your mammogram or find on the ductectomy, but the tissue I removed this week definitely shows it. We're doing some additional tests on the tissue sample now to determine exactly what kind of cancer it is, but the extra test results won't be back until next week. I'm so sorry.

"There is something else. Even though the sentinel lymph node was negative on the frozen section during surgery, the pathologist has looked at the specimen in more detail and the final pathology results show that your sentinel node and one other lymph node are positive for cancer. A third node had a really small tumor, a 'micrometastasis' that is too small to count, but they saw it under the microscope. You'll definitely need to see a medical oncologist."

I shook my head, trying to think clearly. I was wide-awake, alert, and sitting up when I heard Dr. Cooper say "cancer" at the start of the conversation. It was like my brain was running on two channels. One path heard the entire conversation with Dr. Cooper about the cancer, and the other one was having its own conversation, *"But he said that I didn't have cancer, it was just some pre-cancerous cells! And this couldn't be right when I had a negative mammogram in March; that was only five months ago! They must have confused my pathology report with someone else. This can't be happening to me."*

I don't know how much time had passed before I heard Dr. Cooper's voice again, "Agatha?"

I decided that my questions of doubt and despair would have to wait, and focused instead on the practical conversation.

"Yes, I'm here, Dr. Cooper. But what does this mean? Do we wait until the final results come back next week? Does this mean that I have to have chemotherapy and radiation?"

"Actually, the tissue sample we took this week still has cancer cells around the outside; it's called a 'positive margin'. It means that we'll have to do surgery again in about three weeks. You'll need time to heal before the next one."

"Another surgery? That will be three in eight weeks. Are you sure?"

"Yes, I am. We'll discuss it all when you're here for your office visit on Tuesday. I am so sorry for you, but Dr. Rodes and I will take good care of you. I've already called him and he'll make sure he's available for your next surgery."

"Thank you, Dr. Cooper."

With that, I hung up the phone and quietly burst into tears. After fifteen minutes of crying, I decided that I needed to share the news with Curtis. Although a lot of it was healthcare jargon, I needed him to understand that I had cancer, needed another surgery and probably chemotherapy and radiation. I got up slowly and walked into the living room. Curtis spoke first, "What's wrong? What did Dr. Cooper say?"

"I have cancer and I have to have another surgery," I said quietly, my eyes still misty with tears and shock.

"Cancer? But he said that you didn't have cancer! Another surgery? What kind? Why?"

"I don't know any more details, but they have to do more tests. He said that we'll discuss it next week at my office visit."

"Well, I'm definitely going with you this time."

I longed for Curtis to cross the room and take me in his arms. I don't know why I couldn't ask him for the embrace that I needed so badly. *Was it because I was afraid of being rejected?* I didn't want to take the chance. *Why couldn't he be the one to figure out what I needed? Why did I always have to ask for affection when it wasn't associated with sex?*

I stared into space for a few minutes. "Thanks. I'm going to take another Vicodin and go back to sleep now."

I lay back down, but it wasn't a deep sleep. I couldn't get the image and voices out of my head. More surgery. Cancer. *Why was God punishing me?* Then I felt more guilt about how selfish I was. David and his family were at Jason's gravesite in North Carolina. *Why did I have to have three surgeries in eight weeks?* Nothing about my life was fair, and this fit right in.

℥ ℥ ℥

I slept through dinnertime, and around 8 p.m. I was awakened by a voice gently calling my name. "Agatha."

I was resting pretty comfortably on my right side, facing away from the door. "Curtis, thanks, but I'm still not hungry. Go ahead and eat without me."

There was no response, and I realized that it wasn't Curtis' voice I'd heard. I peered out from beneath the covers and was startled awake by an apparition at the foot of the bed, a figure in glowing white.

"Agatha, I know you've had a difficult day and are grieving for David and his family, too."

"Who are you?"

"I've come because I have a question for you."

40

"What question? Who are you?"

"Jason was willing to die for me, are you?"

Was it the pain medicine talking? But then I felt a cool breeze and I was too frightened to speak. The apparition moved closer and repeated the question, "Agatha, Jason was willing to die for me, are you?"

I'd always heard lots of voices playing constantly in my mind. Long ago, I learned to hold my tongue, but I still have a restless unruly mind, and often my thoughts defy my will and make me second-guess what I know to be true. It had always been just voices, but this time was different. I could see a glowing shape and feel a presence in the room. *Was this apparition real, or was it just my overactive mind playing tricks on me when I was emotionally overwhelmed with fear and sadness?*

I was wide-awake now and was angry when I realized that it was Jesus standing before me. *How dare he ask a question like that when he hasn't been there for Jason or me in such a very long time? How could he ask me to give up my life when I begged him and he still didn't spare Jason?*

"I'll have to get back to you on that, Jesus," I said loudly, just so there would be no mistaking that it was me answering through my own voice. With that, I turned my head back to the wall and closed my eyes.

I slept fitfully, waking up with pain every time I turned over. I was a mess of emotions with things darting in my head: uncontrolled pain, despair over Jason's death, cancer, another surgery, and now a heavy-duty question about dying for Jesus. I finally fell asleep but awoke with a start around midnight. There was no one in the room, but again I felt the cool breeze. I peered into the darkness and said, "Jesus, I have an answer for you. Yes, I am willing to die for you. Do you hear me? YES! I am willing to die for you."

"Yes, my child, I hear you."

With that, I fell back asleep. I couldn't possibly tell Curtis what had just happened. I didn't want him worrying about me dying, and he wouldn't have believed me anyway.

❧ ❧ ❧

The next two weeks were a whirlwind of doctors' visits, tests, and sleepless nights. I had appointments with a medical oncologist, a radiation oncologist, a plastic surgeon and more visits with Mark Cooper. I had blood work drawn, an MRI, two CT scans and a PET scan. Every day was exhausting; every night I stayed up late, researching chemotherapy, radiation and surgical options. It seemed like the treatment course depended upon what type of tumor I had, and the final pathology report still wasn't back from the specialty lab.

How could I ever figure out the right answer? In addition to all these tests to determine how far the cancer had spread, I also had to decide on my next surgery. Mark said it was my choice, but within the next three weeks, I would be having either a lumpectomy or a mastectomy.

I came up with another approach. I was convinced that I was going to die in six months, or why would Jesus have come personally to ask me that question? I was worried about another surgery, losing my hair and throwing up from the chemotherapy and radiation. Maybe the right decision was to not have chemotherapy or radiation and focus on enjoying the next six months with family and friends. The initial pathology had showed a slow-growing, unusual tumor. After all, it hadn't shown up on a mammogram just five months before and all breast exams were negative, even the ones done by the doctors. With every ache and pain, no matter how small, I was convinced that the cancer had spread and that my diagnosis would show the final stages of metastatic disease.

I alternated between wanting to spend my last few months in happiness, and wanting to live forever. I was frantically glued to the Internet, researching any and all approved and experimental treatments. Curtis went to sleep at 9 p.m. each night, but I'd be up long after, looking at website after website, hoping that the next one would have the answer.

I would catnap between 2 a.m. and 6 a.m., and started having a rather strange recurring dream: a pretty little girl with white hair and a yellow and white gingham dress was playing in a meadow of spring flowers. She was carefree, laughing and giggling and running in circles. There was a man in the dream, but his back was to me so I couldn't tell who he was. He did seem to be older, dressed as he was in a suit and highly polished shoes.

The little girl would keep running in circles, just out of the reach of the man. He'd chase her and when he was just about to catch her, she'd dart away from his grasp, laughing. Each morning I would wake up, exhausted and in a cold sweat, just as the figure was about to catch the little girl. During the day I'd pray that the dream would stop and I'd go back to sleeping peacefully throughout the night. I needed to be well rested if I was going to start a rigorous cancer treatment, but each night the dream returned and the happy little girl delighted in being just outside the man's reach.

ço ço ço

In the spring of 2006, Curtis and I had started the Ph.D. program in Public Administration at Tennessee State University. I'd continued working full-time for HCA and Curtis worked part-time for the State of Tennessee. I had only been attending school part-time, but now, with this cancer diagnosis, I had a decision to make. It seemed useless to continue in classes when I would never finish the degree. I wanted to concentrate on living to the fullest my last six months. It was pointless to learn more knowledge than I would ever use.

Still, it was a hard decision. I'd wanted to continue my education right after my undergraduate degree, but with Mom all alone after Dad died in 1980, medical school was out of the question. Other degrees looked appealing over the years, but most of them would have required me to quit my job and go to school full-time. I'd never had the economic resources to do that; I'd worked full-time since I graduated from high school. This Ph.D. program at TSU was local and the first I had come across that was designed for full-time employees, with night and weekend classes.

Despite my past dreams of higher education, I hadn't gone back to school for me. Instead, I'd gone to encourage Curtis. His lifelong dream was to teach at a university and he couldn't find a decent teaching job with a Master's degree. But he was afraid of failing, especially at his age, and it took my encouragement (and some harassment) to get him to take the Graduate Record Exam and enroll. We were the first couple ever to be in the same Ph.D. program at the same time at Tennessee State University.

But now this decision had to be about me, and what I wanted. I enjoyed my two spring classes in Organizational Theory and Public Policy and even though it was a struggle during the summer with my first surgery, I'd made it through a Research Methods class. It was fun being back in school and I'd received three "A"s my first two semesters. But facing a third surgery and an uncertain future, I knew that the right thing to do was to withdraw. I reluctantly placed a call to my class professor and advisor, Dr. Rodney Stanley, to tell him that I had just been diagnosed with cancer and had to drop out of school.

"I'm so sorry to hear about your health. Are you going to be starting chemotherapy and radiation? I had an aunt who had breast cancer ten years ago and it was rough-going for awhile, but she's fine now."

"I don't know what's going to happen next. We're still waiting for final pathology results to come back and I've been having tests for the last ten days. I just have a feeling that it won't be good news. I'm pretty worn out from not sleeping, too."

"Well, I have a suggestion. Rather than you dropping out, why don't we take it one day at a time? Curtis will be enrolled in the same classes in the fall and can take notes for you if you can't make it. I have office hours three days a week if you need extra help. Let's just play it by ear."

"Really? Are you sure, Dr. Stanley? I'm really enjoying my classes, but I'm overwhelmed right now. I just don't know what the future will bring."

"I know that there is a graduate school rule that you can't miss more than two classes in a semester, but I can make an exception for an illness. I'll talk with the Dean and get his permission, but let's see how it goes. You are a good student and I hate to have you drop out of school just yet."

A thought popped into my head: I wanted to ask him to pray for me, but it didn't seem appropriate. He'd once mentioned in class that he attended a Southern Baptist Church in Nashville, but I'd never had a conversation with him about religion. As I certainly wasn't comfortable telling him that I'd had a nighttime visitor and would probably die within months, I didn't have a good reason not to take his advice about staying in school.

"Thank you so much for all your support, Dr. Stanley. I promise to do my best to keep up with the class and I'll keep you posted when I find out more about my treatments. I've really enjoyed school and am looking forward to starting your Advanced Research Methods class in a few weeks. Thanks again."

᳚ ᳚ ᳚

Curtis insisted on going with me to see Dr. Cooper before my third surgery. All the tests results weren't back from the outside laboratory yet, but I had to have surgery before a decision could be made about chemotherapy.

Dr. Cooper said, "I've reviewed the pathology results we have and I feel sure this will be your last surgery, but you need to decide if we are going to do another lumpectomy or a mastectomy. I recommend you have a mastectomy because I want to be sure that I get all the cancer cells this time. My job is to keep you alive; your plastic surgeon's job will be to make you beautiful again!"

45

I laughed through the tension at his joke, but Curtis said, "What do you mean, a mastectomy? Why can't you just take a little more tissue out? Isn't it overkill to have a mastectomy? I was surprised after the last surgery when she came home and her nipple was gone. She hadn't mentioned that was part of the procedure. And I've heard that with a mastectomy you lose range of motion in your arm. She won't be able to play golf again if she has a mastectomy, right?"

"Agatha has two choices for the next step: either a lumpectomy or a mastectomy, but mastectomies have changed in the past ten years. We don't take all the lymph nodes out like we used to, and that's what causes all the problems with lymphedema, a build-up of fluid in the arm. The surgical reconstructions are different too, so we don't have to use the tissue from her back that causes some problems later on. As I mentioned before, I'm interested in keeping Agatha alive and the odds of surviving ten years or getting cancer again are identical whether she chooses to have a mastectomy or another lumpectomy with radiation. It is her decision."

When we got into the car, Curtis said, "You're not going to have a mastectomy, are you? You'll never look the same. Since Dr. Cooper says it's our choice, I vote for the lumpectomy with radiation."

"I don't know; this is all so overwhelming. I need some time to think."

"What's to think about? I thought we agreed that a mastectomy was the last choice."

I was silent. I was trying to figure out why Curtis was lobbying so hard against me having a mastectomy. *Was it because it was a "bigger surgery" with a longer recuperation and blood loss, or because I would be losing a breast and my appearance would change?* Appearance had been a huge part of our initial attraction to each other and I knew that a large chest was a big part of my appeal. I wanted to ask him, *"Will you still love me if I have only one breast?"* but I didn't dare. What if he said, "No?"

46

I decided to stay quiet, immersed in my own thoughts. I couldn't bear the idea that he might only love me for how I looked, and I didn't have the heart to tell him that I was pretty sure that I was only going to live another six months. From that perspective, what I looked like naked really didn't matter much.

ॐ ॐ ॐ

Surgery was scheduled for the following Tuesday, and I called Mark's office on Thursday to let him know that I was opting for the lumpectomy with radiation. I didn't get to talk with him personally, but left a message with the answering service. The decision was final: lumpectomy with radiation. On Friday, my medical oncologist, Dr. Denise Yardley, called to let me know the final results of all my tests: blood work was fine; CT scan showed a spot on my spine (but the MRI scan showed it wasn't cancer); chest X-ray was negative; and breast cancer pathology showed a slow-growing tumor that had probably been developing for at least ten years. Most importantly, the PET scan showed no evidence of cancer anywhere else in my body.

The final summary was a breast tumor slightly bigger than one-half inch that would hopefully be completely removed with one more surgery. There was no other evidence of cancer. Dr. Yardley was thrilled with the test results and said that she'd have copies for me at my office visit on Monday.

ॐ ॐ ॐ

The hematoma was still painful and I was grateful that Mark would remove it during my surgery the following week. My tossing and turning was keeping Curtis up, so he decided to sleep upstairs in the guest bedroom until things returned to normal. As I was drifting off to sleep Friday evening, the little curly-haired blonde girl reappeared in the meadow in the twilight. A tall man was in the distance, but as the little girl ran, he got closer and closer to catching her. She was laughing and playing in the long shadows when a dark cloud came over the field. Startled, I sat up in bed.

I heard the voice again and the white apparition appeared at the end of my bed, "Did you call me?"

"Who's there?"

"I thought I heard you call my name."

I felt the cool breeze again and knew who it was standing before me in dazzling white. "Well, now that you are here, I do have a question. Why are all my tests negative? I thought when you visited me last time and spoke to me about Jason dying it was because I was going to die too, in six months. But based upon the medical tests, it appears that I may live a long life after treatment. I had accepted that I was going to die soon and told you that I was willing to die for you. I even made sure that my will was up-to-date and that Curtis' children would be well taken care of. But if I'm going to live a longer life, why did you put me through all that? Why did you ask me if I was willing to die for you?"

The voice was clear, "I needed to know if you are for me or against me. Now that you believe in your heart that you are willing to give up your life for me at any time, you will not die in the next six months. I have work for you to do on my behalf and I need you on earth to be my eyes, my hands, and my feet."

Tears started to well up in my eyes. I wasn't crying in relief that I would live, instead I was crying because I felt needed. "Really? What could I possibly do for you?"

"Right now, I need you to heal and get well. Love me and feel my healing power as you go through your next surgery. I will comfort you as you rest in my arms. I'll let you know when I need you to do something."

Could I have possibly heard correctly? Could God really want me to rest and heal? I'd been prepared to do anything that He asked, but instead He wanted to delight in me so that I could become whole again.

With that, the apparition disappeared.

～ ～ ～

I fell back asleep with a new joy, not over living longer, but about having a real purpose in life, whatever that was going to be. As I fell asleep, the same dream started over, but this time I could see the little girl's face. It looked just like an old photograph of me when I was three years old. As I ran in circles, I delighted in being just outside the man's outstretched arms. I'd usually wake up just as the man was about to catch the little girl, but this time the dream was different. I began to tire and my running became slower and slower. Just then the man scooped me up into his arms and held me tight as I buried my head into his shoulder.

"Agatha, I love you. I have always loved you. It's time for you to quit running and rest with me."

I awoke on Saturday morning, feeling refreshed for the first time in months. I wanted to tell someone about the dream, but I couldn't tell Curtis that I was going to live, because I had never told him I was going to die.

5

After Surgery

The STRICT FATHER Model takes the view that life is difficult and that the world is fundamentally dangerous. Survival is a major concern and there are dangers and evils lurking everywhere, especially in the human soul. The primal experience behind the NURTURING PARENT Model is one of being cared for and cared about, having one's desires for loving interactions met, living as happily as possible, and deriving meaning from mutual interaction and care.

– George Lakoff

I was scheduled to meet with Dr. Yardley on Monday afternoon to go over my test results one more time before surgery. I'd already seen Dr. Hunt, the radiation oncologist, and he'd echoed Dr. Cooper's words that there was no difference in survival or cancer recurrence between a mastectomy, or a lumpectomy with radiation.

Dr. Yardley was also an old friend from Centennial. I trusted Denise totally and knew that she would have my best interests at heart. Even better, she was well known as one of the top breast cancer oncologists in the United States. Although I'd talked with her by phone the previous week, it was good to see her in person the day before surgery.

"Agatha, I see you've scheduled surgery with Dr. Cooper for tomorrow afternoon and Dr. Rodes will be your Anesthesiologist. Well, you have the two best guys taking care of you; you'll be in good hands. I know we talked about your test results on Friday, but I wondered if you've had time to think about them over the weekend. Do you have any questions?"

"I don't think so. We're all set for a lumpectomy tomorrow and Dr. Hunt will start radiation in about four to six weeks."

"I wanted to ask you about the decision to have a lumpectomy. Are you certain that you don't want to have a mastectomy?"

"But you're the one who first said that the survival rates were the same for a mastectomy, or lumpectomy with radiation. I'm hearing a hesitation in your voice; why are you asking me if I want to have a mastectomy? Did another test come back worse than you thought?"

"No, I still think that survival and cancer recurrence rates are the same. But did Dr. Cooper explain the results he got back from Vanderbilt, after he sent your pathology slides over there to be read? I just got the report myself."

"Yes, Dr. Cooper told me about the report, but the way he explained it, it sounded like it was the same as the first one."

"Well, the Vanderbilt pathology report shows a little more detail as to where the cancer cells are located on the edge of the tumor. Dr. Cooper is going to have to take quite a bit more breast tissue off than we originally thought. He's an excellent surgeon, but I'm not sure that you'll be pleased with the cosmetic results. There won't be much he can do to balance out your two sides. And the radiation on the left breast will change the tissue even more."

"Oh, dear." Just a few minutes before I'd been so convinced that the lumpectomy with radiation was the right decision. "What would you do if you were me?"

"I always recommend breast-conserving surgery, and that isn't a bad choice for you from a survival standpoint. But based upon these new pathology results and purely from a cosmetic standpoint, I'd have a mastectomy if I were you."

A friend of mine who was also going through breast cancer treatment was fond of saying, "You're going to have a lot of doctors looking after you, but you've got to pick a quarterback." Denise Yardley, my medical oncologist, is my quarterback.

"Thanks for being honest, Denise. I trust your advice."

It was a split second decision and with surgery scheduled for the next afternoon, I couldn't take the time to call Curtis and ask him what he thought. Plus, I knew what he would say: "I thought we talked about this and you weren't going to have a mastectomy unless you had to."

"Denise, can you do me a favor? Can you call Dr. Cooper right now and change my surgery tomorrow from a lumpectomy to a mastectomy? I know it's a longer surgery and that I'll have to stay in the hospital overnight, but I've changed my mind and I want to make sure the operating room scheduler gets the message about the change. I won't be able to get through to Dr. Cooper's office until late this afternoon because he's seeing patients, but he'll answer a call from you right away."

Denise left the room to call Dr. Cooper. I said a short prayer that Curtis would understand my decision, but all I could think about was what he would say when I told him. Would he say, "I'll love you no matter which surgery you have," or "We agreed that you'd have a lumpectomy with radiation and you've gone against my wishes?" I couldn't predict his response, but I hoped he was in a good mood when I got home.

ᡐ ᡐ ᡐ

I breathed a sigh of relief when I arrived and realized that Curtis wasn't home. I wondered why there wasn't the usual note in the kitchen, but I decided to start making dinner. I needed to eat early, because at midnight I had to start fasting for surgery. My phone rang and I grabbed it on the first ring, thinking that it was Curtis. Instead, I heard Dyer Rodes' friendly voice. "Hi! I wanted to check on you and let you know everything is set for your surgery tomorrow. I got the message from Mark that you've changed your plans and will have a mastectomy instead of the lumpectomy. The anesthesia is a little different, but very safe. I want you to know that I will be with you the whole time and won't let anything happen to you. I'll be there for you."

"Thanks, Dyer, that is really comforting to hear. See you tomorrow."

Just then, Curtis walked in and threw his car keys onto the table. "Well, it looks like I'm going to have to go to Memphis for work this week after all. I have to leave right after I take you to the hospital tomorrow morning. Do you think one of your girlfriends can give you a ride home?"

"Curtis, I need you to be there. Dr. Yardley and I talked about the pathology results from Vanderbilt, and I need to have a mastectomy. Dr. Cooper already knows of the change, but I'll have to be in the hospital overnight. I realize that I should have checked with you first, but there wasn't time. Please, don't be mad at me."

There was a dreadful silence, then Curtis said, "You need to have a mastectomy or you WANT to have a mastectomy? Which is it?"

"Dr. Yardley explained that I wouldn't look the same; I won't be balanced. If I have a mastectomy I can have reconstructive surgery that will make me look better when this is all over. That is important to me, too."

"I thought we agreed you were going to have a lumpectomy. You should have talked to me about this before changing your mind."

"Really, Curtis, there wasn't time with the surgery tomorrow. I had to let Dr. Cooper know today."

"Well, what's for dinner?" With that, Curtis poured himself a double shot of Jack Daniels, walked into the other room and turned on the TV, settling down in his favorite chair.

I couldn't believe that he had so abruptly changed the conversation. *Did he really not care that I was having surgery the next day and would need to stay in the hospital*? I followed him into the other room, but he was listening intently to a news reporter on the TV.

"But, what about tomorrow? I need you to stay at the hospital with me."

"I guess I'll call the Commissioner and tell him I can't make the trip until Wednesday," he said without even looking up.

I was hoping that he would cancel the trip entirely but I didn't dare ask. He'd been without a job for so long when we moved to Tennessee and I knew that he didn't want to do anything to lose this one. Because he'd asked me not to share my cancer news with anyone outside the immediate family, I suspected that he hadn't told his boss either, so it would be awkward to say that he couldn't go on a business trip without having a good reason.

I finished making dinner and walked back into the living room to tell him we'd be ready to eat in about five minutes. He'd fallen asleep in his favorite chair, snoring. I hated it when judgmental thoughts started playing in my head, but I wondered if he'd stopped off for a drink on the way home from work and that was why he wasn't home earlier. I said another silent prayer of thanksgiving. Once he'd fallen asleep, drinking or not, he was always out until the next morning.

I wanted to call the ladies in the PORCH CLUB, but Curtis's "gag order" had extended to my friends. He'd even told me not to call the church when I wanted to have my name added to the prayer list. I wasn't sure why it had to be such a secret that I had cancer, but I had to respect his wishes. His mother was still being treated for liver cancer, but she was doing well. It had to be hard for him to have his mother and his wife both living with cancer. Maybe his behavior was just his way of coping with the difficult news.

ೀ ೀ ೀ

The next day was hotter than expected, but I was packed and ready for surgery. I said another silent prayer and told the dogs I'd see them soon. I was nervous and tried to make small talk on the way to the hospital, but Curtis said he hadn't slept well and wasn't in the mood to talk, so we rode most of the way in silence. He did say that he was postponing his trip to Memphis for one day since I had to stay overnight in the hospital. I was relieved when Dr. Cooper and Dr. Rodes walked into the pre-op room and assured me that everything was going to be fine, even though they were running behind schedule from the morning surgeries. Since I was staying overnight and Curtis wasn't going to Memphis, it didn't matter how late I got out of surgery. Dr. Cooper had already reserved a hospital room for me.

Everything went as planned in surgery and Mark came to visit me in the Recovery Room, saying the surgery went great and that I was a wonderful patient. Then a nurse told me that when I was waking up I'd taken a swing at one of the other nurses. How embarrassing! I did remember asking for more morphine for the pain, and hoped it hadn't contributed to my bad behavior. I was glad that I didn't remember anything else from the surgery. Dyer came to see me in Recovery and said that he'd gone out to the waiting room to tell Curtis everything was fine, but couldn't find him. He had left a voicemail on his cell phone number.

"That's strange. Curtis didn't have anywhere to go. I wonder why he wasn't in the waiting room." I told Dyer I was worried that Curtis wouldn't be able to find me, as I was going to a room in Main Tower, instead of in the Women's Hospital like we'd originally been told.

"Well I hope he can find me when he gets back. He's got my iPod and my clothes."

Dyer assured me he'd keep trying to reach him by phone until they connected, but for now I needed to rest and not worry about anything except healing.

"Sounds good," I mumbled as I drifted off to sleep, the morphine kicking in. I was hopeful that Curtis hadn't left the hospital and was at a local pub, but I was in no condition to go look for him. The next thing I knew, I was waking up in a hospital room with a nurse taking my blood pressure.

"Have you seen my husband?"

"He was here for a little bit and dropped off your suitcase. He said he was going out to get something to eat and would be back after dinner."

Around 7:30 p.m., Curtis came into the room and asked how I was feeling. I wasn't in any pain but was pretty groggy from the medication. "Okay."

"Well, it looks like they're taking good care of you here. I'll head home and feed the dogs some dinner and be back to get you in the morning."

"Can't you stay for a little while? I need some company."

"Well, the dogs haven't eaten and it's almost eight o'clock. I really need to get home, but I'll be back tomorrow." With that, Curtis gave me a peck on the cheek and left. That's when the tears started. I didn't know if it was a reaction to the morphine, but I felt cold and very lonely. I just wanted to be held and there was no one there. My mother had been gone for fifteen years and Curtis had just walked out of the room and vanished.

I rang for the nurse. "Can you get my iPod out for me, please? I need some music."

I drifted off to sleep being serenaded by Josh Turner's *Your Man* from his *Long Black Train* album, followed by Alan Jackson's *Red Like A Rose*. I hit the repeat button and played the two albums over and over again until I fell asleep around 2 a.m.

ھو ھو ھو

The next morning I awoke with just mild pain and was anxious to get home. Curtis arrived around 10 a.m. and was annoyed to find that the discharge paperwork hadn't been completed.

"How come we have to wait? It's not like you didn't know she was scheduled to go home today."

I held my tongue because the nurses had been wonderful. I'd eaten a little bit late in the evening, and then they had given me pain medication throughout the night so I'd be comfortable. Dr. Cooper made rounds early in the morning and said everything was okay for me to go home. I had no complaints about the care I'd received, but it would be good to sleep in my own bed.

The long list of discharge instructions were written down for me: no shower for forty-eight hours and I had to keep all the bandages on until then. Report any fever or uncontrolled pain to the doctor immediately. The biggest surprise was the two drains that were coming out of my left side; they hurt worse than anything, and were draining a bloody, awful-looking fluid. The nurse said I'd have to measure it and record the amount every few hours so Dr. Cooper could look at the log when I saw him in the office the following week. The drains were definitely the worst part.

Throughout the night the nurses had taken care of the drains, but now they were my responsibility. I was sure that Dr. Cooper had mentioned the drains during my last office visit, but I couldn't recall that conversation at all. Curtis left the room as the nurse was explaining the drain instructions. He couldn't stand to see the sight of blood.

I tried to be brave, but I was resentful again that I was going through this alone. I really wished Mom were here to take care of me. I was tired of being the strong one all the time.

When we got home, Curtis told me that he hadn't talked his boss out of the Memphis trip and would need to leave first thing the next morning. Because of the drains, I was going to have to sleep upright in a chair, so that night I got settled into the living room with extra pillows and the TV remote control. "I guess I'll be okay while you're gone. These drains are 'icky' but the nurse said that's normal. They'll be out in seven to ten days, so it won't be forever. I'll see if the next door neighbors can check on me."

As I drifted off to sleep that night, I wondered what I would look like when the bandages came off. As my mind wandered, I realized that I hadn't thought about Jimmy once since the surgeries started over eight weeks ago. Curtis and I hadn't even been to church in almost two months. I fell asleep wondering if Jimmy still read at the lectern during the early Mass.

I slept fitfully throughout the night, afraid to move for fear of dislodging a drain and bleeding to death. I got up groggily the next morning and measured the drain output, noting that it was a lot more than I thought it should be. I debated whether to call Dr. Cooper, then decided to wait another day before I panicked. I called my next-door neighbor and explained that I'd just had surgery the day before and Curtis had to leave on a trip to Memphis. I was relieved when she said that they'd be in town for the whole week and to call if I needed anything. Curtis packed and left for Memphis around noon, saying that he'd be back sometime on Friday after his meetings were done.

Around 4 p.m., the doorbell rang. It was a girl from work bringing chicken soup and chocolate chip cookies. I welcomed the company and someone to talk with to take my mind off the surgery and the pain. I hadn't asked my boss to keep this last surgery confidential, and news traveled fast. A huge plant was delivered from friends in Bethesda, Maryland, and David called to say that his family and his whole church were praying for me. I was amazed at the outpouring of love from everyone, particularly people I didn't know that well. My co-workers had sent food, the ladies from the PORCH CLUB brought gifts and food, and near and distant friends were calling and sending well wishes via email.

I realized that I hadn't heard from anyone from our church. I had told Curtis that I wanted to be on the prayer list and called the church that Monday afternoon when I realized that I'd be in the hospital overnight. Maybe they had lost the message. It was a huge church and it was probably hard to keep track of all the families.

I picked up the phone to call the church again, but was interrupted by the doorbell. It was another plant from my former coworkers in San Antonio. They'd heard through emails that I'd been diagnosed with breast cancer and wanted to send their love. Mark and Dyer both called to check on me that evening, and I prayed eagerly that night in thanksgiving for such wonderful friends and doctors. I felt loved, not because they were family and had to love me, but that they loved me because God loved them so much. I was amazed because I had done absolutely nothing to deserve this outpouring of love. I had always been the one that cared for family members when they were ill, and this was the first time that I was the recipient.

Over the next three days, my mood swings were tremendous. I was relieved when Dr. Cooper said that he thought they had gotten all the cancer, but I was still anxious because the final pathology results wouldn't be back until Monday. On the one hand, I was glad that Curtis was out of town so I could rest; on the other hand, I wanted to have him here to comfort me with a hug and tell me what he was feeling. When I first told him that I had cancer, he seemed withdrawn. He never said he was upset, worried, or anxious. I wasn't sure life would ever be the same again and I wondered if my relationship with Curtis would change. We'd been so close, physically and emotionally, those first years of marriage, but it was different now. If I could only figure out what was wrong, I'd fix it. I wanted to live the rest of my life fully alive, and I wanted to share that fire with Curtis.

ᏜᎧ ᏜᎧ ᏜᎧ

The shock of having my nipple removed was nothing compared to what I felt during my first post-surgical shower that Friday morning. After removing the bandage, I looked in the mirror and saw the concave hole where my left breast had been. I burst into tears, and was relieved that Curtis wasn't there to see my chest, or to see me crying. I'd seen pictures of mastectomies but it is totally different when it is you. I'd chosen a "delayed reconstruction", which meant I'd have to wait eight weeks before plastic surgery started. I kept reminding myself that it was only two months, my body would have a chance to heal, and that the important thing was that I was alive. But I still felt extremely ugly. I knew I had made the right choice with the mastectomy, but I wondered if it would have been better to have both breasts removed. At least then I wouldn't feel so lopsided.

When Curtis got home late Friday evening, I asked him how his trip was and if he wanted to see the incision. "No, you know how I hate blood. I want to remember you the way that you were. It will be awhile, but I know that your plastic surgeon will have you looking as good as new in no time."

That night, I came to bed and started to snuggle with Curtis. "I missed you this week. The girls were here from the PORCH CLUB and the next-door neighbors came over to check on me every day, but I still wish you had been here. It was a tough week."

"Well, you know that I have to work out of town sometimes, in fact, I have to go to Knoxville on Tuesday next week and won't be back again until Friday. Why are you sleeping in bed, don't you still have to sleep sitting up with the drains in?"

"Dr. Cooper said that it was okay to lie flat now as long as I'm careful, and I missed you."

I snuggled closer, hoping that Curtis would understand that I missed him physically as well as emotionally. "It's been over a week since we've had sex. I always miss you when you are out of town."

"I don't think it's a good idea for us to have sex just yet. I'd hate to have something happen and dislodge the drains. I better sleep in the guest room until you get the drains out and things are back to normal."

"Look, I even printed this from the Internet. There's a very helpful website that discusses different positions and well, options, during these two weeks after you've had a mastectomy. Some of them are the ones you like. I promise it will be okay."

"I'd never forgive myself if you bled to death."

"Two weeks is a long time for us not to sleep together."

Curtis didn't respond; he just gathered his pillow and headed upstairs to the guest room. I was totally confused, because this had never happened before. We'd always thought that sex was the cure for any problem and had liberally applied the treatment. I couldn't help but wonder if he was having an affair. It would explain the recent increase in his trips to Knoxville.

ৡৡ ৡৡ ৡৡ

It was a very long two long weeks, but the drains finally came out. That was a huge milestone in my recovery and I felt 100% better. I knew it would make a difference for Curtis, too.

Friday evening after dinner I said, "Do you want to see the incision now? The drains are out and everything is starting to heal."

"Will I be grossed out with the way you look?"

"I don't know, but let's go into the bedroom and I'll take my shirt and the prosthesis off slowly so it won't be as much of a shock."

Curtis stared at the hole that had been my left breast and said nothing. I looked into his eyes as if I could see his thoughts. After a few minutes, he left the room, went upstairs, and turned on the TV. Feeling lost and alone, I got dressed and wondered what to do next. I'd read a lot on the Internet about the emotional aftermath of breast cancer and how husbands react. Sometimes it takes a while for them to realize that their wife is going to recover and normal relationships can be resumed. I just hoped that it didn't take too long for Curtis to realize that I still loved him. And I hoped that he still loved me.

Music has always soothed my soul, and I let Alan Jackson sing to me from my iPod for the rest of the evening.

❧ ❧ ❧

The following Monday, I returned to work with Dr. Cooper's blessing. He'd suggested I take it easy my first day back, but said it was up to me to pace myself. After being off almost two full weeks, I was anxious to get back to work, see friends, and get caught up on things in the office. It was better to be active than to mope around the house agonizing over the way I looked. On the way out the door that morning, Curtis told me that I needed to come home at noon.

"I'll see how I feel. Dr. Cooper said it was okay to work a full day if I felt like it. I just won't know until I try, and besides, I want to see everyone. My boss and the staff have been wonderful throughout all my surgeries, sending me notes that they're praying for me. I want to thank everyone."

In truth, I just needed to feel like things were getting back to normal and thought that working all day would be a good start. I hoped he would understand that.

"I said that I want to see you home at noon. I don't want you working too hard and getting tired out on your first day back. I'll be home waiting for you."

When I got to work I made the rounds of the offices, thanking everyone for their prayers, then I dove into getting caught up on email and a few notes on my desk. Before I knew it, it was lunchtime. I felt great and made a quick call home to tell Curtis that I was going to work a little longer. I left a message when he didn't pick up, "Feeling great and decided to work all day. Should be home around 5 p.m."

When I got back to my desk around 1:30 p.m., however, I started feeling queasy. I didn't know if it was something I ate, but I was still having some intermittent pain where one of the drains had been. I didn't want to take any pain medication since I still had to drive home. I thought about calling Curtis to come get me, but decided to sit quietly until I felt better. Around 3:00 p.m., I went to my boss' office and told her that I was headed home for the day. I thanked her for her kindness through all the surgeries and how glad I was to be at work again.

"It's good to have you back. See how you feel in the morning. If you need to take the day off or come in late, just give me a call."

What a great boss! No lecture about not finishing the whole day. I thought about it a lot on the way home. I didn't remember being compassionate with my employees when they had problems. I was raised in the management style that employees should park their problems at the door and not bring them into the workplace. After all, if you start making exceptions for one person, then everyone has something going on in their life that interferes with work. Pretty soon, none of your staff is working a full shift.

I was surprised that these thoughts still popped into my head. I was so appreciative of my boss' compassion, but I certainly didn't measure up when I had been in the boss' chair. I knew that today wasn't the day I would reconcile that conflict. Years of management training couldn't be undone just because I was the one that needed the exception.

Finally, I pulled into the driveway, relieved that I would be lying down soon. I could feel the exhaustion rising in my shoulders.

When I walked in the door, Curtis said, "You look awful. I thought I told you to come home at noon and it's already almost 4 p.m."

With that I burst into tears. "I do feel awful. The pain kicked in after lunch and I felt too sick to drive home. I would have been home before now but I was afraid to drive. All I wanted was to spend a full day at work so that I could feel normal again, like I'd never had cancer. Please don't yell at me."

"If you'd come home at noon like I told you to, you wouldn't feel so bad. I told you not to work a full day."

I was shocked that he was so unsympathetic. I was softly crying and he didn't seem to care. "I'm too sick to eat dinner. You can eat by yourself. I'm going to bed and don't wake me when you leave for Knoxville tomorrow."

With that, I went to bed. Strangely, my crying stopped. Instead, I resolved to focus all my energies on getting my strength back. After all, I still had more surgeries in the future, when I would start the reconstruction. Maybe then my marriage would be back to normal, too.

৯০ ৯০ ৯০

I continued to feel better each day, and before I knew it, it was December, and time to start the next phase of surgery. The PORCH CLUB had been wonderful, getting together every month for lemon drop martinis at Maggiano's. They were so encouraging and such good friends.

David also called and emailed to offer his support. He had become a special friend, and since he'd been through cancer with Jason he knew how tough it is. One day, when I met him in the cafeteria for lunch, he asked a particularly insightful question: "What did you fear most about the cancer? Was it a fear of the pain, of losing your hair, or of dying? Everyone has a different fear."

"That's a great question, and I've had a lot of time to think about it over these past six months. The first few days, my biggest fear was all that you've mentioned: having uncontrolled pain, losing my appearance (especially my hair), or even the unknown of dying. But by the next week I realized that my biggest fear was that I would lose my faith. I knew that as long as I trusted God I would be okay, no matter what happened. I was so angry after Jason's death, but the day I was diagnosed with cancer, I finally understood. I don't control anything, and God controls everything." I took a deep breath and decided to plunge ahead and tell David about my two encounters with Christ.

64

"I've never told anyone this, David, not even Curtis. But I feel like I can share this with you since you and Jason are connected to the story. You know last August, on the first anniversary of Jason's death when you and your family were in North Carolina? That's the day I got the call from Dr. Cooper that I had cancer. I was still off work recuperating from my lumpectomy and had been grieving your loss all morning. With Dr. Cooper's call, the attention turned right back around to me. I believe that I got that call on the one-year anniversary for a reason."

I hoped that David wouldn't think I was crazy, but I thought, *Gee, it really happened, so why am I worried about telling the truth?*

I continued, "I wasn't sleeping well that afternoon. I was grieving for you and your family in North Carolina and upset about my own diagnosis. I was alone in the bedroom when I heard a voice and saw a white figure at the end of the bed. I couldn't make out who it was, but I felt a presence. First there was a cold breeze and then the figure spoke. It said, 'Jason was willing to die for me, are you?'"

We both had tears in our eyes. It took a few minutes to compose myself, and then I told him that I had answered "Yes" when the figure returned later that evening.

David started to speak, but I interrupted him.

"I know. It's a pretty phenomenal story, but that's not all. I was in a whirlwind for the next two weeks, undergoing tests trying to determine the extent of the cancer. I was preoccupied with preparing myself to die in six months."

"Why six months?"

"It just seemed like everything I'd read about really serious cancers said the life expectancy was around six months."

"But Jason lived longer than that. We had him with us twenty months after he was diagnosed."

"I know, I wasn't thinking very rationally at that point. I just knew I was going to die soon."

65

"So, I'm confused. You responded to this figure that you were willing to die in six months and that was three months ago. You seem awfully calm for someone who's going to die soon."

"Well, there is another part of the story. I had a second visit from the same figure."

"When was this?"

"About two weeks after the initial call from Dr. Cooper. I was getting ready for my third surgery and was still convinced that I would die within six months, even though all the tests were coming back negative. My blood work was fine, I had a CT scan and MRI scan that showed no cancer, and even a PET scan was clean. I didn't know what it meant."

"So, did you talk with the doctors about the tests?"

"Yes, but I decided to pray to God, too."

I told David about the second encounter, when the figure told me that he needed me to be his eyes, hands and feet on earth and that I wouldn't die within six months.

I swallowed hard before asking the next question. If anyone would understand, it would be David.

"Do you believe that I actually saw Christ?"

"From what you've told me, yes. Christ walks with us every step of the way, and as the human form of God he takes on our characteristics. Yes, I believe that it was Christ."

"Then what did he mean by, 'I have more work for you to do?'"

"That's the question that we all ask. I can't answer it, but Christ can. You'll need to be patient. He'll give you more information when the time is right. Didn't he say that he wanted you to 'heal' first? You're just starting reconstructive surgery and that will take at least six months. Maybe he wants you to go through that before he'll visit you in person again. Or, maybe the healing that he spoke of is more emotional or spiritual, rather than physical. But I'm confident that he'll pay you another visit, but it will be in God's time."

I then told David about my recurring dream about the little girl who had repeatedly escaped from the unknown man in the meadow. David's eyes widened when I revealed that in the last dream, the little girl looked like me and was finally caught by the man. And it all happened the same night that I been visited by Christ.

"Do you think that little girl is me and the man was my father?"

I hadn't shared a lot about my childhood and how strict my father had been, so I now gave David a quick description so he'd understand the reason for my question.

"Agatha, I'm not convinced that the man in your dream was your father."

"But who else could it be? In every dream, it was my father's build and stature. Even though I couldn't see his face and the figure never spoke, it 'felt' like my father. Strangely though, I never remember playing with him like that, and never in a meadow. It was the last dream, when I felt a wind and this figure scooped me up in his arms. It was so wonderful, like I had finally found a home. If it wasn't my father, who could have been?"

"I think that was God the Father, as the Holy Spirit."

I was sobered by the possibility. David had given me a lot to think about.

୨୦ ୨୦ ୨୦

That dream never recurred, but it was replaced by a new dream in which I was traveling to a faraway place to help take care of some people I didn't know. I didn't recognize any faces, but there were lots of little children, all of them hungry for food and attention. In my dream, I would try to talk with them, but they answered in a language I didn't understand. I knew a little Spanish from living in San Antonio, but it didn't sound like any Spanish words I knew.

୨୦ ୨୦ ୨୦

67

I had surgery in December to place an expander in the left breast tissue; it would remain there for three to four months, and was slowly expanded with saline injections until there was a pocket to accept an implant. I was excited when I woke up from surgery and I no longer had a "concave" hole. The expander was making a little "bump" that gave me hope and made me feel a little better about the way I looked. It was uncomfortable, but I figured it was well worth it to be on the road to recovery.

The following week, I met David for lunch. I told him about my new dream and asked if he had any idea what it might mean. He'd just returned from a mission trip to Guatemala and had been to Honduras many times. I asked him what it was like to travel overseas and care for others. I'd only been to Canada and Mexico, so I had no idea what the rest of the world looked like, except what I had seen on TV, online, or in the newspapers. David's face lit up as he shared some of his incredible experiences, serving as a pharmacist in makeshift medical clinics in faraway places.

It was on Saturday the week before Christmas when I had a vision that I was compelled to get a passport so I could do some international mission work as a pharmacist. I eagerly told Curtis and suggested that we drive to the post office that day and apply for passports together. Curtis was skeptical that I was being called to serve in a foreign country, but if that was what I wanted to do, he said wasn't going to stop me.

"It would be great if this is something we could do together. I know that it would enrich our marriage and spiritual life. I'm so thankful to be alive and we have so many things to be grateful for. I just want to give back, to help others who need it."

"I'm okay with you going if that is what you feel you need to do. I might help raise money here, but I'm not at all interested in traveling to any foreign countries. It's too dangerous. Why don't you call the church on Monday and see if they have any mission trips they're planning for next year?"

"Great idea, Honey."

It would have been better if Curtis and I served together on a mission trip. There were plenty of opportunities to help people in Nashville, but I was feeling restless. David and I often talked about his medical mission trips to Honduras and Guatemala. He always said that he got much more out of serving than he ever left behind.

Foreign travel would have to wait, however. It was the first Christmas after my diagnosis and I wanted everything to be perfect for the holiday. We were flying to Oklahoma to be with Curtis' family, but it was bittersweet. His mom had died of cancer just a few months before. Everything in life wasn't perfect, but I kept reminding myself how fortunate I was to be alive.

6

Back to Church

"There's nothing in the world so demoralizing as money."

– Sophocles, in Antigone

Curtis and I had only been to church a few times since my cancer saga had started in July, and he wasn't interested in going without me. The only time in my life that I hadn't been a faithful churchgoer was during college. When I returned to church I had promised that no matter where I lived, I'd show up whenever the doors were open. I never thought that I would be too sick to go to church and I had missed the forgiving power of the Eucharist.

Since we hadn't been attending church, our financial contribution was less than usual and I wanted to make a larger donation to make up the difference. The Christmas Dinner Dance scheduled the Saturday before Christmas was also a fundraiser for the youth group, so I suggested to Curtis that we give a "catch-up" donation. Curtis agreed, so the Monday before, I stopped by the church office to see if there were still tickets available. I was looking forward to going; I was feeling pretty good after the surgery, and I was also hoping to meet some people, as we hadn't really gotten to know anyone in the two years we'd been attending.

As I wrote out the check to cover the missed donations, a thought crossed my mind: *I wonder if Jimmy will be there?* As quickly as the thought appeared, I chastised myself for even thinking it. I needed to focus on rekindling the romance in my marriage, not on romantic thoughts about other men.

"Ma'am, for that amount of money we'll give you ten tickets," the church secretary offered, "That's a whole table. Maybe you'd like to invite your friends?"

"That's okay, we only need two tickets. You can use the rest as a donation. We don't know eight other people from the church to invite." I volunteered the story of my breast cancer diagnosis and how thankful I was just to be alive for another birthday and Christmas. The receptionist said she was glad I was okay, adding, "God bless you," as I walked out the door.

The phone rang a few hours after I arrived home. "Are you the lady that just gave the large donation to the dinner dance?"

"I guess that's me; I was just by the church and did write a check for tickets to the dinner dance."

"I wanted to thank you, because I'm the chair of the committee that planned the evening as a fundraiser for the youth. We were short money for the band and food and since the event is this Saturday, we were afraid that we were going to have to take the deficit out of the church's general fund. Father told us that unless we sold enough tickets to cover expenses we couldn't hold the event next year. Your check was the exact amount that we needed to cover the expenses, with a little left over. I just wanted to thank you and to tell you that it is a sign from God that you stopped by to give us this money. I'm really looking forward to meeting you and your husband on Saturday night."

I was so excited on Saturday. I had shopped all week to find a formal dress that was flattering and wouldn't show the breast prosthesis. After three days, I found the perfect dress: a short black skirt with a white bodice that only needed a slight alteration in the V-neck. The dinner was scheduled to start at seven, but I was dressed and ready to go by six. I wanted so much to feel attractive, to dress up and go out for a night on the town

71

after all I'd been through. Curtis was ready at six too, and we decided to have a cocktail before heading to the church. Curtis didn't particularly enjoy meeting new people, and I knew that he was hoping the liquor would calm his nerves.

"You look great in your new suit, Curtis!"

"I just hope everyone else is in a suit too, and not a tuxedo."

"I'm sure we'll be just fine. I'm in a short party dress, and when I paid for the tickets the receptionist said tuxedos were not required."

As we drove to the church, I noticed the tiny snowflakes dancing in the air. It was a crisp night, and a magical one. "Curtis, I'm just so thankful to be alive. Thank you for taking me to the dinner dance tonight. I know it's not something that you particularly like doing. I'm grateful."

"Well, let's hope it's not too stuffy."

The church hall had been converted into a land of enchantment, with bubbling fountains, red Santa Clauses and green elves serving drinks and hors d'oeuvres. As we checked in, the lady at the registration table said, "Your table is number two, right in front of the bandstand. You've got a great table with interesting people. The man who plays the piano at the early service on Sundays and his wife will be sitting with you. Have a great evening."

As we made our way to Table #2, I silently hoped that it wasn't too "upfront". Curtis didn't like to be the center of attention, preferring to hang out in the back of the room. I hoped for this one night it would be okay. I rationalized that everyone would be eating and dancing and it shouldn't matter where we sat.

Almost all the guests had arrived when the Master of Ceremonies indicated that everyone should take their seats for a few announcements. As I sat down, I noticed that there was a menu card at each place with the buffet menu on one side and a list of "Sponsors" on the reverse. To my surprise, Curtis and I were listed as a Silver Sponsor for the evening. *How efficient*, I thought. *I*

72

only gave them the check on Monday; they must have had them printed up since then.

Just then, Curtis turned the card over and saw our names under the "Silver Sponsor" group. Under his breath, he growled, "What's the meaning of this? Exactly how much money did we give to the church?"

I responded calmly, "Let's not discuss it here. What's done is done. We can talk about it when we get home tonight."

"We're going to talk about it now. How much money did we give?"

I was frightened when I saw the look in his eyes. "I'm not going to talk about it now."

"Well, you know that I can look it up in our bank account online and see the cancelled check, so you might as well tell me now."

"I said we'd talk about it later." Just then I heard the MC announce our names, asking the three Silver Sponsors to stand and be recognized for their contribution. I stood, but Curtis stayed glued to his seat, glaring up at me.

When I sat down, I said, "Curtis, let's not ruin the evening. We talked about giving money to the church for all the Sundays we missed when I was sick. I'm grateful I'm alive and we can afford it. Remember, we talked about it before I went by the church office this past Monday and gave them the check. You told me it was okay."

The explanation wasn't enough. Curtis decided that the best way to handle his anger was to be silent to me and to everyone else. He wouldn't speak when spoken to and when our table was called to go through the buffet line he mumbled something about not being hungry. In the meantime, he used all the drink tickets we'd been given when we checked in.

The gentleman to my right at the table asked me if Curtis was feeling sick since he wasn't eating. I stammered something about him having a big lunch that day and hoped that the others wouldn't notice that Curtis was the only one in the room that still had an empty plate. The servers were just getting ready to clear all the food from the tables so the dance could start when Curtis decided that he wanted something to eat. He jumped up from the table, grabbed his plate, and then started complaining that there was no roast beef left and only turkey for the hot entree. Holding back tears, I decided that it was time to go home and skip the dance.

When we got outside, I realized that Curtis had drunk too much wine to drive, so I drove home in a light snowstorm. It was hard to manage since I'd just had surgery and my left arm was still painful. The roads were slick, and the icy trees that had looked so magical just a few hours before now looked ominous. I managed to navigate the short two miles to the house by driving twenty miles an hour, but I burst into tears the minute we were inside.

"How could you embarrass me like that? Refusing to stand up and be recognized for giving money to the church and then not talking to me or anyone else all evening, like you are mad at the world and everyone in it. How could you complain about the food choices after you refused to go through the buffet line when it was our turn? Do you realize that everyone at our table asked me if you were sick because you were acting so strangely? Your behavior was awful and ruined this special night for me. I told you that I wanted to get dressed up, go out with my husband, and feel beautiful just one more time in my life. I wanted tonight to be special to celebrate the miracle that I'm still alive. If you ever pull the silent treatment stunt in public again, I will divorce you. You can count on it."

"Is that a threat?"

"Take it however you want."

Could I have just threatened my husband with divorce? I had no answers on how to repair my marriage. With that, I went upstairs and slept in the upstairs bedroom, alternating between anger and tears.

♫ ♫ ♫

I needed six months of saline injections to expand the tissue of my left breast enough to accept a silicone implant. I was thrilled with my plastic surgeon, Dr. Donald Griffin. He'd come highly recommended and was reassuring at each visit. Every month he injected more saline into the expander. Even though I'd have back spasms for a few days, I didn't care. I was anxious to get the implant on the left side and to have a smaller implant on the right to "balance" everything out.

Three months into the "expansion" phase, I decided to try to play golf again. I'd played varsity golf at the University of Oklahoma and continued playing for fun after college, but I hadn't played in the nine months since this whole ordeal had begun. I called up Dr. Maikis, my OB/GYN, and made a date to play in an EWGA get-together that Saturday. I knew that with my doctor along, I'd be in good hands should anything go wrong when I swung a golf club with the expander in.

I got up early, excited about playing golf. I didn't have any expectations of shooting a really good round, I was just thankful to play. I had taken a shower and was getting dressed when I remembered that I needed to print a $10.00 off coupon for the golf course. As I sat down at the computer, I was horrified to see that the last opened browser was a picture of a voluptuous girl without any clothes on. It was definitely pornography, not art. I was too shocked to speak. I thought (or had hoped) that all that was over when the Playboy subscription had lapsed the year before, but apparently I was wrong.

I forgot all about printing the coupon, and couldn't bear to face Curtis, who was in another room. I called out to him that I was leaving and headed out the door. I was so angry by the time I got to the golf course that I immediately confided in Dr. Maikis. She was right when she said that I had to confront Curtis, but it wasn't going to be easy. Our sex life had been pretty dismal for the past year.

When I got home, I tried to remain calm as I told Curtis that we needed to talk. I burst into tears when I told him that I had seen the pornography on the computer and tried to explain that I felt ugly enough without him looking at other women, especially those without any clothes on. Curtis said, "What pornography? I haven't looked at that stuff in months. You must have dreamed it."

"I know I didn't dream it, it was right there on the computer when I went to print a golf coupon."

"Prove it. I bet it's not in the browsing history because it didn't happen."

With that, I started sobbing uncontrollably.

Curtis said, "So are you saying that God put that website on the computer so you'd get upset? Because I certainly didn't do it and we're the only two in the house."

"No, I'm not saying that God put it there, but I saw it and I want you to know how it makes me feel."

"But if I didn't do it, then I'm not responsible, so you shouldn't feel bad about it."

I left the room and came back a few minutes later with some pillows. "So you say that you didn't have anything to do with that being on the computer and it's all in my imagination? Well, I'll just be more comfortable moving into the guest bedroom until I sort all this out. I'm sure you'll understand."

ço ço ço

I monopolized the next meeting of the PORCH CLUB. I'd always been guarded when sharing personal stuff about my marriage, but this time the first thing I told them was that I'd moved into the spare bedroom because of the naked woman I saw on the computer. At first they didn't offer much advice, but I was grateful for their sympathy. Kim spoke, "I just can't imagine how you feel. Do you think this is payback because you had a mastectomy instead of a lumpectomy and changed the surgery without consulting him?"

"No, not really. We've had issues with pornography since we got married. He said that it was his 'bachelor' subscription to

Playboy and that he subscribed because the articles were so good. There was no arguing with him about his motives. He'd get angry if I suggested that he bought it for the centerfolds. And then there were the B movies. Shortly after we got married, he suggested that we watch some movies together. Mostly people having sex, sometimes three together, or two girls together. He said it turned him on so he'd be a better lover.

"I was pretty lost and didn't know what a good Christian wife should do. I didn't have anyone that I could confide in, so I watched. After a while it struck me that it was wrong even for a married couple to be watching those movies, so I refused. I wonder if he didn't keep watching them alone when I wasn't home. I never go through his desk; that's his private area. But I'll bet he put the movies there after I protested.

"Thinking back on the past few years, I just buried my head hoping the problem would go away. Now I can see that it was always there. I'm so ashamed to be telling you this. Why would a husband have to watch those kinds of movies or read Playboy to have sex with his wife? And all this was before I had the mastectomy."

Carol put a sympathetic hand on my arm, "I'm so sorry for you."

"I just don't know what to do. I feel like I keep ending up back in the same place. When my first marriage was dying, I didn't try at all to make it work. I just wanted someone to love me. Instead of suggesting counseling or trying to save my marriage, I just started the affair with Curtis and filed for a divorce three months later. Dave didn't even contest it. By that time, we weren't talking at all and getting lawyers involved didn't help.

"I'm telling you all this because I've come to realize that my relationship with Curtis started with sex as the foundation. It was an attraction, a lust, arms that were willing to say, 'I love you' when I felt insecure in my marriage. It was based upon sex and never really moved past that. We were both hung up on the way we looked, we exercised and dieted all the time and even gaining a few pounds would send me into the doldrums until I lost them.

I wanted to have a real marriage, where two people confide in each other, trust each other, and love Christ together, but we always ended up in bed. We'd even joked before we got married that as long as the sex was still good, we'd never get a divorce. How sad is that.

"Our marriage was fun at first, but a few times when I was lonely or insecure, Curtis made it worse by telling me that he didn't need 'drama' in his life. I got to the point where I wouldn't share anything but good news with him because it made me look weak in his eyes. But when the cancer hit, I had no choice but to tell him. How fitting that I got a form of cancer that changed my appearance and interfered with our sex life! I can't imagine what it would be like to have a husband who loved you even when you had only one breast.

"I don't know if there is any way to repair our marriage. I feel so useless, like I'm damaged goods. We haven't had sex since I moved into the spare bedroom a few weeks ago and all we do is argue. He starts drinking early in the evening, then wakes me up at 2 a.m., bellowing, 'You're not going to divorce me are you?' I have to get some sleep; I'm working full-time, going to school part-time and still have more surgeries ahead. I'm exhausted all of the time."

Jackie said, "Don't you think it's time to go visit a priest for some counseling? You are on a very rocky road and you need some outside help. I know how much you love Curtis' family and the children. Don't throw it all away over this pornography thing. It must make you feel awful, but you can overcome this if you're both willing to try."

"I don't know, Jackie. I suggested that we go for counseling when I first moved to the spare bedroom, but Curtis was resistant. Then I suggested that after church each Sunday, we talk about the sermon or the readings. I think what we need is more God in our relationship. But even that has turned out horribly. The last few weeks we've ended up in these huge fights over Scripture. We have very different views of God. His view is that God is a 'STRICT FATHER' who has rules and likes to catch us breaking them. When God finds out, He exacts punishment, trying to get His people into line. Curtis brought up the example of Adam and Eve in the Garden of Eden and how they were banished from the Garden, with harsh punishments for all of mankind.

"My view of God is so different. My God is a God of Love, more like a 'NURTURING PARENT' who has rules, but who keeps taking us back with grace and mercy every time we mess up. I don't believe that it gives us a license to keep going out and sinning, but it does give us freedom from the guilt Satan uses to trap us. We go from trying to play by the rules and failing every day, to wanting to be good people to please God, to make Him happy. It's a totally different way of looking at life.

"Curtis and I can't seem to break through the differences. I'm not a rule-breaker either, but I'm studying how Jesus treated people and I see nothing but love for everyone. Although he rebukes the woman at the well in the Gospel of John, he does it in private way. Instead of scolding her, he shows her a better way, a 'living water' that will make her life so much richer with him, instead of all the adulterous relationships she's had. I relate to the woman at the well, because it is me. Jesus treated me with kindness and forgave all my sins, and now I want to please him."

Kim said, "Wow! That sure is a mouthful of revelation, but I'm really worried about your marriage. Have you always been so apart on your views of God? Is this a change from when you were dating?"

I paused, swallowing hard. *Could I trust the PORCH CLUB with the truth of my stupidity?*

"I've never admitted this to anyone, not even myself. When I met Curtis and he was Catholic, I thought that all I needed to know was that we were raised in the same religion. My first marriage was in a Southern Baptist Church, and I appreciated the fellowship and Bible Study there. But when my marriage was falling apart, I knew I would have to leave the church, so it made sense for me to go back to what I knew from my childhood: Catholicism.

"Curtis and I never talked about God or how we viewed Him, and we never read Scripture together. All I knew was that we'd attend church together and that was that. I thought that my faith was strong enough for both of us so it didn't matter. It wasn't until months after we married that I realized that Curtis didn't even own a Bible. I offered to give him one of mine, but he wasn't interested. He said that he'd read it before and knew what it said.

"I was so naive to think that one faith is good enough for two people. Unless both people love God first, a marriage will eventually fail. Do you think I'm stupid for never having discussed my love of God with someone I wanted to marry? I was star-struck, in lust, and lonely without any family. He had five brothers and sisters and two children, and I married all of them. I thought that God had sent him to me to ease the loneliness of not having a family. Sometimes, when we want something so badly, we can read the signs wrong; we hang a 'FROM GOD' sign on them even though we know in our heart that they aren't good for us."

I felt better having confided in the PORCH CLUB and ordered another martini. I didn't usually drown my sorrows, but maybe this was the night that I would get a little tipsy. Surely one of the girls would drive me home.

After the third round of martinis were delivered, Jackie asked again, "So are you going for counseling?"

"I don't know. Curtis acts just like his view of God: a 'STRICT FATHER'. He can't believe that his wife has moved into the spare bedroom. I've told him that it's been hard on both of us through this breast cancer journey and maybe we did need some help, but to him that would be like admitting defeat, like he couldn't keep his wife happy. It seems like just when my heart starts to soften and I want to love him completely again, he wakes me up at 2 a.m. to ask me about divorce. I just feel that I'm in a downward tailspin that I can't get out of. I have to get some sleep. I'm physically and emotionally exhausted."

Jackie said, "It is draining when a relationship isn't working. I've certainly had my share of bad ones, you know, when you aren't communicating well enough to get over the rocky phase. You're both wounded and some days it seems like you're intentionally trying to hurt each other. I hope things work out, but it sounds like you need some counseling. Hopefully Curtis will agree."

"I know that you are going to try to make your marriage work," Carol said, "but you haven't mentioned Jimmy in a long time. Does he still go to the same church?"

"Yes, but I haven't talked with him since I started having all these surgeries. We had a children's pageant last Sunday and he was there with his two boys. He did tell me last year that he'd divorced right before he joined the church and was still a little uncomfortable dating with children so young. My heart skipped a beat when he mentioned dating, even in a general sort of way. But now that I've had all these surgeries, I don't feel attractive anymore."

"Don't talk like that!" Kim exclaimed. "You're still facing more surgery and it will take awhile, but you'll feel a lot better about yourself when the reconstruction is over. But I do think you need to sort out your marriage with Curtis before you strike up another relationship. Showing interest in Jimmy will just confuse you even more.

"Sounds like that's one of the mistakes you made the first time around. The world teaches that when we hit a rocky spot we can just get a divorce and move on to someone else, but the problem is that the divorce doesn't change *us*. The problems with *us* are still there. God intended that we'd be married to the same person for life, with both of us loving Him and serving Him. When we run into rough patches, He expects us to run to Him for help. Sounds like you may have some things out of kilter, in how you relate to people *and* how you relate to God."

Carol said, "Kim has some good advice for you. You've been through a lot and it would be easy for you to run for comfort to the arms of another man. But that isn't the answer."

81

I realized that Kim and Carol were right. I did have things wrong with God and my relationships. But I couldn't deal with it all right now.

"Enough about me!" I said, pasting a smile on my face. "What's going on in your lives? It's your turn to talk."

7

Foreign Lands

"Pain insists upon being attended to. God whispers to us in our pleasures, speaks in our consciences, but shouts in our pains. It is his megaphone to rouse a deaf world."

– C.S. Lewis

I called the church after the first of the year to ask about mission trips. In fact, I made multiple calls, to both the church and the diocese office, over the next few months, but I always heard the same answer: "Donations are down because of the economy, so we've had to cut back on our outreach money. There are no trips planned. We'll let you know if we hear of any." In May, I thought I had a lead on a trip to Guatemala, but when I called I was surprised to learn that it was a doctor from somewhere in Ohio. They were planning a medical mission trip to Honduras with doctors and nurses from Cleveland, but they weren't sure if they needed a pharmacist. The organizer was nice enough and invited me to "come along", but I wanted something a little more definite and I really wanted to go with a group from Nashville.

Part of the reason I felt God was calling me to serve on a mission trip was so I could meet people from our church who might help me and Curtis grow in our faith, and who might mentor us to lead a God-filled marriage. The PORCH CLUB was great support, but Curtis was even starting to complain about the time I spent with them. I found myself telling him I had to "work late" when I was meeting the girls for a drink, because it didn't cause as much tension or require further explanation. It was hard for me to lie to him, but I rationalized that a little white lie (or two) wouldn't hurt, and it would prevent a fight.

Lately he had seemed more despondent about his job and his coworkers, but work was work and we needed to make the house payment. With all the debts paid and the kids out of college, we'd started to enjoy other things again. I was thankful that my six-month follow-up tests were negative, and overjoyed that we'd gotten through those dark days. But Curtis still didn't seem happy. There was always something wrong and I couldn't seem to fix it.

In June, there was a break-through in my quest. I was having dinner one Friday evening with Priscilla, a coworker at HCA, and complaining to her about the difficulty in finding a mission trip. "I can't believe that someone who already has a passport and is willing to pay her own way can't find a volunteer trip." Priscilla was sympathetic and promised to let me know if she heard of any opportunities.

The following Monday, Priscilla sent me an email that her church had planned a mission trip to South Africa in the fall. The trip hadn't filled up with their own church members, so they were asking everyone to spread the word that there were still slots available.

Her message had a link to the church website with information about the trip. I was amazed when I read the bottom of the page: "For more information, contact Dyer Rodes through the church office." *There couldn't be two people in Nashville named Dyer Rodes.* My anesthesiologist and good friend was coordinating a mission trip to South Africa! It seemed like too much of a

84

coincidence and I wondered out loud if this was the trip that God wanted me to be on. I paged Dyer immediately and he promised to send me a DVD from the previous year's trip. The deadline for the deposit wasn't until August 1, but they only had a few spots left. I told him I'd watch the video and then call him.

My every five-year class reunion was coming up in just a few weeks, and I was anxious to get back to New York and tell Mom and Dad all that had been going on in my life. Ever since I was a small child, I've believed that the saints before us are always with us. There was something about being able to go back home and visit the cemetery that made the conversations feel more real. I could only take two days off work, so I made plans to stay at the Abbey of the Genesee.

The Abbey is a Trappist Monastery and the quietest place I know. The guesthouse is silent, and there are services at the chapel five times a day to feed the soul. It was just what I needed: to get away for some quiet time to think about my health, my marriage, and what God wanted me to do for the rest of my time on earth. Three days wasn't much time, but it was all I could spare. At least I'd have time for a visit to the cemetery to talk with Mom about breast cancer, the trip to South Africa, my marriage, and how thankful I was to be alive.

Curtis was less than enthusiastic about both the trip to South Africa and my trip to New York. "I don't understand why you're going without me. And you know how I feel about traveling to foreign countries. I'm not going. Why would you go on a mission trip with a group that wasn't from our church, and an Episcopal Church, at that? I know what's going to happen. You're going to go to South Africa and then come home and want to join that church. I won't have any of that. We're staying right where we are."

I explained that I was only going to New York for three days this time and it was too expensive for both of us to make the trip for such a short time. What I really wanted to tell Curtis was that I needed the time to be alone to talk with God about what it meant to have breast cancer, and how it had brought me closer to

85

my faith. I also needed to hear from Him whether the mission trip to South Africa was the one He wanted me to go on. And I admitted that I needed to talk to God about my marriage.

When I married Curtis, I'd promised God that this time around it was a promise to Him, not just a promise to another human. I'd pledged to stay married and faithful, no matter what. Curtis and I had dreamed of sitting together on a front porch in two rocking chairs until we were both too old to rock.

But things had been so awful lately. I still had another surgery to schedule, and I was having hot flashes and joint pain from the medications that I was taking to prevent a recurrence of cancer. I had also developed blurry vision in my right eye; it started the night before my implant surgery in May. My doctors said it had nothing to do with the medications, and I had seen the best ophthalmologists and neuro-ophthalmologists in Nashville and no one could find anything wrong. Mark Cooper had even ordered a Brain MRI that, thankfully, came back negative. I kept reminding myself to be grateful that I was alive, but clearly I also needed to sort some things out. I was physically, emotionally and spiritually drained, and the only real answer was to turn to God. I prayed that Curtis would somehow understand, but it was as if he saw God as competition, that I would need him more if I relied on God less. I desperately needed a few days in the quietness of the Abbey.

Resolute, I booked my trip to New York. I was eager when the day arrived as I finally boarded the plane. The Abbey of the Genesee is only five minutes from where I grew up in Geneseo, New York, and I have always gone to the monastery for rest and solitude. I'd become a fan of the Abbey during the late 1970s, after reading *The Genesee Diary* by Henri Nouwen. Nouwen wrote it when he was admitted to the monastic community as a temporary Trappist for seven months. He was fascinated by the discipline and simplicity of the monastic life. I've read most of his books and knew that he too had struggled with emotional turmoil, writing *A Cry for Mercy* when he was at the Monastery for a second time. It would be good to be back in New York for a few days, catching up with old classmates and hopefully finding answers to the nagging questions that kept running through my head.

My flight was late landing at the Rochester airport, but I knew if I took the back roads I could make it to the Abbey in time for Vespers at 4:30 p.m. I arrived just in time to dash into the bathroom at the Chapel and change from shorts into a dress. I slipped into the chapel, and took a seat in the first of the three rows of pews. As I waited in the darkness for the monks, I prayed a sincere prayer that I would find healing on this trip: healing from breast cancer, healing for my broken marriage, and discernment on my call to serve others through a mission trip.

The monks filed in and the lights were turned up just enough for us to read the three Psalms in the Psalter. I looked at the celebrant's board and saw that Psalm 62 was posted as the first reading. I found the page and closed my eyes until the chant of the monks began, "Only in God is my soul at rest, from Him comes my salvation."

I didn't hear the other hymns that evening. The first line of Psalm 62 repeated over and over in my head. *That was it. What I needed was rest. Rest from physically feeling bad, rest from Curtis waking me up at 2 a.m., and rest from trying to be the perfect wife and stepmother.* I was worn out from living the wrong life, and here in one sentence was the answer: only God could give me rest. The verse from the Psalm danced in my head as I lay in bed that night. *Could it be that simple, that God was the answer to everything?*

I was deeply disappointed when the morning sun brought nothing but more questions. *I knew that I needed to renew my faith, and to change my life to be more faithful to God, but how? I couldn't believe that divorce was the answer, but what did I need to do to lead a God-filled marriage? And what about the South Africa trip? If Curtis refused to go, would that be another thing that drove us apart? What if God asked me to go and not Curtis? Would I be a bad wife to do something on my own to serve God?* Instead of receiving answers, I'd never wrestled with so many questions before.

Over the next three days, I attended four services a day at the Abbey: Lauds, Sext, Vespers and Compline, asking each time: *"What is it you want me to do, Lord? I am your willing servant."*

Every time, God said, "Be patient my child. I will speak when you are capable of hearing. For now, just rest."

There it was again, the command to "rest."

On my last day in New York, I made my every five-year visit to the cemetery. I talked about my breast cancer and surgeries, and told Mom how much I had wished that she had been there.

"But I *was* there, you just couldn't see me. I went through all the pain and heartache with you. "

I hadn't experienced her presence at the time, but her saying that she was there all along was strangely comforting. I gave some more details about the surgeries that I'd had and the hot flashes, but I wasn't prepared to explain the rocky road my marriage was on. I hoped Mom wouldn't bring it up in front of Dad.

Instead, Mom said, "I have some news too. Your father quit drinking two years ago. Well, he has a glass of wine with dinner, but he doesn't get drunk anymore. The even better news is that he doesn't *need* to get drunk anymore; he's a changed man! He is kind and thoughtful, not just to me, but everyone we meet. He's always trying to help someone, or even give them money. Remember what a tightwad he was when he was on earth, making you buy your own car when you went to college? He's completely changed. We go to church every Sunday and he even leads a men's Bible Study on Wednesday nights."

"But Mom, I never saw Dad in church, not once."

"He went once in a while when I would drag him, but he quit going altogether when your brother died. He was depressed but wouldn't get help. I tried to love him through it, but nothing seemed to matter to him after we lost your brother. He just became angrier and more withdrawn. You want to hear another funny thing? Remember how your dad used to hate to travel? Well, we just went with our Sunday School class to South Africa.

We met Archbishop Desmond Tutu in Cape Town. He's incredibly impressive and funny. What a wit! Of course, no one else could see us, but he is such a spiritual man that he could sense our presence immediately. We had a lovely conversation about forgiveness and loving your fellow man. Your dad was nodding in agreement the whole time!"

"Mom, I know that you won't believe this, but I have a chance to go to South Africa this fall! I've known for six months that I am called to go on a mission trip, but Curtis doesn't want to go. I'm torn about going without him, but I need to concentrate on deepening my own faith and following God's will in my life."

"Yes, my child. At times it is difficult, but you must always put your relationship with God above everything else."

Mom and Dad seemed so incredibly happy, giggling as they told me what their days were like in heaven. They were totally different people, nothing at all like they were on earth. Silently, I vowed to be a better wife, to be more understanding, and to suggest that Curtis and I go get counseling. If Curtis wouldn't go, then I'd go myself. There were some deep dark secrets that I needed to work through, either with him or without him.

I vowed to forget about Jimmy, too. An affair is never an answer to marital problems, and I knew it. I had to be strong. I'd made a promise to God when I got married the second time and I wasn't going to break it. I thought for a moment about sharing all this with my parents, but I was still cautious, fearing an inquisition from Dad. *Could it be possible that people changed so drastically after they got to heaven?*

"Mom, I am so thankful that I've lived a whole year after being diagnosed with breast cancer. Thank you for being with me through it, even though I didn't know you were there. Because of the cancer, I have a new life and I feel like I'm making up for lost time. I'm anxious to get on with this business of serving God."

"Yes, you are learning that He loves you very much and wants the best for all His children. Keep your eyes focused on

Him alone. Don't let anything worry or distract you. I know it is time for you to go. Bye, my darling Agatha, I love you."

"Hey, I love you, too!"

"Is that you, Dad?"

"Yes, it's me! I've changed. I still let your mother do most of the talking, but I'm not at all the man you used to know, who was constantly angry and ridiculed your mother about every little thing. I know that I was demanding, never listening, just barking orders. I wish you could know me now, but you will know the new me someday. I am no longer there on earth to care for you, but put all your trust in the Lord and He will protect you and guide your path."

"Hey, Mom, Dad--I love you both!"

9o 9o 9o

I returned to Nashville with a renewed spirit and enthusiasm for my marriage and mission work, but I still wasn't sure about the trip to South Africa. *What if I had heard wrong and it was just a coincidence that Mom and Dad had visited there recently?* Curtis was still insistent that he wasn't going. Each time I tried to talk about it, he'd change the subject.

In my doubts, I began to pray in earnest for my marriage and what I was supposed to do with my life. Curtis and I went back to attending church each Sunday, but we'd end up in the same argument about whether God was a God of punishment, or a God of love. Sometimes Curtis wouldn't want to talk about the service at all. In the early days of our marriage, I looked forward to Sunday mornings; we'd get up early, go to Mass and then often have sex before making brunch. But after the pornography and my ongoing reconstructive surgery, the sex had stopped completely. I didn't know what to do to make things better. All I knew to do was pray.

The deadline for the South Africa trip deposit came and went and I still didn't feel that I had clear direction from God.

Maybe it wasn't the right time to leave Curtis when we weren't communicating well. He never wanted to be alone, always traveling with me on business trips unless he couldn't get off work. When he didn't go, he'd be sullen for days after I returned. I had a trip coming up in the next few weeks; Curtis couldn't go and I was dreading his response when I got back.

"Honey, you've got to trust me when I go out of town. I have to travel for my work and I'm seeing people I've known for years. I swear that they are just old friends, nothing more."

"But you'll be having dinner and drinks with men alone and staying in the same hotel. It isn't right for a married woman to have dinner with another man except her husband. After a few drinks, no telling what might happen. It's not the way a Christian wife acts."

"Curtis, you've got to trust me. A marriage built on judgment and suspicion has a rocky foundation. I have never been unfaithful to you, and I never will. Please trust me."

૭ ૭ ૭

I was grateful that I had some time alone to think and pray on my business trip. I had received no word from God about the South Africa trip, yet for next few days, my mind kept wandering back to it. It wasn't until the plane ride home, however, that I realized the call was real. I couldn't wait to get home and tell Curtis that I was convinced that I should go to Johannesburg and help feed children orphaned by AIDS.

"Thanks for picking me up, Curtis. It was a good pharmacy meeting, and I learned a lot, but I have other news. I want to go to South Africa. I've prayed about it and believe that God has asked me to go on a mission trip there. You know how much I love to cook and there's the opportunity to go with Dr. Rodes' church and help feed children. Do you want to go with me if there's still room?"

"Absolutely not. I told you I'd help raise money for a mission trip, but for our church, not another church. And you know I won't travel overseas. It's too dangerous. I don't want you going either."

"But Curtis, they went last year and Dr. Rodes said it was safe. They partner with a church there and the parishioners open up their homes. It's not like we'd be out on our own. Plus, I found out that Archbishop Desmond Tutu's daughter is coordinating the trip. She lives in Nashville. She'll make sure we're safe."

"I'm still not interested in going, but you do what you have to do. I think it's a stretch to say you have a sign from God that you are supposed to go. I think it's what you want to do, and you're trying to make it 'God-inspired'. No one actually hears God's voice."

I was quiet. It was futile to explain how I was sure that God wanted me on this mission trip. Since Curtis hadn't forbidden me outright, I decided that silence was best. *I wanted to be a good wife and follow Curtis' leadership as the head of the family, but what if God was calling me to do something that Curtis didn't approve of?*

I'd never considered this question before: "What do you do when you feel called by God and another human interferes with that calling? How do you reconcile that?" I would definitely take up that topic in my next prayer time. The words of Psalm 62 came back to me: "Only in God is my soul at rest; from Him comes my salvation." I knew that with everything I was going through, I needed to continue to rest and pray.

What to do about the deadline for the trip deposit? The next morning, I called Dr. Rodes from my office. While the phone was ringing, I played the conversation through in my mind. *What would I say if the trip was already full? What if the deposit deadline couldn't be extended? What if they had decided not to take anyone who wasn't a member of their church?* I had to leave a message, and as I waited for Dr. Rodes to call back, I said a silent prayer of thanksgiving for being alive. I told God that I was okay with whatever He decided was best for me, whether that meant going to South Africa or not.

"Hi. Agatha, this is Dr. Rodes. Are you okay?"

"Good morning, and yes, I'm fine! Didn't mean to worry you, but I do have a question. Has your trip to South Africa filled up yet? I know that the deposit deadline has already passed."

"Why do you want to know?"

"Please, Dyer," I said laughing, "Just like a man to answer a question with a question! Is your trip full?"

"No, it isn't full. Do you want to go?"

I paused for just a few seconds, "Yes, I do."

"I don't know what to say! I am thrilled and I know that it will be a life-changing trip for you. It was for everyone who went last year, and most of us are going back again this fall."

"I can drop a check off at the church this afternoon after work. How much should I make it out for? Is the whole amount due or just the deposit?"

"Don't worry about the check. I'll call the office and tell them that you're going. We have an organizational meeting with Naomi Tutu scheduled for this Sunday at 4 p.m. Can you make it? You can meet everyone who's going on the trip."

"Yes. That would be great. Can I bring my husband too? He's a little reluctant to let me go by myself, but I told him I'd be in good hands with my doctor along."

"Sure. Everyone would love to meet him. He's welcome to join us on the trip, too. I'm thrilled you are going, and I want to share something with you. Our whole group has been praying for weeks about this. We had twelve people committed to go, then one girl had to drop out when she couldn't get off work. So we've had eleven commitments for the past eight weeks. We've prayed, we've made announcements, and we've even put up posters. We've done everything we could think of to promote the trip, but no one has stepped forward. So you'll be number twelve."

"Is there a special significance to having twelve people on the trip, like the twelve disciples?"

"That's funny, I hadn't thought about the connection between twelve pilgrims to South Africa and twelve disciples! But you are right, that may have a special significance. But we also learned a few weeks ago that in order to ensure our group rate for the flights, we had to have a minimum of twelve people going. Since we only had eleven, each person was going to have to pay an additional $300 and the amount was due next Monday. So by you coming along on the trip, everyone is saving $300 in airfare. That's more money we'll have to donate to the Feeding Scheme program, which is our main project in Johannesburg. I can't wait to tell the others. Agatha, blessings on your decision. I know you won't regret it. I guarantee it will be life-changing."

I called Curtis to tell him the good news and that we were invited to join the pilgrimage meeting on Sunday at 4 p.m. "You'll know Dr. Rodes from my surgeries, and I'm sure everyone else will be nice, too. After all, it is a church group."

 confidence ❧ ❧ ❧

For the next few days, Curtis and I didn't talk much about the trip. I didn't have many details to share, but thought we'd get more information at the meeting. But when 3:30 p.m. came on Sunday, Curtis decided that he wanted to stay home and watch golf on TV instead.

"Don't you want to meet the people I'll be traveling with? You know Dr. Rodes, but even I don't know anyone else. I'd feel more comfortable if you came with me."

"This is your trip, not mine."

I wondered what excuse I was going to use this time. Dr. Rodes had even sent an email over the weekend, reminding me of the meeting and specifically inviting Curtis to come. It seemed that every time I was excited about something, Curtis put a damper on it. After the cancer and surgeries, I was emotionally drained. I still didn't trust my emotions and I didn't want to begin my relationship with these people by lying.

I arrived on time and Dyer was there to greet me. ""I thought your husband was coming with you today. I know I met him when you were in the hospital, but everyone else would like to meet him, too."

"Something came up and he couldn't make it today. Maybe he can come for the second meeting right before we leave." I was hoping that "something came up" was general enough that God wouldn't consider it an outright lie. Why couldn't I just say, *'Curtis didn't want to come because he's home watching television'*? That would be the truth, but then it would sound like there was something wrong with our marriage. All these nice people didn't need to get involved in my problems. It was a wonderful meeting with Naomi Tutu, and I immediately felt like I had ten new friends.

ço ço ço

I was excited the whole week before the trip, and made a list of everything I had to pack. I knew Curtis was still apprehensive about me going to a foreign country, so I tried to spend as much time as I could with him after work. On Friday, I suggested we go to a local restaurant in Franklin, where there was a watch party for the Oklahoma University Sooners, my alma mater. Curtis loved to watch Big 12 football and it was hard to get the games on Nashville TV since they usually ran the SEC games.

I got home a little late from work and was tired, but I knew that Curtis was looking forward to watching the game, even if he was less than enthused about the watch party. He didn't like to meet new people and was uncomfortable even around people we knew because he was constantly comparing himself to others. As soon as I got home, I guessed that something was wrong. Curtis seemed argumentative about every little thing I said, and when we got in the car, he suggested that I drive.

"Curtis, can you drive this time? My right eye hurts even worse when I'm tired." I had been living with blurry vision for four months, and although the pain was better, I still couldn't see well and driving at night was particularly hard. I thought it was a reasonable request, but then I realized that I needed to drive, because Curtis had been drinking. I went into the kitchen, opened up the pantry and found four empty beer cans on top of the trash.

"Okay, I'll drive tonight. It's not worth fighting over. Did you have some beer this afternoon?"

"Maybe with your vision problems you shouldn't be going to South Africa after all."

"Well, I am going and we leave tomorrow. Let's just go watch the game, meet some people, and have a good time. It's the last time we'll be together for twelve days."

We were halfway to Franklin when Curtis said, "I just have one question about your trip."

"What's that?"

"Well, we haven't been doing very well lately in the bedroom department. In fact, with you sleeping upstairs, we haven't had sex in months. A man has needs you know. Are we going to have sex tonight before you leave for South Africa, or not?"

I was stunned. I thought that we had been getting along a lot better the past few weeks, taking things slowly and trying to repair our relationship. I'd suggested that we go back to when we were first dating and learn how to love each other again. When I was relaxed, I felt myself falling back in love with him. It was good of Curtis to let me go on this trip to South Africa alone, but now this comment. I guess sex had been an unspoken issue all along.

"I can't believe that you just asked me that, like women don't have needs too? I thought we were getting along better and we'd agreed to take it slow and try to fall back in love. What changed tonight?"

"Well, if a bomb blows up in the Johannesburg airport when you arrive, you'll die and I'll never see you again."

"I can't believe that you just said that. If I die on this trip, it is God's will, with no strings attached. Let's talk about this when we get home after the football game."

We walked into the restaurant and immediately recognized the OU section by the red banners and flags. We sat down at a table, and I introduced Curtis and myself to the other couple sitting there. When the waitress asked for our orders, Curtis said, "I'm not hungry" and, closing his menu, ordered a beer. I ordered food and a beer and told him that I'd share if he got hungry by the time the food arrived.

I asked the other couple about their time at OU and suddenly realized that Curtis wasn't participating in the conversation. "*Oh no! Not this again. It can't be the silent treatment again! This can't be happening to me!*"

But that is exactly what was occurring. Curtis didn't speak a word, even when the other couple asked him a direct question.

"Is your husband, okay? He looks pale. Are you sure he's okay? He's sweating and looks awful."

"No, I'm sure he's fine, just a little tired. He had a hard day at work. We'll probably leave at half-time."

When the food came, I offered Curtis part of my hamburger, but he just glanced at me and didn't speak.

Enough is enough. We're leaving at half time, I told myself. I needed to finish packing anyway.

With that, Curtis ordered another beer.

True to my word, I stood up at half time, said goodbye to the couple at the table, and headed for the door. Curtis followed close behind.

"I'll drive," I said. "You are in no condition to get behind the wheel of a car."

"What do you mean? I'm fine."

"Right. You weren't in any condition to drive on the way down here and you've had three beers since then. Get in the car. We're going home."

As I pulled out of the parking lot, I started crying. "How could you embarrass me like that? You have no social skills or you wouldn't pull a stunt like that in front of other people. What were you thinking in there?

"I was thinking about our previous conversation."

"So do you think the silent treatment is going to punish me into loving you? If you think that sex is on the agenda for tonight you are sadly mistaken. In fact, I told you last December that if you ever pulled the silent treatment on me in public again, I would divorce you. When I get home from South Africa, I'm contacting a lawyer and drawing up the papers."

I cried all the way home and Curtis said nothing.

৯০ ৯০ ৯০

We hardly spoke the next day, but Curtis agreed to take me to the airport. We were almost there when Curtis said, "Were you serious last night? Are you going to file for a divorce when you get home?"

"Curtis, I don't know about a divorce, but I do know that our marriage is in serious trouble. South Africa is the land of forgiveness. I'm hoping to learn more about forgiveness and mercy on this pilgrimage. Please just let me go on this trip and then we'll talk when I get home. I don't want a divorce any more than you do."

Curtis unloaded my suitcases at the curb, gave me a quick peck on the cheek, and pulled away.

Why did I always feel like he had the upper hand? I wanted him to be proud of me for serving the Lord, but instead our parting words had been about divorce.

I needed someone to share the thrill that I was feeling. In a little over two hours, I was leaving to serve in a foreign country! I texted the PORCH CLUB, "Love you girls! Off to South Africa," before turning off my phone.

8

South Africa Bound

*Many people ask me what I have learned from all of the experiences in my life, and I say unhesitatingly: People are wonderful. It is true. People really **are** wonderful.*

– Archbishop Desmond Tutu

Excited and with my passport in hand, I was anxious to get the trip underway. A priest from St. George's, the Reverend Timothy Jones, was going on the trip, and he gathered us at the airport gate to pray for safe travels and that God would be glorified with our work. They sure were a praying people in this Episcopal Church.

It was a short hop from Nashville to Atlanta, but the next leg of the journey, from Atlanta to Johannesburg, South Africa, would be eighteen hours. I was delighted to find myself sitting next to Father Tim, and I shared a long re-cap of my recent battle with breast cancer and the feeling of being called by God to do mission work.

I decided against sharing with him about Curtis and the current state of my marriage because I was confused and couldn't put my feelings into words. I had pledged to be a devoted wife and really did love being married and having a family. I couldn't understand why Curtis seemed to be negative and unhappy all the time. We'd both had our share of burdens, but we also had each other. I was sure that God would give me clear answers about my marriage when I was in South Africa.

In the past, I'd hidden truths out of embarrassment or fear, but this was different. My feelings about my appearance and intimacy had been such a roller coaster since the cancer diagnosis that I needed to sort them out before I could talk with anyone about them.

It turned out that Father Tim and I shared a love for Henri Nouwen's writings, and I was impressed that Tim had written and published a dozen books; he had even spent time poring over Henri Nouwen's archives in Toronto for the book, *Turn My Mourning Into Dancing*. We spent the first nine hours of the flight comparing notes on Nouwen, and spent the last nine hours sleeping. Even with the excitement of my first international flight, I was able to get a good night's rest.

Arriving at the Johannesburg airport, I was bear-hugged by Father Xolani and Joffe from St. Thomas Anglican Church, the church that St. George's partners with in Kagiso, a township just outside of Johannesburg. They embraced me as if we were old friends and I listened to the excitement in their voices as they shared our schedule for the week.

The first few nights we would be staying in Soweto, where high school girlfriends of Naomi Tutu had bed and breakfast accommodations. They all turned out to greet us, and of course everyone in the airport knew Naomi, recognizing her as Archbishop Tutu's daughter. I was excited to hear that her parents still had a house on the same block where we'd be staying in Soweto, and that she'd made plans for us to have dinner at the Archbishop's home later in the week.

ℰ ℰ ℰ

Naomi said it would be important for the group to understand the history of South Africa, particularly the apartheid period that existed when she was growing up in Soweto. After a good night's rest, we departed early in the morning for tours of Nelson Mandela's home and the Apartheid Museum. I was horrified to see the entrances to the museum marked, "Whites" and "Blacks" and, even worse, everyone was issued a ticket marked either, "White" or "Black", and directed to separate but certainly not equal, entrances that matched the cards. It was shocking to see how different life was during apartheid if you were black, white, or colored. We spent four hours in the museum and exited in silence. When Naomi asked what we thought, I said, "I was transported back to 1976, when I was a college student, and I realize now that I was totally oblivious to the brutality of apartheid. I had no idea the government was forcing students to learn in a language that they didn't know. How come I wasn't aware that my fellow man was being crucified halfway around the globe?" I thought back to the frivolous life I was leading in the "wild '70s" and was embarrassed by my ignorance of another culture's plight.

During our nightly debriefing time, Naomi explained that communication from South Africa had been blocked to the rest of the world, so it would have been hard for us to really understand what was going on. Naomi's explanation didn't lessen my guilt any. So many people have been oppressed for centuries because of their gender, skin color or religious beliefs. I didn't sleep well at all my second night in South Africa.

᧏ ᧏ ᧏

The next day dawned with a light rain shower, and I was anxious to get started "serving." But first the parishioners from St. Thomas held a breakfast reception for us. Each person from St. Thomas hugged us as we were introduced. I have never felt so loved! I had never met these people, yet I was warmly embraced.

They didn't want to know what I did for a living, or if I was married or single. *Could I ever be as loving to others when I returned to Nashville, loving without judgment?*

After greetings and breakfast, we went to a place called Soul City, outside of Kagiso. It was where the poorest of the poor live in little shacks made out of cardboard and scrap aluminum. We were all horrified to see one spigot of running water for every hundred homes, where the women would go to fill up their jugs for the day. A few port-o-potties were available in the back of the settlement, a long walk in the heat of the day. We visited the empty dirt space where we would be building a house later in the week. It would be a new home for a grandmother, her two daughters, a cousin, and children. There were fifteen people in all. Their previous three-room house had blown down in a windstorm a few weeks before. We wondered aloud how fifteen people could live in three rooms.

We boarded the bus again and traveled to a suburb, Kliptown. Kliptown has a high rate of unemployment, and poverty is the primary source of the temptations and challenges faced by the youth. A high rate of HIV/AIDS, alcoholism and substance abuse puts these young people at risk as they try to shut out the world around them.

We were walking along a dirt street, taking in the sights, the sounds, and the despair of Kliptown, when I saw the huge brown eyes of a beautiful little girl staring up at me. Instinctively, we both reached out our hands, my right hand to her left. I instantly felt the warmth of our touch. After walking a few yards, she took my hand and placed it in the hand of another little girl, almost half her size. The older girl scampered around to the other side of the younger girl, grabbing her right hand. The three of us continued to walk together, with the littlest girl in the middle.

After twenty steps in silence, another member of our group, Joanna, joined us. The older girl reached up her right hand to hold Joanna's left hand and the four of us walked hand-in hand. Joanna asked, "What is your name?"

The older girl replied, "My name is Maria."

Joanna spoke again. "How old are you?"

"Nine years old."

"And what is her name?" Joanna continued. "How old is she?"

"This is my sister, Sarah. She is four. I take care of Sarah," Maria said with a wide grin.

We walked on in silence, but I understood. At first I had thought that when Maria had passed my hand to her sister it was because Maria didn't want to hold my hand any longer. Instead, she'd let her little sister feel the touch of my hand. I knew that I had just traveled halfway around the world so that a nine-year-old girl named Maria and her four-year-old sister, Sarah, could teach me to care more about others than about myself. When we love others unselfishly, we are willing to freely give up what we want the most so that others can experience love.

I was amazed at how trusting the two little girls were, and I realized that because of the trust that they had shown in me, I felt a responsibility for them, like we were somehow connected. I even had a flashing thought that I'd ask Curtis about adopting Maria and Sarah and bringing them to America! Then a second thought flashed through my head: *How would it change my relationship with Curtis if I did the same thing? What if I trusted him to protect me and be responsible for me? What if I spontaneously reached out my hand to take his, not to manipulate him or as a prelude to sex, but as a sign of me trusting him?* I couldn't remember the last time we'd held hands as friends. I'd kept a journal for years, and that night I wrote, "Day Two–South Africa–Maria & Sarah–show Curtis that I trust him. It might be the first step in repairing our marriage."

ço ço ço

As we worked side by side with teachers and students in the vegetable garden, I eagerly absorbed information about the country and basked in the incredible warmth and acceptance of the South African people. The goal was to expand the planting

103

area, as they needed more vegetables to feed the children after school on Tuesday each week. We were clearing a large patch of ground when a boy came up to me and handed me a small rock. "For you to take back to America. To you from me."

"Thank you so much. What's your name?"

"Here my name is Kagiso. In America, my name would mean 'Peace.'"

"How beautiful, thank you, Peace."

I thought, *Yes, Peace. That is what we all long for in our lives. And I'm finding it here in South Africa.* I couldn't wait to write about Peace in my journal that night.

ᖇᖇᖇ

On Tuesday evening, our group had dinner at the Tutu home. Although the Archbishop and his wife were staying in Cape Town, we were thrilled to be in his home with his daughter, Naomi, and son, Trevor. The Tutus provided a wonderful meal and we were encouraged to roam throughout the home and take pictures of the wonderful art collection. I even took a photograph of the 1984 Nobel Peace Prize prominently displayed in the living room.

After dinner, we enjoyed a fascinating conversation comparing the current United States government with the post-apartheid government of South Africa. Naomi's cell phone rang and she stepped into the kitchen to answer it. She returned and told me I had an emergency call from America.

My heart started racing even before I heard Curtis' voice. "What's wrong? Naomi said there was an emergency."

"There is an emergency. Dick's in the hospital with a heart attack and is scheduled for surgery in the morning."

"Dick?"

"Yes, you know, my golfing buddy."

"Oh, no. What happened? What hospital is he in?"

"Skyline Medical Center."

"I don't know many people who work at Skyline. Have you been to visit him?"

"No. Susan just called to tell me a few minutes ago."

"Well, I'm not sure there is anything I can do for him from here, except pray. Tell Dick and Susan that I'll keep them in my prayers tonight."

"Yes, I'll tell them. One other thing, are you going to divorce me when you get home?"

It took a minute for Curtis' words to sink in, but my heart sank with embarrassment as I realized that Curtis had been drinking, and this probably was the "emergency" that had sparked the call. Not that I didn't doubt that Dick was in the hospital, but why bring up divorce?

I lowered my voice as I stepped into the hallway so that the others wouldn't hear, "Curtis, you've been drinking again. I'm six thousand miles away and I'm not having this conversation with you over the phone. I appreciate you telling me about Dick, but I'm not talking with you about our marriage tonight. This phone is supposed to be reserved for emergency calls only."

"But I need to know tonight."

"Curtis, I'm hanging up now. We can discuss our marriage when I get home."

I returned to the dining room and felt my face blush a hot red, wondering if anyone could tell how upset I was. Naomi asked if everything was okay and I stammered that a friend was in the hospital with a heart attack and having surgery in the morning. Dyer asked everyone to pray for my friend in the hospital as he ended the evening in prayer.

ç§ ç§ ç§

I couldn't sleep that night, the unanswered questions once again cascading through my head like a waterfall. I felt so much love here in South Africa from all these strangers. It was more love that I'd ever felt in my life. *Could the warmth that I felt be an*

105

outpouring of their tremendous capacity to forgive? That an entire country could forgive the atrocities suffered under apartheid was a dramatic lesson. Little children forgive easily, but adults harbor resentment for a lifetime. I still found it hard to believe that the prisoners at Robben Island could forgive their captors. When I thought of the times that I had been "wronged" in my life, the wounds were pale in comparison.

I was embarrassed when I thought about how angry I could be with Curtis for the slightest wrong. Not only would I be angry at the presumed insult, I would flare its fire by playing it over and over again in my head. One ember that had slowly burned away our love was an issue over the money in our joint checking account. It had happened when we were first married, but it's amazing how Satan can rekindle an old memory and fan it into a raging fire.

I had been furious and accused Curtis of either having an affair or sending more money to the kids than we'd agreed upon. He denied both at first, and then finally admitted he was helping his son with car payments. I'd threatened to divorce Curtis for keeping secrets and although I'd never mentioned it again, I realized now that I'd never really forgiven him. It was 3 a.m. that night in South Africa when I got up and wrote in my journal: *Forgive Curtis for buying the kids the car, forgive him for drinking, forgive him for everything. It's not up to you to judge him.*

I went back to bed, but couldn't fall asleep. I realized how judgmental I'd been, not only of Curtis but also of everyone in my world. It was a horrible feeling, as I'd always thought of myself as loving and easygoing, but the vision that I saw when I stepped away was very different. I needed to feel superior and righteous and I could only do that by putting other people down. What a blow to my ego, and a sobering thought that I wasn't the "good" person that I tried to portray. Now God was showing me the sinner I really am. I guess that's what happens on mission trips: you learn about a new culture and people, but God also meets you there to reveal your true self.

෨ ෨ ෨

The next two days were taken up with working in the garden and cooking for the children. Given my love of cooking, it was my favorite part of the trip, especially when we saw the smiles on the faces of the seventy children we fed that Tuesday afternoon. One of the children was asked to say grace and shouted out loudly at the end, "...and God bless our friends from America!"

෨ ෨ ෨

After hugging all the kids goodbye, we split up into two cars to head back to Soweto. During the drive, my mind drifted back to the message from the previous night. If I was going to learn to serve God, I needed to work on myself first. In trying to determine what my purpose in life was, I'd criticized others who didn't share the same gifts or calling. *How could I judge another person's value?* That was reserved for God alone.

We were on the highway when the other car pulled next to ours and motioned for us to pull over. After both cars had stopped, Naomi came over to our car and said, "Agatha, you have another emergency call from America."

With my mind racing with shame, I scrambled out of the back seat and took the phone from her outstretched hand. I looked at my watch and realized that it was 7 a.m. in Nashville. My heart began to race with fear; this couldn't be good news.

"Is Dick okay? What's happened?"

"I just wanted you to know that I've taken the dogs to the kennel. You can pick them up there when you return."

"What do you mean? What's going on? Do you have to go to the hospital to be with Dick? Do you have to go out of town for work?"

"No, Dick's surgery went well and I don't have any business trips this week."

I was still trying to figure out what the emergency was.

"Are the dogs okay?"

"Yes, the dogs are fine, but someone has to care for them until you get back."

None of this conversation was making much sense, and then it dawned on me why. "Curtis have you been drinking? How could you? The dogs are depending on you."

"That's why I'm taking them to the kennel. I won't be here when you get back."

My compassion turned to anger. *Why could I not even go on a church mission trip without this burden? What did this mean— that he was leaving me?*

"You're drunk. I'm not having this conversation with you."

"That's fine. I knew you wouldn't care. Just remember these words, 'I won't be here when you get back.'"

I heard the click of the phone and the conversation was over. I didn't know what to say, but handed the phone back to Naomi with a soft, "I'm sorry for causing so much trouble." I climbed into the back seat of the car. Don, one of my traveling companions, asked, "Is everything okay? You look white as a sheet."

I thought, *It's not fair to involve my new friends in my problems. How embarrassing that my husband is leaving me while I'm on a mission trip.* I wanted to be anywhere but in that car, and my mind took me away to a time when I was five years old and I'd run next door in the snow to the neighbors for help. My father was drunk and standing over my mother with a kitchen knife, threatening to kill her. But when I returned with the neighbors, my father and mother were quiet. "Nothing's wrong," they said. "She has an overactive imagination for a five-year-old." My mother's voice from forty years before echoed in my head, reminding me that family matters meant family-only matters.

I snapped back to the present when Don repeated, "Is everything okay?" It was a split second decision. *Should I remain quiet bearing this burden myself, or should I confide in my new friends?*

Everyone seemed so nice and understanding on the trip, like I'd read about Jesus in the Gospels. Jesus seemed to always know when someone was embarrassed or needed to be comforted, and he never condemned them. I blurted out, "That was my husband and it sounds like he's been drinking."

Don looked at his watch, "But it's 7 a.m. in Nashville!"

"I know. He called to tell me he wouldn't be there when I get home, and that he's taking the dogs to a kennel. I guess he's leaving me."

Dyer had listened quietly, but now he softly said, "Sounds like he's doing you a favor."

Don said, "I am so sorry for the pain you are going through, but you know there's nothing you can do from here, don't you? We will care for you."

I wanted to cry, but instead I was comforted by the show of love from my new friends. For the first time in my life I wasn't keeping a secret to hide my embarrassment at a failure. These people cared about me in spite of what I was going through. I guess I would expect that from the priest on the trip, but everyone else exhibited that same type of love, too. I knew my marriage was over and I resolved to learn about forgiveness and judgment and make some changes in my life. We climbed out of the cars when we reached Soweto and I realized that this mission trip was less about me serving the people of South Africa, and more about what I could become by learning to love God and accepting His love.

ᖁ ᖁ ᖁ

It was hard to concentrate through the closing devotional that evening, and I was grateful when Dyer closed us in prayer and asked for "comfort for all those who are going through tough times." I knew that he was talking about me, but I wondered if maybe there was someone else who had sorrow in their life too. That night as I crawled into bed, I begged God for restful sleep. It had been months since I'd slept well, with all the emotional turmoil in my marriage and my health. I didn't want my marriage to end this way, but at least it was closure and I definitely longed for healing to start. I was so relieved to know that these faithful friends were praying for me and hadn't judged me for failing. As I drifted off to sleep, I wanted to remember this feeling of being wrapped in God's loving arms forever.

9

The Most Important Thing

*...left to ourselves we lapse into a kind of collusion with entropy,
acquiescing in the general belief that things may be getting worse
but that there's nothing much we can do about them. And we are
wrong. Our task in the present...is to live as resurrection people in
between Easter and the final day, with our Christian life, corporate
and individual, in both worship and mission, as a sign of the first
and a foretaste of the second.*

– N.T. Wright

I was relieved for a change of venue as we boarded the plane to
Cape Town, but then I was upset again on our visit to Robben
Island where Nelson Mandela spent eighteen of his twenty-seven
years in prison. After seeing the jail cell and the yard where they
had tediously crushed stones, I found it unbelievable that the
prisoners could have forgiven their captors. But many men from
the church at Kagiso were imprisoned at the same time as
Mandela and they told the same stories: "God commands us to
forgive. Not when people ask for forgiveness, but because God
has forgiven us first."

On the boat back to Cape Town, I vowed silently that I would forgive Curtis for leaving me and would start a new life, this time walking with God. I knew that the hardest part was going to be giving up Curtis' family. I'd longed for a family of my own and with Curtis, I married into a huge one. But now the kids were twenty-seven and had their own lives to live. It was time I started serving God instead of myself.

I heard a knock at the bedroom door and found Naomi pinning a message at each of our rooms: Father will be celebrating mass at the Cathedral at 7:15 a.m. If you are up, please join me and I'll introduce you.

"Are you kidding, a chance to meet your father? Of course, I'll be there," I said as I read the note aloud.

❧ ❧ ❧

As promised, Archbishop Tutu celebrated mass, and his homily recounted his recent trip to the Sudan as Chair of The Elders, an independent group of global leaders who work together for peace and human rights. He described the horrors that he had seen in the Sudan, referring to it as a "new apartheid".

How could this be happening again? I thought. *Won't humans ever learn to love each other and quit destroying each other through power and greed?*

Along with his sobering message, we received a lasting memory when Archbishop Tutu posed for a group photograph with us. If only I could learn to have his quiet spirit, his incredible intelligence and most of all, his intense love for his fellow human beings. His small stature was eclipsed by his spirituality, and I understood how he had been able to talk with Mom and Dad on their recent trip to South Africa, even though they'd been dead for decades.

I worked through the next few days with a renewed interest. My guilt was gone, and I finally understood what it is like to be a beloved Child of God.

❧ ❧ ❧

On Saturday afternoon, we flew back to Kagiso. Parish families had graciously agreed to take us in pairs to stay with them overnight. Suzy, another traveler from St. George's, and I stayed with Tshidi Gunguwo, a businesswoman and the wife of a doctor in the township. What a wonderful evening we had as we learned firsthand about family life in post-apartheid South Africa. It was interesting to hear Tshidi's two teenagers discuss the challenges they face; they were so similar to those faced by youth in America: the pull of success, sex, drugs, and other distractions.

The unemployment and high school dropout rates only exacerbated their worries, as most South Africans weren't able to go to college. Many ended up in a vicious cycle of alcohol, illicit drugs, and indiscriminant sex, leading to the explosion of AIDS. Tshidi's family was particularly touched because, as a doctor, her husband saw many people who couldn't afford their AIDS medications or didn't get routine healthcare. Tshidi wanted to start an orphanage to provide food and daycare for those who had no family.

Suzy and I were overwhelmed by her hospitality. We finally got to bed at 3 a.m. after talking and laughing into the night. I'd learned so much during this trip about oppression, forgiveness, and reconciliation, but it had been the conversations with Tshidi about caring for others that were the most meaningful. I vowed that even if I no longer had a chance with Curtis, I was going to look at all my relationships through different eyes when I got home.

We arose for a full breakfast in the Gunguwo household, briefly meeting Tshidi's husband who had been on call at the hospital all night. Suzy and I had a chance to recap our week and the lessons that we'd learned. We told Tshidi about our house project in Soul City and planting the garden for the school feeding

113

program. I told her how much I enjoyed cooking and that it was a joy for me to help prepare food for the children.

Tshidi listened intently as we told about our work and how excited we were to meet all the people from the church. She in turn told us of her family's involvement and how important the church and its ministries were to the community. But then, after an awkward pause, Tshidi said, "We appreciate all you have done for us this week, but you know that it is not the most important thing, don't you?"

Suzy and I looked at each other with a blank stare. Neither one of us knew what Tshidi meant. I ventured, "Tshidi, what do you mean, that the garden and house aren't the most important thing? Tell us what you are thinking."

"We are very appreciative of the house that you built for the grandmother and her family, and your contribution to the garden and feeding program is a visible demonstration of your work for God's glory. But there is something far more important to us. Twelve of you have spent a lot of money and taken time from work to travel halfway around the world to be with us. Just your presence here gives us hope that tomorrow's South Africa will be better than today."

I couldn't speak as tears started to well up in my eyes. *Could I believe what I had just heard?* My whole past had been consumed with "doing" things and many of them were "good" things. But here my new friend from South Africa was telling me that just my presence was enough. *Could my "being" be valued so much that it truly is enough? Could it be possible that I didn't have to build anything, donate money, or start a feeding program or an orphanage, but I could still have value?*

I had always been focused on the here and now of the material world, but Tshidi and my new friends from South Africa were focused on the eternal truth that we are God's beloved children; they recognize that He knew our goodness long before we were born. We don't have to do anything to earn God's love. I swallowed hard, but then a smile came to my face. Yes, the most important thing was showing others God's love, and for Tshidi, just our being there was evidence enough that God existed and was present in South Africa. I guess I had known it in my head all along, but now I was ready to accept it in my heart. My musings were interrupted when Tshidi looked at her watch and said we had to hurry or we'd be late for our last church service of the trip.

ço ço ço

It was a huge celebration, a traditional Anglican service filled with glorious African music. Afterwards, the parish treated us to a potluck luncheon on the lawn as our official send-off before we headed back to Nashville.

I couldn't believe that the time had flown by so quickly, or I had learned so much. I worshiped a week ago as a visitor, but today we shared bread and wine as friends. Amid hugging and tears, I said good-bye to Mbali, Lorraine, Dipuo, Tshidi, Joffe, Father Xolani, Mama Sheila and all the wonderful people who I had met just eight days before. It felt like we had known each other our entire lives. I was definitely coming back next year.

The suitcases were packed into the fifteen-passenger van and then we all piled in. As soon as our driver began to pull away we knew something was wrong. We got out of the van and looked in dismay at the crooked trailer that was half-on, half-off the roadway. The previous night's rain had softened the grass, and with the added weight of the luggage, our trailer had jackknifed, with one wheel off the road sunken deep into the swollen grass. .

"We'll never make it to the airport on time," someone said. The chatter continued with, "I wonder when the next flight out of Johannesburg is?" and "There aren't any tow trucks available today, it's Sunday. We probably can't leave until tomorrow." And another person said, "I have to be back to work tomorrow. What are we going to do?"

The grumbling began to accelerate as visions of missed flights crowded into our heads. The only vision in my head was one of returning to an empty house and the reality of my new life back in the States. I was consumed with my sadness for a few minutes, and then I heard a low hum. It started as a low rumble, and then grew louder. It was one of our South African friends, and it sounded as if he were tuning a symphony orchestra before a concert. Within a few moments, the pitch was picked up and joined in by all the South Africans. I couldn't believe it--they were singing an Anglican hymn of praise, giving glory to God!

They were beautiful voices, but I was trying to make sense of it all. *Were they joyous because they didn't want their American friends to leave so soon? How could a jackknifed trailer filled with fifty suitcases be a blessing?* But then I listened to the words they were singing, "Give praise and glory unto God, the Father of all blessing...with balm my inmost heart He fills, His comfort all my anguish stills. To God be praise and glory."

As I looked at the twisted trailer, I understood: everything brings glory to God, the bad as well as the good. Our South Africa friends continued to sing, raising their hands high to the sky and swaying back and forth in a gentle rhythm! The only thing I could do was cry.

How could I be so self-centered about my health issues and my marriage when God still loved me more than anything in life, loved me even when the situation looked devastating and hopeless? My tears flowed freely down my face, and I didn't care how I looked or who noticed. *Only one question remained: Could I ever get to a place where I would sing a beautiful song in bad times, as well as in good?*

By then, the men had unloaded the luggage from the van and were looking over the back tire mired in the wet mud. Joffe brought some cardboard from the church and placed it under the back tires. It didn't look very promising, as the wet ground engulfed the pieces in mud. As the men gently rocked the trailer backwards onto the cardboard strips, our driver got back in and slowly put the van into gear. All I could hear were glorious voices still singing praise to God. The tires took hold and the van slowly pulled out of the wet ground. The singing got louder, with all hands held high into the air.

With a final groan, the van pitched onto the solid surface of the roadway and a cheer rose up from everyone! We scrambled to hug our South African friends with more tears all around.

"Goodbye, my new friends, until we meet again!"

ॐ ॐ ॐ

I snuggled into my plane seat filled with a spirit of wonder at the goodness of God. I vowed that I would forgive Curtis for everything. Maybe with God's help we could still be friends. I just wasn't sure how I would find him.

10

Coming Home

"You can't, in most things, get what you want if you want it too desperately: anyway, you can't get the best out of it. . . The time when there is nothing at all in your soul except a cry for help may be just the time when God can't give it: you are like a drowning man who can't be helped because he clutches and grabs. Perhaps your own reiterated cries deafen you to the voice you hope to hear."

— C.S. Lewis

An eighteen-hour plane ride gives you plenty of time to wrestle your thoughts to the ground. The gentleman next to me wanted to talk about a book he'd written on his imprisonment on Robben Island, but I was grateful when he finally nodded off. I was on emotional overload and exhausted. Sleep was elusive.

I tried to concentrate on warm memories, especially the last embraces from my new friends. The cultures are different, but their genuine love reminded me that we all have the same Spirit within us, making us one. The phrase, "brothers and sisters in Christ" was no longer just a contemporary euphemism, but a realization that we all have the same Father. It would take some adjustments in my life to live out the idea that my "neighbor" was also my family.

My thoughts drifted to the people that I'd traveled with from Nashville. Incredibly successful as businessmen and women, they attributed everything they had to the glory of God. I'd been in churches where the rich felt "chosen" and the poor experienced a dreary life. This group from St. George's was different. They were willing to serve God with menial tasks and big projects alike. There was nothing too small to honor God. It was fun being with them as they served the Lord. I had searched a lifetime for joy, and I found it in the friendship of these eleven people.

I wanted to put my past twelve days in South Africa on continuous replay, but it was hard to put Curtis out of my mind. *Had he gone to Oklahoma, where his family was?* It was with sadness that I realized that we hadn't seen any of his family since Christmas last year. His mother had died ten weeks before, and the holiday hadn't been the same without her.

My thoughts always got stuck in the middle of a great debate. I wanted to be a good Christian wife and support my husband through "better or worse", but then I would think about my unsettledness and guilt over a divorce. *What had happened in our marriage that we couldn't seem to talk without fighting?* Our young desires for happiness were now a distant past. I had wanted everything to be like when we first started dating, but you can't turn back the hands of time just because the path you chose didn't lead you to the enchanted castle.

It was around the time we stopped to refuel in Dakar, the halfway point home, when I noticed my throat was scratchy and I felt feverish. My lack of sleep on the trip had caught up with me. The world always looks worse when I'm sick and I needed all my energy to make decisions when I got home. I retrieved two aspirin from my bag in the overhead bin, and snuggled up against the window. As I finally drifted off to sleep, I dreamed of a new life with a renewed faith and service to my neighbor.

ော ော ော

We landed in Nashville and I definitely was sick with a sore throat, earache, and fever. One of the girls from the trip offered to take me home from the airport and all I could think about was a hot shower and going to bed. I'd just have to track Curtis down tomorrow.

I remembered the dogs were at the kennel, so we swung by to pick them up on the way home. The dogs are always so excited to see me, eager to share their unconditional love. As I paid for their stay, the girl at the checkout desk asked, "Is your husband okay? He looked pretty sick when he brought Rachel and Bridget in."

Details of the last phone call from Curtis when I was in South Africa were still crystal clear, but there wasn't any point in sharing them. Maybe I had been wrong and Curtis had been sick instead of drunk. I was grateful to be headed home and to bed.

I unlocked the front door and was surprised that the alarm wasn't set. I let the dogs out into the backyard and went into the kitchen to get a glass of water for more aspirin. As I walked into the bedroom, I was shocked to see Curtis covered up in bed.

I shook him gently. "Are you okay? I thought you said that you'd be gone when I got home."

"I expected to be gone."

It wasn't a clear voice that answered, more of a guttural sound. I moved closer and looked at Curtis' face.

"What happened to you? Were you in a fight? You have huge black circles around your eyes. Did you fall?"

"Yes, I fell."

"Oh, dear. Let me get some cool water."

In a hurry, I spilled water on the kitchen floor. I opened the pantry door to discard the used paper towel and discovered a trashcan filled with empty liquor bottles of all kinds: Johnnie Walker Black, Grey Goose Vodka, and Maker's Mark Whiskey. I counted ten full-size bottles of liquor and two empty wine bottles. I knew they weren't in the trash when I'd left twelve days ago.

This could not be happening to me again. Why was I always the caregiver? I wanted to be back in South Africa, letting my new friends take care of me.

I returned to the bedroom and laid the cool towel on Curtis' forehead. He'd fallen asleep and seemed to be resting comfortably.

As I sat in silence in the living room I decided that I'd go to a motel for the night to get some rest. I gathered my thoughts: *If I had some help, maybe things wouldn't look so bad. If someone else would talk to him about his drinking, maybe he'd go for some counseling and we could make a go of our relationship.*

I called Curtis' four brothers and sister, asking if anyone could come to Nashville and help me. I even offered to pay their airfare, and pay for everything while they were here, but everyone was too busy to make the trip.

Next I thought about calling the kids, but they hadn't been to visit their dad in over a year. They hadn't even gone to Oklahoma for their grandmother's funeral, so I hadn't seen them in almost two years. It was awkward because I didn't want them to think less of their father, but I needed help. I struggled and decided against calling them. At twenty-seven years old, it was clear that they had their own lives to live.

Michael was the one brother who I hadn't reached, and I suspected he and his wife were in Guadalajara, Mexico, visiting her family. Michael was always my favorite in-law, and I hoped that he would call back before I went to the motel to sleep that night. A quotation came to mind, but I couldn't recall the author. *"It isn't the struggle itself that is the most difficult; it is when we struggle alone."*

I walked back into the bedroom to tell Curtis that I was going to a motel for the night and would call him tomorrow. After all, I was sick and I needed to get some sleep. My head was starting to throb and my sore throat was getting worse. "Curtis, I'm going to a motel. I'll call you tomorrow after I've had time to get some sleep. I'm sick, I have a cold and I don't want to make any decisions or have a conversation tonight."

He started to get out of bed and began weaving. I looked into his eyes and realized that he hadn't sobered up at all since I'd walked in four hours ago.

"Curtis, you need to get back into bed. Have you been drinking? "

"I don't remember anything since you left to go to South Africa. I'm glad you're home. It was awful without you."

"Can you walk? Can you get in my car? I need to take you to the Emergency Room. Are you willing to go to the hospital and have a doctor look at you? You look beat up."

He was sitting up unsteadily on the side of the bed and I realized he had bruises all over his body, with deep, black circles around his eyes. When I'd worked in the Intensive Care Unit back in Oklahoma, patients looked that way when they had bleeding in the brain; we called it "raccoon eyes". As much as I wanted to run away, I knew I had to get Curtis to the Emergency Room.

"No. I can't make it to your car."

"Go back to bed. I'm calling for an ambulance for you to go to Centennial Medical Center. They will help you there. You need to rest."

When I'd worked at Centennial, the staff suspected that Curtis drank heavily. I thought I'd hidden it from everyone, but occasionally Curtis would call when I'd have to work late and the staff would answer the phone. No one ever asked me directly, but I could tell that there were whispers about us. We'd often turn down invitations to socialize because I didn't know what condition he would be in when the weekend rolled around.

I swallowed hard because after today it wouldn't just be whispers. But Curtis needed the best care and that was at Centennial. I remembered back when I was in South Africa and had told people I hardly knew about my marriage. They had helped me understand how comforting it is to have others stand with you when you're in pain. Even when your life is a disaster, people will help you if you give them a chance.

My hand was steady when I dialed 911. "I've just arrived home from a trip and my husband can't stand up. I think he's been drinking, but he has bruises around his head like he's been beaten up. He needs to go to the Emergency Room and I can't get him into my car. Can you come and take him to Centennial? He's not in immediate danger, but I can't get him there by myself."

I got an overnight bag together for Curtis and started praying. The ambulance came within minutes, along with a fire truck escort. It was 9 p.m. and the commotion rustled my next-door neighbor, who realized immediately what was happening. "We are so sorry you have to go through this. Will you please let us know what we can do for you?"

I can be pretty stoic when I have to be, but rather than make the same tired excuses, I was honest this time: "Thanks, but there's nothing you can do right now. Curtis has been drinking and I'm afraid he's been hurt. I'm taking him to the Emergency Room. Did anything unusual happen at the house while I was in South Africa?"

"No, nothing that we saw or heard. I'm so sorry for you. Please let us know if we can help."

ços ços ços

It was a long ride to the hospital. A few employees remembered me from when I had worked there, so the proverbial cat was out of the bag. Everyone would know that my husband was an alcoholic. It actually felt good not to have to hide the facts any longer.

The Emergency Room doctor was busy with two other patients, but he stopped to tell me that he had ordered lab work and Curtis would be moved to Radiology for a CT scan to make sure there was no brain damage. It seemed impossible that just twenty-four hours before I had been listening to South African voices, with their hands held high, praising God. My throat ached and I knew the fever was back. All I knew to do was sit in the small chair in the Emergency Room bay and pray.

After taking a swing at one of the nurses, Curtis had been sedated and was resting comfortably. He'd exclaimed to everyone who came behind the curtain, "Tell her, Doc; it's not my drinking, it's my deviated septum. If I could just have surgery I'd be a different person. Look it up on the Internet. My depression would be gone if I could breathe again. It doesn't have anything to do with drinking, I just need to get my nose fixed and I'll be a new person. Tell her, Doc."

At 2 a.m., the doctor pulled the curtain back and said, "We do have some good news. We just got the CT scan results back and there is no damage to his brain. The bruises look like they are days old and there's no sign of any internal bleeding. However, we are concerned about his troponin level; he may have had a heart attack, but it's too early to tell. We're going to admit him to the CCU and move him there in a few minutes. All his other laboratory work is normal except for a few electrolytes; he was probably dehydrated. Oh, and, his blood alcohol level was 0.35 when we drew it around 10 p.m. last night. When was the last time he had a drink?"

"Oh, my! I'm not sure, but I know he hasn't had anything to drink since I got home around 1 p.m. yesterday. I've been in South Africa for twelve days."

"Well, he needs to be detoxed carefully with an alcohol level that high. But we'll take good care of him in the CCU for a couple of days. Our bigger concern is this heart enzyme. We'll be watching him closely.

"Should I stay with him?"

"No, you need to get some rest. We'll call you if anything changes. We should have another level back before 9 a.m. Why don't you get some sleep and come back around 10 a.m. or so? Since he hasn't been seeing a doctor regularly, the hospitalist will take care of him while he's here."

The transportation technician held the elevator door for me as he was moving Curtis from the ER to the CCU on a stretcher. The doctor was right that I needed rest, both physically and emotionally. It was 3 a.m. and I knew in my heart that I was going to divorce Curtis. All I could feel was relief that the nightmare was going to be over.

The technician looked at me and said, "I'm so sorry for you, Ma'am." I fought back the tears; I hadn't had sleep in over thirty hours and I was definitely sick. I felt awful. But it was nice to have a stranger care.

"Thank you for your kindness."

"No problem. I really admire you, Ma'am. You're a saint for sticking by him. Most wives would have dropped him off at the Emergency Room and headed home."

I felt numb. I couldn't accept false praise. I wasn't a saint, far from it. It wasn't that I didn't love Curtis anymore; I just couldn't take care of him any longer. The phone call in South Africa played through my head: "I won't be here when you get home." It was obvious from the last twelve hours that Curtis hadn't meant that he was leaving me to live somewhere else. He'd planned to drink himself to death.

It was 4 a.m. when I finally crawled into bed. I said a prayer of thanksgiving and asked forgiveness. This was the final chapter of my marriage and this time there was no turning back. I was resolute to start the divorce process as soon as I could find a good lawyer.

$$\text{\ensuremath{\wp}} \quad \text{\ensuremath{\wp}} \quad \text{\ensuremath{\wp}}$$

I slept for six hours and went back to the hospital, hoping to catch the doctor on morning rounds. I knew that David and Dyer would already be at the hospital and I'd sent a quick email to them about what had happened and asked for their prayers.

When I got to the CCU, Curtis was combative, shouting, "Are you going to divorce me? I have sleep apnea, you know. It hasn't been diagnosed, but that's what's wrong. It makes you depressed. You can't leave me now. You promised to love me for better or worse."

125

The nurse came in to give him another Valium injection. "I'm sorry, Ma'am, but I've got to give him more medication to calm him down. The doctor has already made rounds this morning, but I'll get him on the phone so you can talk with him."

The nurse handed me the phone. "Here's his doctor."

"Thank you for all you're doing to keep Curtis comfortable. He doesn't seem to have changed much since I brought him into the Emergency Room last night. Did he have a heart attack?"

"No, the first laboratory test that was elevated turned out to be a false positive. When the second one came back normal this morning, I had them re-run the sample from the Emergency Room last night and they got a different result. I'm so sorry, but it appears that everything we're seeing is related to his alcohol level. We're going to have to take a few days to detox him and then we'll go from there. Don't get too far ahead of yourself and try not to make any decisions today. We'll take good care of him."

"Thanks. I appreciate your kindness and care."

When I got to the CCU waiting room, I was grateful to see David sitting there. His words were comforting, but his willingness to be present with me meant the most. He stayed for almost an hour and said that he would pray for Curtis' recovery, for my health, and for wisdom for me in decision-making. I didn't realize how good it felt to have someone say, "I'll pray for you."

ॐ ॐ ॐ

The next three days were touch-and-go as Curtis had around-the-clock sedatives to keep him from hurting himself while we waited for his alcohol level to slowly come down. I was relieved when I'd visit and he would be asleep. When he wasn't, all he'd say is, "You aren't going to divorce me, are you? You promised to love me for better or for worse."

My sadness was growing and my own sickness had turned into a full-blown bout of bronchitis, complete with coughing,

126

chills, wheezing, and a headache. I'd gone back to work to distract me from the mess my life was in. I faithfully made hospital visits morning and evening, but the more I tried to love him, the more I couldn't.

On the morning of day four of Curtis' hospital stay, I was relieved when I saw his brother, Michael's, phone number on my caller ID. He apologized for taking so long to call back, but he'd just returned from Mexico. "I'll be there tomorrow, but what's going on? We heard Curtis had a heart attack."

"Not exactly. The heart attack turned out to be a false alarm. But he did have a blood alcohol level of 0.35. I don't know what to do next. They are talking about discharging him tomorrow or the next day. Thank you for coming to help me."

"You bet. I've already checked flights and I'll be on the Southwest flight that arrives at 11 a.m. tomorrow."

It was a huge relief to have Michael on the way. I had made up my mind that I was going to file for a divorce, and I didn't want to tell Curtis alone.

ço ço ço

On my way to the airport, I found myself drowning in a lifetime of self-pity. As a little girl, I'd wedge myself in between my parents when they were fighting, trying to distract my father from physically abusing my mother. Later it seemed like getting straight "A's" in school was the only thing that was rewarded. Now I was faced with more tough decisions and my life was a mess. I had more surgeries to go through, and my marriage was over. I said a prayer that Michael wouldn't judge me, but my decision was final. I hoped that Michael would understand that I needed to be alone and get my relationship with God straightened out.

We went straight to the hospital from the airport. Curtis started the conversation saying, "It's sleep apnea. Nothing else is wrong with me. I just need surgery and I'll be fine."

"Curtis, do you remember drinking while Agatha was in South Africa? The laboratory results don't lie. You were pretty drunk when the ambulance brought you here."

"I don't remember that. Can they schedule my nose surgery before I go home? I've read about it on the Internet. I have all the symptoms. I don't sleep well at night, can't breathe when I sleep, and I'm depressed."

"If you're depressed, why don't you see a doctor and get some medication? I have a friend in Houston that was depressed and the doctor gave her some medication. She's a different person," Michael offered.

I knew Michael was trying to be helpful, but it was a conversation that I'd had with Curtis more than once: "*If you are depressed, go see a doctor, and get some help. There is nothing to be ashamed of, but these demons are ruining our life together.*" Maybe the advice would be different coming from someone other than his wife.

"I don't need pills. I need surgery and then I'll be fine.

I was so appreciative that Michael had come to help, but he couldn't stay forever. In fact, he was going back to Houston on Saturday. I continued to pray in earnest, as I knew all the decisions would eventually fall back on me. I wasn't well enough to take care of Curtis and he wouldn't admit that he needed help. Curtis transferred to an inpatient rehab facility the next day, and Michael and I went to visit him in the outdoor picnic area at lunchtime.

Curtis seemed glad to see us and thanked Michael for coming to visit. "But all I need is surgery and I'll be fine."

Michael said, "Curtis, you've got a drinking problem and you need help. You may need surgery too, but that isn't going to cure your drinking problem. I don't believe you've ever apologized to Agatha for everything that you've put her through with your drinking. It would be a great start on a new life."

Curtis was silent and I wondered if he'd even heard his brother. Curtis had never said he was sorry to anyone for anything, and today was no different. There was always an excuse or someone else to blame. I was disheartened when Curtis finally looked up and said, "Michael, you are a good brother, but this isn't really any of your business. I hope that you can come and visit us again soon. Goodbye."

We all stood up as Curtis silently walked back toward the main building.

"I guess that sums it up, Michael. I'm sorry, but I've made up my mind. I'm divorcing Curtis. I have the name of a lawyer and I'm calling him on Monday. It is too painful to see him when he's drinking. There is nothing I can do to help him.

A flush rose in my cheeks as Jimmy's image flashed in my mind. I quickly pushed it back into the dark depths of my memory. "There isn't anyone else Michael, I promise. I just can't go on living my life with Curtis like this."

"I understand," was Michael's response.

ço ço ço

I dropped Michael off at the airport on Saturday morning and told him how thankful I was that he had come to help me.

"I didn't do anything really. It sounds like you'd already made up your mind about the divorce. I hate to lose you as a sister-in-law, and I really don't see how Curtis will make it without you; he does love you."

"He sure has a funny way of showing his love." I felt tears start to well up in my eyes when I thought back to when we were first in love, but I shifted back to the present. "You won't lose me as a sister-in-law; I'll always be a part of the family. It wasn't that you did so much while you were here, you just showed up when I called. It was so good to have someone know what I was going through. It made it easier to bear. Thanks again for coming."

It was a lonely ride back to the house and I had most of the weekend in front of me. I would have to get used to a big house for only the dogs and me.

❧ ❧ ❧

I started moving the trash can to the curb for Monday morning pick-up and realized that it just wasn't the ten bottles of liquor in the pantry trash; there were more empty bottles in the large trashcan. That explained the blood alcohol level.

It was late Sunday afternoon and I needed to talk with someone who I trusted. I dialed Kim from the PORCH CLUB. All the girls had sent me an email when I returned from South Africa, but I hadn't had time to fill them in on everything. The initial report was that Curtis had a heart attack and that is what I had texted them. I said that I'd fill them in when I knew more.

I openly shared my thoughts, and my sadness. "Kim, I'm filing for a divorce on Monday. I can't take this anymore."

"Let's talk about that, girl. It doesn't sound like Curtis has had the capacity to encourage you to love God; in fact, if anything he's interfered with you getting involved at church or studying your Bible. I don't see that it's going to get better and he hasn't apologized or said that he would change. It's like he's trying to compete with God, and doesn't understand how important our individual relationship with God is. I can't believe that I'm going to even suggest that divorce is the right answer, but I need to ask you to think about why you feel this way. You know I love you and you can't go on like this. You've still got more surgeries to face and you need people to surround you with love, not people who are dependent upon you for all their emotional needs. I'll pray for you, but it may be God's will that you get divorced."

"But God hates divorce. How can I know what the right decision is?"

"You'll know the answer, just keep praying."

❧ ❧ ❧

I prayed all week, but when I got up the next Sunday, I couldn't face going to the Catholic Church alone. I didn't want anyone asking where Curtis was, and I certainly didn't want to share that he was in inpatient rehab. My friend Priscilla had sent me an email asking me to sit with her at the 7:30 a.m. service at St. George's Episcopal Church. I knew that I needed to go to church somewhere, and receiving communion always made me feel renewed. I walked into the foyer of the church, but instead of seeing Priscilla, I was hugged immediately by one of the guys from the South Africa trip, Larry Trabue.

"We knew we'd convince you to visit!"

I managed a weak smile but I was bolstered by his enthusiasm. Someone was actually glad to see me. I decided to share the short version of what had happened since I'd returned from South Africa, and he invited me to join him and his mother for brunch at Belle Meade Plantation after the service." We'll see you at the restaurant; bring your friend too if she can make it."

Why were people I hardly knew so friendly? I felt the same way here in Nashville that I had when I was in South Africa: warm and cared for, like I belonged. It must be their faith in God, because there was no other explanation for the joy that I experienced when I was with people from St. George's.

That night I prayed again that I would receive some clear direction in my life. I was resolute that I was filling out the questionnaire the divorce lawyer had emailed during the week. I didn't relish being alone in the world again, but I felt that God was telling me that it was important for me to be single again. It would allow me to rekindle my relationship with God without the responsibility of caring for a husband and a family.

On Monday at noon, I called my lawyer and explained that I wanted to be fair and split everything 50-50. Now that both of the kids were out of college it would be easier. Since we were out of debt, Curtis could live comfortably on his own income and I could live on mine. I dropped by the inpatient treatment facility on the way home from work and told Curtis the news that I had completed the paperwork for the divorce, and that when he was discharged he'd have to find another place to live.

"So, this your final decision?"

"Yes, it is, I just can't go on like this."

"You know I'll never stop loving you. But if you file for a divorce, we don't have anything else left to discuss."

So it was going to end like this. Without any fanfare or attempt at reconciliation. There was a part of me that still wanted to hear him say, "I love you. I'll do anything you say to keep you. Just name it. Give me one more chance." Instead, there was an uncomfortable silence between us.

I didn't know what to say except, "I'm sorry, Curtis."

గ్రా గ్రా గ్రా

The final divorce paperwork was ready in a few weeks and the administrative assistant emailed me a copy to review before I went by the office to sign the original. I was at work and printed the copies at our shared printer, but when I got up to retrieve the documents, a wave of nausea came over me. I couldn't be pregnant; I knew it was just nerves and the voice in my head making me feel guilty: *How can you file for a divorce? He hasn't committed adultery or left you as a non-believer. You call yourself a Christian? Good Christian wives don't divorce their husbands.*

I sat down at my desk again and prayed to God that the decision I was making was the right one. I got up for a second time to retrieve the divorce papers from the printer. As I was hurrying to the printer room, I stopped abruptly when I felt a rush of air. It felt like someone had bumped into me coming around the corner. Startled, I turned around but no one was there.

"You shouldn't stop suddenly like that; one of us is going to get hurt."

It was clearly a voice.

Another whisper, "You should watch where you're going; you're the one who was walking too fast."

I knew the words were all in my mind, but they were just as real as if they were spoken out loud.

"I'll be with you every step of the way."

"Who are you? What do you want from me?"

"I said, 'I'll be with you every step of the way.' It won't be an easy road that you are going down, in fact it's going to be very rocky and you'll have a lot of sadness. But it is the right road, and I promise, I'll walk right by your side. Now slow down and take a deep breath. I don't want to get my robe caught in the door when you take corners so fast!"

I knew that I hadn't been sleeping very well and this had to be my tiredness showing through. *But what did the comment about the robe mean?* The night that I had the visits from Christ, the apparition appeared dressed in a white robe. *Could it be one and the same?*

It wasn't something I could figure out today. I knew I was tired, but it was comforting to think that Christ would always be with me, protecting me.

I grabbed the paper from the printer and headed back to my desk to make sure there weren't any errors in the Marital Dissolution Agreement. I had time to go by the lawyer's office the next day to sign everything so that a court date could be set.

ഗ്ര ഗ്ര ഗ്ര

It was a tough six weeks until my birthday. I was worrying about money and being alone. I'd applied for a second mortgage so that I'd have enough money to pay Curtis his share of the equity and keep the house. Half of our art collection would go to him, and we'd keep our own retirement accounts. I knew that material possessions shouldn't be important, but I was thankful that I had a good job or divorce wouldn't be an option.

The Tuesday before my birthday, I got a call at work from an old friend, a Cardiologist I hadn't seen or heard from in decades. I'd trained as a cardiology pharmacist straight out of school and did research in the Cardiology Divisions at both University Hospital and St. Anthony Hospital in Oklahoma City. I was delighted to hear that a subcommittee of the American College of Cardiology was holding a meeting in Nashville and my friend would be visiting for a few days. He'd found me through LINKEDIN and then called the switchboard at the HCA Corporate Office. It was so good to talk with him and hear a "Happy Birthday!"

"How about dinner tomorrow evening? Our subcommittee meeting is over at 7 p.m. and we could eat here at the Opryland Hotel. There are some great restaurants here. How about if we meet at the Old Hickory Steakhouse? I'll make a reservation for 7:30 p.m."

I rationalized that it would be okay, after all, I'd filed for a divorce and it would be final in another month. I really wanted to see him. It would remind me of a happier time in my life.

I was excited at the thought of a relaxing evening with an old friend. I even caught myself humming when I was driving out to the Opryland Hotel. I laughed because I was always dancing to music that was playing in my head while I made dinner. Curtis would be critical, like he wasn't in on a private joke, but I have always loved music and there is always a tune in my head. I valet parked and was delighted when I approached the waiting area in the bar at the restaurant and heard, "Agatha, you haven't changed a bit; you are just as beautiful as I remember you." I blushed a little as he kissed me lightly on the cheek, but I warmed to the compliment. I hadn't felt beautiful since that first surgery eighteen months before.

We settled in with two vodka martinis while we waited for our table. I was surprised to learn that he'd relocated his practice to Texas in 2002 and that for a year we'd both been in the same State. Of course, it's a big state and our paths had never crossed. We traded stories of the people we remembered, and the great times we'd had. It was a much happier time for both of us. He'd gotten married right after moving to Texas, but I was a little uncomfortable when he shared that they'd been in counseling for the past year. "Ever since the twins were born three years ago, things have been different. She doesn't want to go out anymore and our whole life revolves around the kids. It's almost like I don't exist."

Our lively conversation continued through dinner and dessert and another pair of vodka martinis. As he was paying the bill, he said, "This has been a great evening! I've got some Courvoisier in my room. Would you like to come up for a nightcap?"

I'd already had plenty to drink, but the night had been so much fun. It was nice to have a handsome guy care about me again. Surely one drink couldn't hurt! I laughingly said that I'd call a cab if I weren't able to drive home.

We got to his suite and he poured two healthy portions of cognac. The conversation was as warm as the liquor. There was a pause and he said, "Agatha, I've always thought you were beautiful, but you were always dating someone else when we were in training. We worked on research projects together and I wanted to ask you out, but I was afraid you'd turn me down. What would you say if I asked you to spend the night?"

"But, you're married! I couldn't possibly stay."

"But you can't drive home. You're in no condition to get your car from the valet. You're going to have to spend the night. It can be on your terms." With that, he poured another cognac. He crossed the room to hand me a fresh glass, but paused for a long sweet kiss.

I didn't resist and tasted another. After all, technically he was the one that was married, not me. If there was sin involved it was his and not mine. More than likely, I'd never see him again. No one would ever know.

"I've shared with you about my breast cancer, but my reconstruction isn't complete. I'm still deformed."

"I don't care. You've always been beautiful to me, and always will."

I wondered for just a moment if it was the liquor that was making me feel warm, but then I willingly fell into his arms.

ভ ভ ভ

I was thoughtful on the drive home the next morning. I wanted to feel guilty, but instead I felt loved. I was still physically deformed yet an old friend had made me feel beautiful again. How could that be wrong?

11

Strangers

Over the years I have learned that the greatest gain from the healing of my own soul has not been relief from pain, though sometimes my pain has diminished. Nor has it been the end of all my struggles, though at many points I have been strengthened. Trial and temptation we have always with us, until Jesus comes again. The greatest gain has been the increase of my capacity to know, understand, and love God. The healing of the soul is for the setting of love in order.

– Rick Richardson

Predictably, I found myself in emotional swings from guilt over sleeping with a married man to euphoria for feeling desirable again after breast cancer. I blamed part of my distress on nightly hot flashes from the Lupron shots that I received to prevent a recurrence of breast cancer. Instead of my life recovering from its tailspin, it was spinning faster and faster.

I was grateful that another semester in school was complete. I'd dropped one class after I got behind in my assignments when Curtis was in the hospital, but I'd finished my health policy class on schedule. I'd always sought solace in intellectual pursuits and I was determined to finish my degree no matter how long it took. The faculty had been so supportive during my surgeries, and I couldn't let them down.

What I hoped was my last surgery was scheduled for the day after my final. It was a short outpatient procedure for nipple reconstruction and tattooing, and a coworker had offered to take me to the hospital. I was grateful to have a friend that lived close by. I'd thought about asking someone from St. George's, but I'd only visited a few times and didn't want to impose.

The Saturday before my surgery, a small group of church members were having coffee after the 7 a.m. service at St. George's. As I got ready to leave, I told them that I was having a "short outpatient procedure; nothing to worry about" the following Friday, and that I wouldn't be there the following Saturday.

"Can we pray for you?"

"No, that's okay, it's just a little procedure; nothing to worry about." I hadn't told them about the cancer, and it was hard for me to accept prayer for such a minor thing.

൭ ൭ ൭

I was back home by 1 p.m. after surgery, resting comfortably and watching television when I heard the answering machine pick up, "This is Seawell, your friend from St. George's. Wanted you to know that we were thinking about you and if you need anything, here's my phone number. Get well soon!"

I knew I wasn't dreaming. I'd only met Seawell a few times at St. George's, yet he'd called to check on me. Must be Priscilla had given him my phone number.

It was a warm feeling as I fell asleep on the couch watching the movie, *"Ghost"* for the fifth time. I didn't wake up until late evening and realized that my voicemail light was blinking on my phone. The messages were from my new friends from St. George's, calling to see if there was something they could do to help! I replayed Seawell's message first, and then it was Priscilla, Bob, and Monica, all wishing me well and praying for a speedy recovery.

Wow, if this is how they treat visitors, I wonder how they treat members? I had never felt so loved by a church community, and I admitted that I had never needed it more.

ɕ� ɕ� ɕ�

The six weeks leading up to the divorce were awful. Every shadow in the night had a fright behind it. I was barely getting four hours of restless sleep each night. The worry was beginning to take its toll, and I knew that makeup would no longer hide my sorrow. Curtis had moved into an apartment and kept making frequent arrangements to come over to the house to pick up a "few things", but it generally ended in a fight.

"So, who's the guy?"

"What guy, Curtis?"

"The guy who's moving in as soon as my stuff is out of here. There has to be a guy. I know you too well. You wouldn't go without sex, so if you're getting rid of me, there has to be someone else."

"I told you that there's no one else. I just can't take care of you any more. I've got to have some sanity in my life so that I can get well."

"I don't believe you. There must be a guy. You know that if you go through with this divorce and ever remarry that you're committing adultery. Read your Bible. You know the chapter and verses I'm talking about."

I was stunned. I'd never seen Curtis open a Bible, let alone read one. *How could he have known those verses and used them against me?* I knew some churches taught that there were only two reasons for a legitimate divorce: adultery, and when the non-believer wanted to leave the marriage. My divorce didn't fit either situation. But I'd resolved that I'd rather be alone in my silence with God, than with someone who was keeping me from my faith.

The word, "adultery" struck a sour note in my head. It was impossible that Curtis had found out about my night at the hotel just a few weeks ago. I felt the same guilt that would plague me whenever I'd failed and disappointed God before.

My mood swings were running rampant and it was easy for me to blame the Lupron shots. One day I wanted to withdraw the divorce proceedings and just try harder at the marriage, and the next day I was resolute again to go through with it. I knew I was afraid of being alone and lonely, but then I wasn't well enough to deal with Curtis' moods. I recognized that the fear of being alone had kept me in my marriage for quite some time, along with my desire to not disappoint God.

My birthday came and went without celebration. I made it to the 10 a.m. service on Christmas at St. George's. Strangely, it was peaceful to be resting in God's house, even as I sat alone.

§o §o §o

The week before the final divorce hearing in January, there was no turning back. Maybe time away from each other was what we needed and we could still be friends. It was an awful thought, but I was glad that Curtis' mother had already passed away. I had loved her and wouldn't have been able to face her when I was divorcing her son.

The Friday before the divorce was final Curtis came over to get his remaining things out of the garage. "So, you're going through with this, huh?"

"Yes, Curtis, I have to. For my sanity, as well as my health. I don't love you anymore."

"You call yourself a Christian and here you, are divorcing me. I don't want this, you know. You can never remarry or it will be adultery. I'd think that would be important to you. You do realize that you'll never see the kids again, don't you?"

"What? What did you just say?"

"I said, 'You'll never see the kids again.' In fact, I've told the whole family that if you go through with this divorce, they are never to talk with you or see you again. I'm the oldest and my word goes. You'll never have any contact with any of them again if you sign the final paperwork. It's your decision. You can change your mind before Monday."

So the line had been drawn in the sand. I blushed because I knew how important family was to me, but instead of making me change my mind, it just made me angry. I felt the color rise in my cheeks as I remembered all the times that Curtis had tried to manipulate my emotions. Every time we'd fight, Curtis would say, "Oh, I never said that, you must have been dreaming," or, "I was only joking, can't you tell when I'm not being serious?"

Was it possible that if I went through with the divorce I'd never see the kids again or hear from anyone in the family? I swallowed hard but my anger rose. "Take the last of your things and get out. I'll take my chances on no one ever talking to me again. It will be better than having all these emotional threats all the time."

"Just remember that you have no family; you'll die poor and alone." With that, Curtis picked up his last box and slammed the front door in my face so hard that it rattled the front window.

Displays of anger just made me calmer. I wasn't going to be in a relationship anymore with someone who wasn't free to love me. I was sure there were demons involved, but they weren't mine, and my love wasn't powerful enough to overcome them for Curtis. I'd been mistaken all along that one faith was strong enough for two people.

ဖော ဖော ဖော

The day for the final divorce hearing had arrived. I put on my gray suit and wondered why I didn't feel better. I knew it was the guilt that was weighing me down. Plenty of pastors' and politicians' wives had "stood by their man", even after an affair.

What was different about their resolve? Curtis had indicated that he wouldn't be present for the hearing, so after three questions and ten minutes, the female judge pronounced that I was no longer a married woman. I walked through the front door of the courthouse into the bright sunlight and felt relief that a caged bird had been set free.

ॐ ॐ ॐ

Two weeks later it was time for my every three-month check-up with my oncologist, Dr. Yardley.

"How are you doing, Agatha? Are you sleeping okay? How are the hot flashes; any better?"

"I'm doing okay, Denise, but the hot flashes still wake me up a couple of times every night. Do you think I should take some sleeping pills for awhile and see if that helps?"

"We can consider that, but only if you really need them. They won't do anything for the hot flashes and you may be groggy in the morning."

My breast exam was normal, but every time I went to the doctor there was always the chance of bad news. With doctors' visits every three months, a new cancer would be caught immediately, but it didn't make the possibility any easier.

"Agatha, let me measure your arms."

"What's wrong?"

"Well, it looks like you've got some swelling. I want to check for lymphedema where you had the lymph nodes removed during your mastectomy.

"Sure enough, your left forearm is 2-1/2 inches larger than your right. Have you been having any pain in that arm?"

"Well, yes, but I didn't think much of it. My left hand started hurting about eight weeks ago and then one day I woke up and the pain was mysteriously gone."

"Probably what happened is the lymph fluid went down into your hand. Your index and middle finger are swollen too. I'm going to order physical therapy treatments for you for the next six weeks. You'll go two or three times each week, and they'll give you a special massage to relieve the pressure. Then they'll bandage your arm to prevent the fluid from accumulating again. They're going to wrap your arm in bandages from your fingers to your shoulder, and it will be uncomfortable at first. But you've got to do it, and then learn to wrap your arm yourself. Lymphedema is going to be a life-long battle for you."

I'd anticipated an uneventful doctor's visit and wasn't prepared for this. I didn't know if I could endure painful therapy visits, and I'd have to take more time off work. It seemed like my health was getting worse instead of better, and now I had a new complication. It was just another thing that I was going to have to deal with.

୨୦ ୨୦ ୨୦

After an initial assessment, the physical therapist gave me a massage, and then wrapped my left arm in tight bandages to prevent fluid from getting into my arm again. She said it was normal to hurt a lot at first, but would gradually get better with more sessions. The only relief from the pain was to elevate my arm during the day and sleep with it on pillows at night. The first two weeks of physical therapy were the worst and I was thankful I had a few Vicodin left over from my last surgery.

୨୦ ୨୦ ୨୦

On the third week of therapy, I slept in past the 7:30 a.m. Sunday church service at St. George's. I just couldn't face the day. I wanted to go to church, but I felt awful. I'd had trouble re-bandaging my arm after my shower the day before, and it felt like all the muscles in my left hand and arm were taking turns throbbing. Vicodin didn't even touch the discomfort.

I'd never been to the 8:45 a.m. service and I wasn't in the mood to meet any new people. I thought about just going back to bed, but I always felt better when I went to church. Whether it was out of obligation or out of desire, I always felt more complete when my week started with worship. I dragged myself out of bed with just enough time to run a comb through my hair and put on a little makeup. I chose a loose blouse and jacket that covered most of the bandages on my left arm, and headed out the door.

I parked in the church parking lot and for a moment thought about turning around and going home. After all, no one would miss me, but I really needed to feel God's presence. As I stepped through the tall double doors a familiar voice rang out, "Agatha, glad to see you!" It was Larry Trabue again. He gave me a big hug and told me I looked wonderful. It was a great sentiment, but I looked anything but wonderful.

Then he noticed the bandage, "What's wrong with your hand?"

I'd shared my breast cancer diagnosis with everyone on the South Africa trip, so I quickly explained that the fluid build-up was a result of my cancer surgery and I was on week three of physical therapy. I thanked Larry for his concern, and then took my place in the back pew as the service began. I was hoping that no one would notice me.

My arm was throbbing and it was hard to concentrate on the sermon. Maybe I should have stayed home and stayed in bed. But the service was coming to a close, and I approached the communion rail. I didn't feel very grateful for my life at that moment, but the Eucharist had always been my sanctuary. The bread and wine had calmed my soul on more than one occasion, and I knew that I would be nourished by it again today.

As the priest made his way down the communion rail, I placed my right hand squarely over my left to receive the communion bread, and hoping to cover up the bandages. I recognized the Rector of St. George's, Reverend Leigh Spruill, as

I'd been introduced to him after worship service a couple of weeks before. Instead of placing a communion wafer in my hands, he stopped before me and gently placed his hand on my left shoulder. He bowed his head and began to pray. "Dear Lord, please comfort your faithful servant and heal her of the afflictions in her left hand. We ask that you give her strength and courage during this difficult time and heal her completely in the days to come. We ask this in your name, Amen."

I was stunned and almost forgot to wait for the wine. I couldn't believe that he had stopped in the middle of communion to pray for me, a visitor to his church. Tears welled up in my eyes as I was overcome with gratitude. Another human being had taken the time to call upon the power of his relationship with the Lord to ask for me to be healed. It was an incredibly powerful emotion as I felt heat rising throughout my body. I was sure that I was experiencing the presence of the Holy Spirit, and the saving grace of healing prayer.

I stood up from the communion rail and realized that nothing had changed physically. My hand and arm still hurt, but I'd been healed emotionally and spiritually. *Was it possible for me to have a close friendship with God and then call upon him to help others through healing prayer?*

I went home and prayed in earnest all afternoon. Although my left arm was throbbing from the bandages, I knew that something important had just happened. I wasn't sure exactly what it all meant, but I knew that this was the church where I belonged.

12

Temptation

No temptation has overtaken you that is not common to man. God is faithful, and He will not let you be tempted beyond your ability, but with the temptation He will also provide the way of escape, that you may be able to endure it.

– 1 Corinthians 10:13

The last thing I felt like doing after work that day was going to a State Legislative Reception. It was week five of my physical therapy visits and I'd worked a ten-hour day with a one-hour physical therapy appointment. I was too tired for words, and my left arm was bandaged again from my fingertips to my shoulder. My fingers ached under the spandex glove, no matter how much cotton I wrapped around them for protection. I'd stopped taking any Vicodin, but was pushing the safety limit on Advil and I certainly wasn't in the mood to eat, drink or be merry.

But I'd promised Sheila, 'I'll see you there' when we'd talked on the phone the week before. Sheila was a pharmacist in Germantown who I'd known even before I'd moved to Tennessee due to our involvement in national pharmacy organization work.

We both were members of the Legislative Committee for the Tennessee Pharmacists Association, and Sheila was on the State Board of Pharmacy. We shared a passion for hospital pharmacy, particularly on patient safety issues, and our paths crossed often.

I wasn't that excited about the Legislative Reception, but I did want to see Sheila. We'd been friends for more than ten years and she'd been a wonderful friend during my breast cancer treatment. It would be good to relax and have a drink with her. My plan was to make an appearance at the Legislative Reception, have one glass of wine with Sheila, and then head home to put my arm on a large stack of pillows and get some rest.

Normally I would hunt for street parking around the downtown Sheraton Hotel, but with a bandaged left arm I was having trouble navigating, so valet parking made sense. The valet took one look at the bandage on my left hand, and offered his arm to steady me as I got out of the car. I had hoped it wasn't too noticeable, but the flesh-toned glove was pretty obvious under my black suit coat jacket.

I made my way to the upstairs ballroom and checked in at the registration table. As usual, the legislators hadn't finished their afternoon session, so there were plenty of pharmacists and pharmacy students, but no legislators. I found Sheila in the crowd and grabbed a drink at the bar on the way across the room. We were just winding up a great conversation over a glass of wine when a huge group of legislators walked through the double doors. The Pharmacy Legislative Reception was noted for having some of the best food, so there was always a good crowd.

I spotted my State Representative, Gary Odom, and took Sheila over to meet him. Although Gary and I don't always agree on every issue, I feel that he is a good listener and votes on issues to support the common good. He seems mindful of the citizens he represents, rather than stirring up controversy all the time. I respect Gary and have voted for him since I've been in Nashville.

I would have never crossed party lines when I was younger, but I'd started listening more to political positions and making up my mind based upon the person's voting record, rather than their party affiliation. I chuckled, as Curtis was a Libertarian and we had long ago given up talking about politics after an embarrassing public exchange of crossfire ten years before. Curtis never knew which candidate I voted for and vice versa. I was sure in many elections I'd cancelled his vote out as his political choices had become more radical and mine had become more moderate.

Sheila and I had a great conversation with Representative Odom about a proposal for a new database that would track all the controlled substance prescriptions filled in the State of Tennessee. Sheila was convincing in her argument that it was a good idea because of the recent increase in drug trafficking, but expressed concern whether the database was robust enough to process the information timely so that it would be useful to a retail pharmacist filling a prescription.

I thanked Representative Odom for his time and was telling Sheila my goodbyes when she said, "Oh, another good friend just walked in. I want to introduce you. His name is Mike Jones. He represents a rural district in the eastern part of the state near Johnson City. He's a great guy, too, and a Republican."

My heart sank because I really wanted to go home and get some rest, but I found myself shaking the hand of a very distinguished looking man with salt and pepper hair and understanding eyes. Sheila had introduced me as a good friend from Nashville that worked at the HCA Corporate office. I knew that Sheila was the Director of Pharmacy at a hospital in Germantown so I asked, "How do you know Sheila?"

"We've worked together on some legislation over the years and I grew up near Memphis. My Dad was a pharmaceutical salesman and called on Sheila at the hospital. It's a pleasure to meet you."

"It's all my pleasure."

"What's wrong with your arm? You didn't hurt it smashing wine glasses in a fireplace, did you?"

I felt a blush coming on, as I never knew what to say when strangers asked about the bandages. I couldn't go through the whole story, but didn't want to lie.

I managed a weak smile. "No, no wine glasses were broken. I'm having some physical therapy and have to keep my arm bandaged between sessions."

"Well, if you ever want to grab a glass of wine some time, give me a call. I'm in town Monday through Thursday each week when the Legislature is in session. Here's my card."

This was a little strange for a first meeting with a State Representative: a wine invitation. I looked down at his card and realized he'd handed me his personal business card, not his legislative one: "Mike Jones, Financial Advisor" and the logo was for Stifel. I noticed the ring on his left hand when he'd extended his card.

"You're a financial advisor? Boy, I could sure use one of those these days."

"Really? I'd love to help you. My office is over at the American Center, just around the corner from HCA. Call me and you could run over to my office one day at lunchtime."

"That sounds great, but I'll have to wait awhile. I'm a little short on money right now." I took a deep breath and wondered if I should divulge that my money woes were due to my recent divorce. But he did seem nice and he was a financial planner. I was sure he'd seen the financial aftermath of a divorce before. "You see, I was divorced six weeks ago and had to remortgage the house as part of the settlement. I don't have any money right now to plan with, or any money to pay you for advice. Maybe I could call you when I get back on my feet financially."

"How about if I don't charge you for the first visit with me? Call me and we can meet in the next couple of weeks. Bring all your receipts and paperwork with you and I'll help you sort it out. We can at least get that done and see where you are. After that if you do need my services, we can talk about a long-term plan. But I won't charge you while we're just getting you organized."

This was such a breath of fresh air! If I admitted it to myself, I was perpetually worried about money. Growing up, my father didn't always have steady employment. I never really wanted for anything, but we didn't lead an extravagant lifestyle. When I got out of college I ran up the usual credit card debt buying a car and my first stereo. I remember thinking that now that I was on my own, everything was so expensive. Having nice things meant spending money. After I got married to Dave, we'd wanted a house and to travel, and credit cards were easy to use. Then, when I married Curtis, I found out how much it costs to raise children with private schools, athletics, and vacations. It seemed like I was always writing a check for something. Just like Dad, both my husbands had had gaps in employment during our marriage.

"Thanks for the offer to help me with my finances, Mike. I'll call you in a week or so."

ᔋ ᔋ ᔋ

On the drive home, I wondered if maybe a budget was what I needed to relieve the anxiety that I always felt about bank accounts, mortgages, and credit cards. Now that I was divorced I had a new worry. I was afraid I might get too sick to work and there wouldn't be anyone to take care of me. Curtis's words came back to me frequently: "You'll die alone and poor." I tried to keep my mind focused on my financial situation and getting all my receipts together, but I couldn't help but wonder what it would be like to be married to a powerful State Representative, or at least to have an affair with one.

I'd been physically faithful with Curtis, but my mind had wandered into the land of temptation every now and again. Well, faithful except for that one-night fling I'd had at the Opryland Hotel. But this was different. Mike was a State Representative, debonair, charming, and out-of-town. I couldn't escape the memories from college of my first affair, when everything was fun. We'd go on picnics and ride on his motorcycle in the summer. It was so carefree. I had to admit that being a mistress had none of the anxiety of the daily grind of married life. What would it be like now that I was single again? It wasn't a long enough drive home for me to complete the fantasy, but I couldn't get the thought of an affair with Representative Jones out of my mind.

My mind was racing as I pulled in the driveway. I knew how wrong those thoughts were. *How could I even think about having another affair with a married man? Hadn't I learned anything in fifty-three years?* Good Christian girls don't have affairs, no matter how much we're tempted. Why did I even have these thoughts? Once again I rationalized that it wasn't really my sin, I wasn't married anymore. The infidelity would be his.

As I scrambled into the house and let the dogs out into the backyard, my mind was still working overtime: *Okay, I'd met a great looking guy tonight and for the first time in months I was attracted to a man again. But he was married, and that was wrong. How could I even think about an affair, when physically, I was damaged goods? I had a bandage on my swollen left arm and scars on both breasts. I might pass in a dark room, but it was obvious that I had had breast surgery. How could I ever sleep with a man again in this condition?"*

Despite all the reasons I had for not feeling physically attractive, I Googled the Tennessee State Legislature website to find out more information about Representative Mike Jones. The first picture that greeted me was a family picture of him, his wife and three children. It looked like it was taken around a Christmas tree and they all looked very happy. She was strikingly beautiful and looked considerably younger than he did. I was actually relieved—he'd never have an affair with me, his wife was too beautiful. I clicked on the next page and his biography was written on a backdrop of a church steeple with the tagline: *Evangelical Christian.*

Oh heavens! I felt like such a fool. In addition to having a young and attractive wife, he was a devout Christian. There was no possibility of an affair. I continued to read his biography and wondered what he meant by "evangelical". The only other time

I'd heard the word was back in college in Oklahoma and my memories weren't warm. It was the "evangelical Christians" who yelled on the street corners that you were going to hell if you didn't "repent" and "get saved". I understood repentance, but had never gotten a satisfactory explanation of what "being saved" meant.

Well, at least Representative Jones didn't raise his voice at the reception that evening. Since a physical affair was out of the question, I thought back to the dismal state of my financial affairs. Maybe I would call him to help with my money problems. After all, he said he'd start out advising me for free. The price was certainly right and it couldn't hurt. After my trip to South Africa and learning more about St. George's, I promised myself that I'd quit trying to do everything on my own and let people help me. It was good to feel that I could reach out for help, but I still was unsure of how to determine whom to trust.

ॐ ॐ ॐ

My arm seemed to hurt even worse during my physical therapy visits that week. I kept thinking that a good cry would help but crying without anyone around to hear me seemed pointless. I was pretty overwhelmed with my illness and my debts, but I kept reminding myself of the most important thing: I didn't have cancer. I really felt that God cared for me, but He was sure taking His sweet time in getting me well.

Other needs were piling up too. The gate wouldn't lock in the backyard and I was afraid the dogs would escape. But I didn't have the money for any fence repairs. It was just going to have to wait until I was financially on my feet again.

I went on Representative Jones' website a couple of times that week, looking at other pictures, noticing that he belonged to a Baptist Church near Johnson City. His website portrayed the perfect life. He was a powerful conservative State Legislator with a beautiful family. He'd mentioned that he was a wine connoisseur when we met and I wondered if it was better to call him to have a drink, or to schedule a time in his office to go through the mess of my financial records. I wasn't sure that I wanted to reveal my personal finances just yet. *Would he question how I'd gotten myself into such a mess?*

But when it was quiet in the evening, I was unsure of my motive for calling him. *Did I really need help with my finances?* There wasn't any money for a financial advisor to manage. I knew lots of people who liked to drink wine. *What was there about him that I couldn't get out of my mind?*

৵৹ ৵৹ ৵৹

I was working on a school paper about health issues, specifically obesity, and how smoking had declined in Tennessee. It seemed too coincidental when I learned that Representative Jones had been the main Legislator to push through a statewide ban on smoking in restaurants a few years ago. I wondered if he would be willing to sponsor a bill to ban sugary snacks and sodas in the public school systems. I looked online but didn't see anything in the legislative database that looked like any "obesity" bills had been filed.

My school paper was a good enough reason to call him and ask for his opinion over a glass of wine. That way I could get to know him a little better and judge if I should share my story of breast cancer and divorce. At least it would explain the state of my finances. If the wine meeting didn't go well, I wouldn't lose anything and embarrass myself in front of a stranger.

Another week went by and I finally got up enough nerve to send him an email: "Dear Representative Jones: I don't know if you remember me. I am a pharmacist in Nashville and met you at the Legislative Reception last month. I'm also in graduate school at Tennessee State University and I'm doing a paper on some health issues. I'd like to ask you a few questions about your work banning smoking in restaurants in Tennessee and what your current position is on banning sugary snacks and sodas in our public schools. Would you be available to meet me for a drink and discuss it?"

I held my breath and hit the SEND button. The minute that I heard the whoosh, I was awash with guilt again. *Exactly why had I sent that email? Did I really care about smoking and obesity, or was I just interested in gauging his interest in me from a more personal standpoint? I'd never get him to leave his wife, but maybe he would be interested in an affair. Why were these thoughts haunting me? Here I was going to a new church and trying to figure out why I'd always failed at relationships. I was going down the same bad road again."*

I wondered what was wrong with me and started praying for wisdom. On the one hand, most of the world thought that affairs were okay when you weren't being nourished in a marriage. After all, it's hard to love someone forever. I was realizing that my long-standing insecurities and fears caused me to crave the closeness and desire for intimacy, clouding my judgment about men. I'd started attending the Confirmation Class at St. George's and knew that they didn't condone adultery. I heard preaching there about God's love, but it was hard to accept that it applied to me with these thoughts running through my head.

There it was, and I wished I could have that email back. My motives were awful. I didn't really need help on any school paper; it was all a lie. But then again, maybe it would be a good way to meet him, to share my story and to ask for his help with my finances. That is what I really needed right now: someone who would help me with my financial needs out of kindness, not someone to date.

I was just climbing into bed when my cell phone vibrated next to my bed signaling that an email had just arrived.

"At Rosemary Beach in Florida. Actually, on the beach. A perfect Zin. And the perfect evening. Sorry that we can't talk about your school paper in person, but call me when you get this message. I'll be up late. Here's my cell number."

I was tired and it was late. I decided that it would be better to respond by email the next morning. I was curious about the message and had trouble falling asleep. It certainly sounded more personal than I'd expected. As I drifted off to sleep, I had visions of Representative Jones relaxing on the beach, drinking a glass of Zinfandel, and me occupying the chair next to him. I wanted to pick up the phone, but it was only in my sleep that I heard my voice, "*Hi, just got your message. Would you pour me a glass of wine, too? I'd love to talk with you.*" With that I drifted off to sleep, smelling of saltwater in the sea air.

I awoke early and wondered if I'd dreamed the whole thing, but no, there was the email, still on my phone. I hastily sent an email back before heading to work, "Instead of a glass of wine at the beach, can you do dinner on the 19th, say around 7 p.m.? Let me know if that works for you." It was two weeks away and I was frantically trying to answer the question in my mind: *Exactly why are you meeting him for wine and dinner?*

Well, I need help with my school paper; I need help with my finances; he's cute and I should be going out with people; he's safe because he's a married man and an evangelical Christian. The little white lies were rolling off my tongue. But in reality, I didn't have any idea why I was meeting him for a glass of wine. I vowed to talk about my cancer, my faith and my need for financial help. This wasn't personal and I needed to just talk about things that related to my wretched financial state of affairs. I needed to get used to admitting my failures, even to strangers.

෧෨ ෧෨ ෧෨

I was glad that the semi-annual meeting of the PORCH CLUB had already been scheduled for that weekend because I needed to talk. Over the past few years, life had taken us in different directions, and the girls had all moved to other cities. I missed them sorely, but it was fun to get together for long weekends and share our stories among lots of wine and food. I was grateful for the chance for some relaxation and was looking forward to the drive to Louisville where Jackie lived.

"Okay, who wants to go first? We've got all weekend to get caught up, but let's break out the wine first." Jackie was always the organizer and party starter. The other three girls went first talking about their families, and their jobs. We hadn't been together since my divorce was final in January, and I wondered how much detail was really important. I didn't want to bore everyone or sound whiney, but it was certainly a tough spot in my life and the PORCH CLUB would understand. On the other hand, I was tired of thinking and talking about my failed marriage.

I shared basic information on the divorce agreement and caught them up on my lymphedema treatments. "Well, have you met anyone new?" Jackie was always the one to ask the personal questions without being offensive.

"No, not really. Well there is one guy, but unfortunately he's married."

"Oh, tell us more!"

So I recounted meeting Mike at the Legislative Reception and how he had promised to help with my finances.

"Sure. That sounds like a good line. Helping with your finances. What did the email from the beach mean?" Jackie was also the one bold enough to cut through any sugarcoating.

Kim wanted to know more too. "Let's talk more about him. Why do you think you are attracted to him? "

That was a good question and it took me more than a few seconds to come up with an honest answer. "Well, I've always been attracted to men with power who are cute and charming. I've dated politicians, physicians, pharmacists, and even some of my bosses. I like men with power and unfortunately some of them have been married. I started dating in the wild '70s, you know."

"So, this guy Mike is just the type of guy that you would normally go after in a crowded room, trying to get him to like you, meeting him for wine or dinner. It sounds like it's your routine response to meeting someone attractive."

"I guess that's true, but when you put it that way, it sounds so shallow." With that, I thought it best to pour another glass of wine for everyone.

Kim jumped back in, "So let's see. You slept with a married man six weeks after you filed for divorce. Now the divorce is final just six weeks ago and you are attracted to a different married man. We need to talk through this."

"Kim, what did you just say?" said Carol.

Jackie chimed in, "What??"

Now that the cat was out of the bag, I thought I better explain, but I was embarrassed even to share the details with the entire PORCH CLUB. "It wasn't like I was withholding information from you guys, but I happened to be talking with Kim before Christmas and she asked how I was doing. I told her about the night in the hotel room in Nashville with my old friend who's married and that I felt awful because I didn't feel guilty. I haven't felt pretty in a long time, even before the breast cancer. But it just seems like you should always feel bad when you are committing a sin. I meant to tell all of you but just haven't had the chance. Every time I think I've made my last bad relationship mistake, I do something stupid again."

"So what are you going to do?" Jackie asked, "Go after this Mike guy, the State Representative? It does sound pretty exciting. I've heard that it goes on all the time with politicians. He probably wouldn't be the first politician that has fooled around on his wife."

"No, I just can't do that anymore; I can't keep leading my life that way. I've got to change, I just don't know how. It is lonely with all of my own family gone, and now that I haven't heard from any of Curtis' family since the divorce, it's even worse. They are treating me like a leper."

As usual, Kim was the voice of reason. "But you can't go on living your life chasing after the wrong guys. Married guys are always the wrong ones. You deserve better than that, to have someone love you that you can have a real, honest relationship with. You aren't going to like this but here is my advice: you are going to have to be patient and wait on the Lord."

"But how will I know when the right one comes along? I fall in love for all the wrong reasons and with all the wrong men."

Kim offered, "You've got to start thinking more of yourself. You are doing the right thing. You are going to church and it sounds like your church family loves you and supports you, encouraging you to dive deeper into your faith. Maybe God isn't going to bring you another husband, not everyone is called to be married. But God does want a relationship with you. Rest in His arms and be comforted by Him. He will never abandon you, and you'll have more riches than you can imagine, if you will just trust Him. It may take some time, but you need to understand that your relationships with men start first with your relationship with God."

I needed to be encouraged that I was on the right track. "So, learning more about God will help me have better human relationships? I need to begin somewhere."

Kim said, "I don't know if we've had enough wine yet for a deep discussion, but I'm reading a fascinating book right now called *Moral Politics* by George Lakoff. Has anyone heard of it?"

Jackie and Carol shook their head, "No," but I said, "There was a book review in the paper a few weeks ago and our Saturday morning after-Eucharist coffee group was discussing it last weekend. I just picked up a copy but I've only read the first few chapters. What does it say?"

"Well, it doesn't really talk about male-female relationships, but it does discuss how our political views stem from our view of God. But as you were talking, I'm seeing other parallels in our interactions with others.

"Lakoff discusses two different ways in which we view God: "STRICT FATHER" and "NURTURING PARENT". There's a lot of information in the book, but I'll give you the short version. The STRICT FATHER is a rule player; everyone has to follow the rules. If you don't succeed, you will be punished. Success comes by sheer willpower alone. For example, if you are married and trying to be faithful, the STRICT FATHER approach says that you ought to be able to just avoid temptation and affairs because God says so and it is wrong. To even think about adultery is a sin and you should feel guilty. Unfortunately most adults fail miserably at this one at different times in their lives, so we carry guilt around with us every day."

"Boy, you can say that again. It's not like I haven't tried hard to avoid temptation," I chimed in.

Kim continued, "The NURTURING PARENT figure sees things differently. This person looks at their spouse as someone to be loved, protected and nurtured. They avoid adultery not because they are afraid of punishment, but because they can't visualize it in the context of what they are called to do: to take care of their spouse and protect them from Satan. See the difference? In one case we have rules to follow and we feel guilty when we fail, in the other case we want to obey God by protecting His children, and because we love Him and want to please Him. Totally different worldviews."

It was then that Kim dropped the bombshell on me, "Was your father a STRICT FATHER demanding that you play by the rules? You've said that he never showed any emotion except anger and disappointment when something didn't turn out the way he wanted."

I wasn't sure how to respond. "I'll have to think about it some more, but do you think I'm attracted to men that were just like my father? You were right, he was a rule player and almost impossible to please. Looking back, I chased after a lot of guys, hoping that if I could be a little more perfect that they'd be pleased with me. Now that you put it that way, it seems that all I am doing is acting out my childhood insecurities, first with my father and now with other men. Is it possible to ever win love from a STRICT FATHER?"

Kim said, "It's hard to overcome our past. No matter how awful it is, it is what we know, and we often repeat the past hoping that we can change it. You said that your father was an alcoholic and Curtis drank too much. What does that tell you about your choice in men? Maybe since you prayed so much for your Father yet it never changed him, you thought you could make it up to God by choosing another alcoholic and then praying him into sobriety.

"Agatha, rationally you know it doesn't work that way. Only the Holy Spirit can change people. And you said that your Dad had an affair. Do you think that is why you are attracted to married men? Maybe you are trying to pretend that it didn't hurt your Mom, although you know it did. You are going to have to let it go. There is only one thing in your life that will ever heal all the hurt you've felt in your relationships, and that is God."

"Okay, enough for the self-examination part of the weekend. We can get back to that later. Let's cook some dinner and watch a movie. We can straighten out Agatha's love life tomorrow," Carol chimed in.

We never got back to the conversation, but I couldn't get it out of my mind. Was I even capable of a real relationship with a guy who was the NURTURING PARENT type? And more importantly, who is God, a STRICT FATHER or a NURTURING PARENT?

13

Picking Up The Pieces

Much of the confusion and pain in fallen humanity's struggle with sexuality stems from the illusions that sexual activity is essential to wholeness, and that other forms of intimacy are inferior to the sexual bond. We can help people by the example of our lives to honor the depth and fullness to be found in the intimacy of friendship.

— The Rule of The Society of Saint John the Evangelist

On the highway back to Nashville, I realized that my wine dinner with Mike was the following Tuesday. I was glad that I'd shared my apprehensions with The PORCH CLUB. They are close enough friends to love me, but also close enough friends to point out when I'm going astray. I had a vision of the PORCH CLUB, sitting at dinner with Mike and me, and it made me smile. *Wouldn't it be great if our best friends could always be with us so that we don't yield to temptations?* That is what best friends are for: not just to love us when we sin, but also to protect us when we are tempted. They have to be really close, trusted friends, and that was the PORCH CLUB.

ᔕ ᔕ ᔕ

My fears of yielding to my desires over dinner were unfounded. Mike talked about his wonderful children, how he ended up in East Tennessee, and how he got involved in politics. I was at ease after my second glass of wine and decided to share about my breast cancer and lymphedema, as well as how the divorce had been difficult both emotionally and financially. Mike was a good listener and insisted on seeing me in his office the next week to help straighten out my dismal financial affairs. It was wonderful to have made another great Christian friend who was willing to help me when I needed it most.

ᔕ ᔕ ᔕ

I spent the next week trying to find all the documents from the divorce and miscellaneous financial papers. I was ready, but apprehensive, when the phone rang just minutes before I was leaving my office to go to Mike's. One of the men in his Weekly Bible Study had died unexpectedly and he was going to have to go back to Johnson City for the funeral. He'd be back around 4 p.m the next day—could we move the meeting to later in the week? Certainly.

When I checked in at the receptionist's desk, I wondered if she knew that I didn't have any money to pay for the appointment. I was hopeful that Mike would "comp" the appointment and then bill me later when I had more money. I kept trying to convince myself that I shouldn't care, but I was embarrassed that I didn't have the money to pay him outright. All my anxiety disappeared when Mike came out of his office to greet me. With a handshake and a warm hug, he said, "It's good to see you again. Come into my office so we can talk."

162

Everything went well and I had almost every document he asked for. He said he'd need to look over the paperwork in a little more detail, but he asked when I was putting the house up for sale.

"I hadn't planned on selling the house; that is one of the reasons I'm in so much debt. I bought out my husband's equity as part of the divorce settlement. I've just taken out a second mortgage so I could pay my divorce lawyer. It's too emotional for me to move right now and I'm not physically able to with all my bandages. I don't want to sell the house."

"I understand how emotional it is for you to move, but it doesn't make sense for you to have a big house when it is only you living there and no family coming to visit. You should sell it and buy a downtown condo closer to where you work."

"I just can't go through that right now. I hope you understand. Do I have to sell it?"

"You've come to me for advice and I'm giving it. Sometimes we have to set aside our emotions to make the right financial decisions."

"I know, but I just can't face moving. Please let me keep the house."

"That's fine, but I'm also advising you never to sign another mortgage with an early pay-off penalty. That's just money wasted."

"I'm sorry. I didn't know any better. I was trying to make the best decision."

"Just remember the next time you take out a mortgage. Here's my number one recommendation: you need to develop a budget and stick with it. Part of your problem is you don't know what your expenses are each month. First, make a list of all your debts, assets and monthly expenses. Before you come back to see me you also need to revise your will. The State of Tennessee will take everything that you have if you don't have an up-to-date will. I won't help you further unless you have these two things: a budget and a will."

"But I don't have any family. What do I need a will for?"

"Trust me, you need a will. You could leave all your money to your new church. I'm sure that they'd be glad to have it. Let's plan to meet again, but don't call me until you've visited with a lawyer."

The meeting was over and we shook hands. I still wasn't sure what I was doing money-wise, but for some reason I did trust him. I'd never been on a budget before, but somehow I was going to have to figure out how to make it on my own.

ൟ ൟ ൟ

By the end of the Legislative Session in May, I drew up a new will and outlined a proposed budget. Mike and I traded emails on my progress. He was so nice not to charge me any money for his advice, and he did move some annuities from fixed to variable after transferring them to Stifel. I didn't know exactly what he was talking about, but he'd filled out all the paperwork and all I had to do was go to his office and sign. There wasn't a lot of money in the annuities, but I was grateful that they'd all be in one place.

When I started tracking my expenses I was amazed to see how much "miscellaneous" money was going out the door each month. Maybe I didn't need as much money to live on as I thought. It seemed like the more things I bought, the more time it took to care for them.

Mike headed back home to East Tennessee the last day of May when the legislative session was over, but he told me to call him on his cell phone if I had any questions over the summer. I'd come a long way from crying each month when I opened my credit card bills.

ൟ ൟ ൟ

I joined St. George's in May. Everyone was so friendly when I visited that I wanted to be part of the community. I was eager to get started on the Sunday School class that had been announced for the summer session. The Reverend Marcia King would be teaching on Philip Yancey's book, *"What's So Amazing About Grace?"* It was a good next step for me to learn about grace after my immersion in forgiveness when I was in Africa. I heard the stories, but it was still difficult for me to believe that people could really forgive injustices, and I wondered if it started with grace. There had been a lot of hurt in my life and I was sure that I was still holding grudges even though I would never admit it, even to myself.

It was strange, but I felt my heart slowly softening towards people in my life, past and present. For the first time, I was beginning to feel that God had really forgiven me, and there is a freedom in passing along that forgiveness to others. My childhood and adult relationships had always been based on the foundation that you had to "earn" forgiveness; it would never be freely given. The priests at St. George's preached so much about God's love, grace and mercy that I was starting to believe in it. There was a consistent message that God really does love us and forgives us even before we ask. It was certainly a new concept for me. It sounded good, but it still seemed almost too good to be true.

I felt awful about divorcing Curtis and wished that we could be friends, but he had made good on his promise that no one in the family would ever talk with me again, including him. I'd emailed my stepson when I was making out my will to confirm his mailing address in New York. In reply, I got this short email: "Thank you for thinking of me, but as you know, Dad has forbidden us from ever seeing or talking with you again. I'm sure you can find a better use for your money than to leave it to me."

෨ ෨ ෨

Some nights I wondered if God wanted me to feel lonely so that I would recognize the importance of my new church family. At this point, they were all I had. On other days, my loneliness made me recognize how important God was becoming in my life. One thing was for sure; He was always there.

In July, I decided I needed a new Bible and went online to search for one. There were twenty more translations since I'd last looked almost thirty years ago. I asked around at church about what kinds of Bibles people read and got a variety of responses.

I was curious what kind of Bible an evangelical Christian used, so I sent an email: "Dear Mike: Hope you are having a great summer. You'd said to contact you if I had any questions and I do have one: what Bible translation do you use? I'm in the market for a new Bible."

A short response: "Yes, having a great summer. Spent two weeks at Rosemary Beach with the kids. I use the New King James version, John MacArthur Study Bible. Can't get a better one than that."

So it was. I ordered one online in maroon leather that afternoon. I couldn't wait to get started seriously reading the Bible again.

Ŷo Ŷo Ŷo

I spent the summer trying to stay on budget and concentrated on paying off the second mortgage. It was the first time in my life that I actually felt good about money. I was giving more money to my new church than I ever had before, even though we'd had two paychecks when I was married. I was learning to align my resources based upon what was most important, and my church contribution was listed first on my budget. It was a huge change from when the church got what money I had left over at the end of each month.

I even sent some extra to the mission in South Africa and designated it for the children's feeding program. I don't know why those kids had touched my heart so. I was already making plans to go back the following fall and inviting friends to go with me. It was a journey that I wanted to share. I had a line item in my budget and if I stayed on target I would have enough money to go back again without charging anything on my credit card. It would be great to return and feel the hospitality of the people there, and it was an important enough desire to keep me on my budget.

୨୬ ୨୬ ୨୬

The Reverend Marcia King's class was over at the end of the summer, but I was developing some personal habits that helped me through the long, hot summer nights when loneliness would strike. I started preparing for Sunday morning worship by reading the Bible readings on Saturday evenings, and every morning during the week I was attending 7 a.m. church services.

My life still felt pretty chaotic, but for thirty minutes each day, God was in control. For the other twenty-three hours and thirty minutes, everyone else was in control, but I was recharged every morning hearing two Bible readings, a short sermon and, most importantly, receiving the Eucharist. It was through the body and blood of Christ that I felt unconditional forgiveness. Hearing about it over and over again, I was starting to believe it in my heart, and not just in my head. I was learning a whole new way of thinking and living. It felt like I was climbing out of a huge darkness into the light. I wasn't at a point yet where I could put all this into words, but I was looking forward to the next meeting of the PORCH CLUB to tell them about the freedom that I was feeling.

୨୬ ୨୬ ୨୬

167

It was late in the year when the PORCH CLUB convened again, this time in Nashville. Nashville is pretty at Christmastime, with Christmas decorations at the Opryland Hotel and musical celebrations at the River. We decided to head back to Maggiano's to relive the very first meeting of the PORCH CLUB almost four years before. We celebrated again with lemon drop martinis, and then headed over to my house for some serious discussion.

"So, how are things going with Mike? " Jackie asked outright.

I started to blush, knowing that Jackie was asking if there was anything more than a professional connection. "Well, I haven't seen Mike since session ended in May. I sent him a note during the summer about which Bible translation he uses and that is how I ended up buying the NKJV John MacArthur Study Bible. I expect I'll see him again in January when the Legislature is back in session. Right now I'm concentrating on the budget he gave me and paying off the second mortgage on the house."

"Good for you," Carol said, "I'm glad you kept the house. I know that you don't need that much space to live in, but where would we stay when we came to visit? Ha ha! I believe you have the gift of hospitality and just like we are here this weekend, you'll open your home up to others in the future. I think that it was God that directed you to not give up the house. I don't care what Mike said, you kept it because you can honor guests with a place to stay."

"So, you've given up entirely on an affair with Mike?" Jackie chimed in.

"Oh heavens, Jackie! There never was an affair; there was an attraction. But like Kim said the last time we were together, I have to figure out why I'm attracted to the wrong guys, like married men. Actually, there is someone new."

"Oh, do tell," Carol entered the conversation again.

"Well, this is totally different. One Sunday they introduced a visitor from another Episcopal Church here in Nashville, St. Bartholomew's. He was teaching one of the Sunday School classes and he is amazing. He has a Ph.D. in Physics from Duke and a

168

Master's from MIT, but he doesn't teach Physics, he teaches on worldview and faith. He gave the most amazing presentation on how we know that God exists. I looked up his Ph.D. dissertation research at Duke and it's very impressive. I decided that I wanted to meet him so I introduced myself after class and asked if he'd like to go for coffee sometime. We've had coffee four or five times and gone to the symphony twice. He's very nice and a faithful man. I'm learning amazing things about my faith from him."

"Great! Finally a new beau?" Jackie said.

"No, not at all! He's fifteen years younger than I am. Although he's cute, it's not a romantic interest. I've figured out that I need to stop looking at men as 'romance' and start appreciating them as children of God. Brian loves to talk about his faith, plus he's very intelligent and I enjoy learning from him. We talk about our spiritual gifts, and how God is using us to restore His kingdom here on earth. He's a great teacher and it is always an interesting conversation. The first time we went for coffee, we realized that 'our Starbucks' was the same one. He lives right around the corner from me, so, no, he's not a beau, he's even better: a faithful Christian friend who is willing to teach me. It is relaxing and fun to be with him."

"Single or married," Jackie asked.

"Single."

"Available."

"Yes, but I've stopped thinking that way. Men are no longer divided into two groups: 'marriage prospects,' and 'not marriage prospects'. I realize how that thinking restricted my relationships. It was an awful way to live: treating men as if they were only good as dating partners. I would take advantage of my 'womanness' by not respecting men for the people they are. Men should be honored and respected as God's children, not either worshiped as idols or put down as slaves. I slip back into that old mode sometimes, but I'm learning. I have a handful of male friends, both married and single, who care more about my faith than about having an 'intimate' relationship with me. It is relaxing to be around them instead of always worrying if I am pleasing them. It's the STRICT FATHER vs. NURTURING PARENT types that we've talked about. They're all NURTURING PARENTs, always willing to teach me more about God."

Carol asked, "Are you learning all this at your church? You talk like you are comfortable with God as a friend."

"Yes, I believe that God is a NURTURING PARENT who loves me no matter what. I'm hearing sermons and Sunday School lessons that keep reinforcing that message. But I've learned as much from people who show me what God's love looks like. It started me thinking that my life could be different. I'm learning to love others with God's love, too."

Kim said, "In this crazy world we can all use more of God's love."

The clock chimed 1 a.m. It was time for one more toast to the PORCH CLUB, and God's love, and then we turned in for the night.

14

Daily Bread

The evidence of the new birth is that I yield myself so completely to God that "Christ is formed" in me. And once "Christ is formed" in me, His nature immediately begins to work through me.

– Oswald Chambers

I wasn't sure how I would make it through Christmas with no husband, no kids, and no family. It was the first Christmas that I was totally alone. I thought about going out of town by myself, maybe to Rosemary Beach, but then I felt silly spending the money when I needed to keep paying off the second mortgage. It was always a tough time of the year for me. Dad had died six days before Thanksgiving in 1980 and Mom had died five days before Christmas in 1990. My birthday falls twelve days before Christmas, so it is always sandwiched between those two memories. As the time grew closer, I didn't know if I should be dreading the loneliness or welcoming the rest from the usual craziness of the Christmas season. I was hoping that God would show me where the happy medium was.

✑ ✑ ✑

On December 1, I went to the mailbox and had a delightful surprise: A Christmas Open House Invitation from Bob, my friend from St. George's. It was the third annual Christmas event and it just happened to be on my birthday, the 13th! I hastily sent a YES to the RSVP: I wouldn't be alone on my birthday after all!

✑ ✑ ✑

I talked with people at the party from St. George's, but I also met new acquaintances, mostly realtors and politicians who were friends of Bob's. By 11 p.m. I was getting a little tired, but I hardly noticed because I was having such a good time. I had started the holiday season dreading both the holiday and my birthday, but Bob's gracious invitation changed my mind. It looked as though 2008 was going to wind down as a good year after all. It wasn't really a birthday party for me, but it was good to be out celebrating Christ's birthday with old and new friends. I grabbed my coat from the master bedroom and was slowly saying my goodbyes. Bob was at the front door and I stopped to tell him what a great time I'd had. I couldn't resist telling him that it was the best "birthday party" I'd ever had.

"Wait, just a minute, young lady," Bob said in his best Santa Claus voice. "I think I have something under the tree for you."

"A present for me? How could that be?"

"Yes, my dear. It is a present with your name on it. Go into the night and put it under your tree to open on Christmas morn'. Merry Christmas, Ho, Ho, Ho!"

I was choking back tears as I got into my car. It had been a hard eighteen months, but the difficulties were all erased by the thoughtfulness of a friend. *Could I ever be that generous in giving to others?*

✈ ✈ ✈

On December 22, I got a call that they were short ushers for the 11 p.m. Christmas Eve service. "Could you help out? Doesn't take much training. Show up at 10:15 p.m. before the Choir starts the Christmas songs and we'll fill you in."

When I arrived, I was delighted to see that Dru Anderson had also been drafted to usher. I'd met Dru on my second South Africa trip just a few months before. It was nice to be with people I knew on Christmas Eve. It felt like I was celebrating with family.

It was almost 1 a.m. when I got home from church, but I didn't care. It was one of the best Christmases ever! I'd been with friends and had an opportunity to serve the Lord at a wonderful spirit-filled service.

Opening the door, I was greeted by my two dogs, Rachel and Bridget. As I bent down to gather them in my arms, I spied the one present that was under the tree. Even though it was 1 a.m., I was grateful to have a present to open.

I unwrapped it slowly and found a book by Oswald Chambers, *My Utmost for My Highest*. I hadn't heard of it, but the cover said it was a devotional with readings for each day of the year. It was late, but I opened the book and read the story for today, Christmas Day:

His Birth and Our New Birth

'Behold, the virgin shall be with child, and bear a Son, and they shall call His name Immanuel,' which is translated, 'God with us' – Matthew 1:23

His Birth in History. ". . . that Holy One who is to be born will be called the Son of God (Luke 1:35). Jesus Christ was

173

born *into* this world, not *from* it. He did not emerge out of history; He came into history from the outside. Jesus Christ is not the best human being the human race can boast of— He is a Being for whom the human race can take no credit at all. He is not man becoming God, but God Incarnate— God coming into human flesh from outside it. His life is the highest and the holiest entering through the most humble of doors. Our Lord's birth was an advent— the appearance of God in human form.

His Birth in Me. "My little children, for whom I labor in birth again until Christ is formed in you..." (Galatians 4:19). Just as our Lord came into human history from outside it, He must also come into me from outside. Have I allowed my personal human life to become a "Bethlehem" for the Son of God? I cannot enter the realm of the kingdom of God unless I am born again from above by a birth totally unlike physical birth. "You must be born again" (John 3:7). This is not a command, but a fact based on the authority of God. The evidence of the new birth is that I yield myself so completely to God that "Christ is formed" in me. And once "Christ is formed" in me, His nature immediately begins to work through me.

God Evident in the Flesh. This is what is made so profoundly possible for you and for me through the redemption of man by Jesus Christ.

Small tears were making their way down my cheeks. They weren't sobs of despair, but droplets of joy. Earlier that evening I had been lonely with no family to celebrate the holiday, but now I understood that my life had been changed. I read, "The evidence of the new birth is that I yield myself so completely to God that 'Christ is formed' in me. And once 'Christ is formed' in me, His nature immediately begins to work through me." It was the best Christmas present ever! I'd received a new life.

I couldn't wait to thank Bob for his thoughtful gift that held the key to my life story. Bob cared enough to want me to grow in my faith. *What more could you ask of a Christian friend?*

ഏ ഏ ഏ

It was an unusually cold January, and on the first day of the Legislative Session I sent a note to Mike, thanking him for his encouragement. He'd been sending a Bible verse or sharing a Sunday School lesson every few weeks throughout the holidays, and I was very appreciative for the inspiring words.

It had been a year since my divorce and my finances had greatly improved. I was getting ready to make the last payment on the second mortgage in just fourteen months. Originally, the loan had been for thirty-six months, but the discipline of a budget had really helped. I hadn't taken any expensive vacations or bought a lot of new clothes, but I really didn't need to. In the past, I shopped and traveled just because I could. Since the divorce, I'd learned to live with less and I was glad that everything was paid off: the car, the furniture, the divorce and the second mortgage. My only remaining monthly payment was the original mortgage on the house. It was the first time in a long time that I could say that I was virtually "debt free" and it was a liberating feeling to not be under such financial pressures. I hoped that I didn't lose my new reality of being able to distinguish between my "needs" and my "wants." It was time to celebrate!

I emailed Mike to tell him. "Do you have time to get together for dinner? I just paid off the second mortgage and would like a glass of wine to celebrate."

"Busy session this year. Not sure I can make dinner, but I'll see you at the Pharmacy Legislative Reception again at the end of February."

I was looking forward to seeing Mike again. He'd been such an encouragement, teaching me that I am a steward of God's

175

money, rather than thinking it all belonged to me, and I could do whatever I wanted with it.

The week before the reception I flew to Washington, D.C. for a meeting at Medicare headquarters in Baltimore. I had just stepped off the plane and turned my cell phone back on when I got a terse text message from Mike, "Don't worry. All your investments are safe. I'll talk with you when you get back. I'll find another job."

Oh dear, I couldn't imagine what had happened. I thought about calling but decided to text. "Are you okay? I'm so sorry. I'm praying for you that everything will work out. I can't imagine what you are going through right now!"

"Yes, I'm okay. I'll fill you in next week when I see you."

ço ço ço

I made it back to Nashville in time for the Legislative Reception on Monday evening. I made the rounds and talked with my State Senators and Representatives, but hadn't seen Mike. As usual, two of the Committees had run late that day and the Legislators were still making their way over to the Sheraton. When I went to get another glass of wine at the bar, I noticed Mike at the door talking with Jim Eoff, one of the faculty members from UT-Memphis College of Pharmacy.

"Let me introduce you to my good friend, Jim Eoff. My dad and Jim went to Pharmacy School together."

"Actually, I know Jim. I'm on faculty at the UT-Memphis College of Pharmacy with him. It sure is a small world."

We talked for a few more minutes about some pending legislation dealing with pharmacy issues, and then Mike said, "It's at times like these when I think it would just be easier to die and be raptured to heaven. The pressure from losing my job is tremendous. I didn't do anything wrong but investments are down with the economy and they had to cut some brokers."

Jim said, "It's hard to know what it all means when you are going through something like this. But be assured that we are all praying for you. We'll see you through this."

I was glad that Mike had wonderful friends to support him. The love and support of Christian friends was all that had gotten me through the past two years.

Mike said, "Thanks for your prayers, Jim. They mean a lot." Then he turned to me and said, "Let's go grab a bite to eat and a glass of wine at Jimmy Kelly's on Louise Avenue. I haven't been over there in awhile."

"Okay, I'll meet you there. See you in a few."

❧ ❧ ❧

Jimmy Kelly's was always a great place to go for a quiet glass of wine and to relax. Late in the evening, it would be deserted and dark in the bar area. I was looking forward to talking with Mike and finding out exactly what had happened at his brokerage office. When I got to Jimmy Kelly's I knew something was really wrong. Only one other person was in the bar, but Mike was pacing back and forth, talking on his cell phone. He acted oblivious to his surroundings. I tried to get his attention, and finally he waved me over to a table in the corner. Mike Kelly owned the restaurant and always waited on the Legislators personally. Mike brought me my glass of wine, which I sipped while I watched Mike pace. I wasn't trying to eavesdrop but it sounded like he was talking with a distraught investment client. Mike finally ended the conversation and joined me at the table. We'd just ordered when Mike's cell phone rang again and he jumped up from the table. "Sorry, I've got to take this one, too."

It was another fifteen minutes before Mike returned to the table and I asked, "What happened while I was in Washington?"

"It's been non-stop for the past week since the news broke about the layoffs and accusations about some of our investments. I have distraught clients who are worried about their life savings, and I've got the media hounding me about my involvement. I actually had a reporter ask me if I was going to resign from the State Legislature over this. I haven't done anything wrong, but now I'm tainted. Your annuities are invested in guaranteed securities and they'll be transferred over to another broker.

"Do you think this is a big enough issue that it will hurt your re-election chances next year?"

"I hope not, but right now everything is up in the air and on the line. It's my integrity that's been damaged. I've just got to pray that all this blows over before election time and I can find another job."

As our salads arrived, Mike made small talk about how busy the Legislature had already been this year. He mentioned that he had been late to the reception that evening since they had their annual basketball game against the legislative interns. As usual, the Legislators won. He laughed about how he had to keep the male interns separated from the female interns to get any work out of them. Just then his phone rang again, and Mike jumped up to answer it.

It was late and I'd finished my dinner before Mike had hardly touched his salad. I hated to leave without hearing more of the story about the layoffs, but I believed Mike's text message that everything with my account was okay. As I got up to leave, Mike finished his cell phone conversation and walked me out to my car.

"Sorry we didn't get to talk much this evening, but being without a job has my head swimming. Jennifer and I have about three months of savings that we can tap into but not more. That was a local reporter wanting to interview me about the firm and the layoffs. I promise that your investments are fine and we'll get caught up soon, okay?"

I drove home unsettled. It wasn't my money that I was worried about, but Mike.

☞ ☞ ☞

I didn't hear from Mike again until April, when he called to ask if I was available for dinner that evening. I'd already made other plans, so we talked for a few minutes and I told him about a new ladies group that I'd joined at St. George's called LIFE (Living in Faith Everyday). I kept the conversation short, as I figured he was too busy for a conversation about my daily routine. He'd probably been in many bible studies, but this was my first serious commitment, with eleven other women for a period of two years. I was anxious to get started and wanted to share with Mike that I was excited about diving deeper into my faith.

ço ço ço

I was busy at work and at school and realized on the last day of session, the third week of June that I hadn't seen or talked with Mike since the Legislative Reception in February. He'd sent a few emails with Bible verses, but not many. I was sure that he was busy in session and the media was still doing frequent stories about the worsening economy.

I stayed up late to watch the last night of the Legislative Session on the Internet, so I knew it ended around midnight. I suspected that all the Legislators had gone out for a night on the town and Mike would be enjoying a glass of fine wine and a cigar until the wee hours of the morning.

As I was leaving the house the next day for the 7 a.m. church service, I knew Mike would be heading back to Johnson City, so I sent him a text: "Have a great summer. I'm coming to visit friends in July in Kingsport. Maybe we can have dinner or a drink when I'm over your way."

I was getting into my car when my cell phone rang. It was Mike. "Say, I'm just leaving for church and then on to work. Can I call you back in about an hour when I get to the office?"

"You don't need to call me back, I just called to ask you to pray for me."

"Pray? Oh no, what's wrong?"

179

Mike's voice was distant, "I don't know how to say this so I'm just going to tell you. Please don't judge me, but I had an affair this past spring. I told Jennifer about it in April and she wants a divorce. She wanted to wait until session was over before she said anything publicly, but it looks like my marriage is over. Will you pray for me and for us? I never wanted this to happen."

"Of course, I'll pray for both of you. Most importantly, you have to win her back. I'll add you to my daily prayer list, starting today."

"Thank you. Please don't say anything. Maybe I can talk her out of it. I promised her that we'd go to counseling as soon as session was over. We just need your prayers."

"My prayers are with you, and your family."

လ၁ လ၁ လ၁

By the end of the day, the shock still hadn't worn off. *How could he cheat on his wife?* It just didn't make sense. I couldn't imagine how she felt.

A range of emotions played in my head. I felt guilty because I'd thought about an affair with him the night we met, but my guilt turned into anger at his betrayal. I admired Mike as a Christian mentor and he hadn't lived up to the pedestal I'd put him on.

I couldn't go to sleep that night, remembering how I'd been let down before by a Christian man who didn't live the same life that he had talked about. We'd dated for three years before I found out about the other woman. When I did, I walked out. No explanation, no discussion. He hadn't lived up to his promises and that was enough for me to leave. I never saw or talked with him again. *Was there anyone that I could ever trust? More importantly, how would God deal with Mike's betrayal? Would He react with punishment or with love?*

๛ ๛ ๛

The sermon the next Sunday mentioned a king who'd taken another man's wife and then had the man killed in battle so that the king would have her all to himself. The story didn't end with a caution against our sinful ways, but instead I heard about how God used King David to do great things after David had repented. I sat quietly in the pew, trying to make sense of the words, and my anger at Mike turned into shame. I was struggling because I felt that Mike should be punished for what he had done, but everything I was being taught at church said the exact opposite: we have to forgive. *Wasn't this the exact lesson that I had learned on two trips to South Africa: to forgive the unforgiveable?*

As I stepped into the sunlight after the service, I wondered, *Could I ever get past my disappointment in Mike?* Deep down in my heart I knew a different question was haunting me: *If Mike can't be forgiven, then why would God ever forgive me?*

Not hearing a response, I suspected that I would get the answers to my questions when God was ready and not a minute before.

As Mike had requested, all I knew to do was to pray.

15

The Aftermath of Sin

Even when sin and misunderstanding burden the common life, is not the one who sins still a person with whom I too stand under the word of Christ? Will not another Christian's sin be an occasion for me ever anew to give thanks that both of us may live in the forgiving love of God in Jesus Christ? Therefore, will not the very moment of great disillusionment with my brother or sister be incomparably wholesome for me because it so thoroughly teaches me that both of us can never live by our own words and deeds, but only by that one Word and deed that really binds us together, the forgiveness of sins in Jesus Christ?

– Dietrich Bonhoeffer

My emotions hung by a dainty thread over the next few weeks. It was my sin, too: lust and adulterous affairs. Most of my guilt was from long ago, and I'd buried it in the pristine wrappings of married life and raising children. I'd thought I'd conquered it, but here it was again in my life, now confronting me from a new angle. Instead of me being involved in the sin, it shone light on the toughest question: *How does a Christian act when another Christian commits a grievous sin?*

ɕ ɕ ɕ

Not knowing what else to do, I prayed. I didn't talk with Mike over the next few weeks, but I wanted to stay in touch so that he knew that I hadn't abandoned him completely. It was a vicious struggle to discern what to do. It would be far easier to walk away from the friendship than continue it during this difficult time. I didn't want to sound judgmental, but all I could think of was, *'What were you thinking? Did you lose your faith?'* Instead of the judgment that flamed inside of me, I decided to send a prayer via email:

"Dear Heavenly Father, I ask that Mike feel Your loving embrace and know that he is Your beloved son and that Your mercy and grace are sufficient in his life. I ask that Mike be willing to admit his weaknesses and give up the 5% of his life that he has reluctantly withheld from You. I ask that he turn his life completely over to Your care, now. I ask that You bless him by giving him the wisdom of the Holy Spirit in repairing his marriage so that he can become the husband and father that he wants to be, and can be, with Your help. I ask that his Christian friends surround him and Jennifer with their love and understanding so that their union will flourish in their midst. In His name, Amen."

It was a short response by email: "Thank you for your prayers."

A few weeks later a text message came: "Jennifer is insisting on a divorce. Please continue to pray."

I knew it was a difficult time for Mike. I sent a hasty text: "I continue to pray for you and your family."

I heard through news clips on the Internet that Mike had resigned from the Legislature. I couldn't imagine what was going on in his life. I struggled trying to reconcile it all. I was so sorry for his wife and their children. But I had flashbacks of the married men I'd been with over the years. Although the wives had never found out, there were always suspicions that surrounded a too-long glance. It was only now, going through this with Mike and

183

his family that I realized how wrong I had been as an accessory to the sin.

I'd rationalized that because I was single, it wasn't a sin on my part. It was obvious that Satan had used me to lure men into sin with the incredible power of sex. I was seeing firsthand what devastation adultery brings to relationships, particularly our relationship with God. I couldn't pretend to be an innocent party anymore. Seeing the relentless aftermath of sin convinced me that God has reserved sex for a husband and wife who have been united as one. Casual sex in any other relationship was Satan's cunning trap.

Weeks went by without any word from Mike. On a Saturday in August, he called to say hello and that he was housesitting in Elizabethton for some friends.

"Housesitting? By yourself?"

"Yes. Jennifer and I have been to counseling but we haven't had any breakthrough yet. We're going to try a separation for a while. The good news is that I'm not too far away and can take the kids to school and pick them up every day."

"What do you mean? Have you found a job yet?"

"No, I haven't had a job for six months now. It's a godsend that I have a place to stay."

"Is this a temporary situation? How long are you going to be housesitting?"

"I don't know."

"I'll keep praying for you. How are you doing money-wise?"

"Living on savings and my 401(k) right now. The press is still trying to figure out why I resigned from the Legislature, but Jennifer insisted if we were going to work on our marriage that I couldn't be traveling to Nashville all the time. It's good news that I'll have more time to spend with the kids, but I need to find a full-time job to take care of them."

"I'm so sorry. I'll keep you and the family in my thoughts and prayers."

৯৯ ৯৯ ৯৯

My daily prayers and Bible reading were spent searching for the answer to one question, *"What do you do when a Christian sins?"* I found plenty about responding with rebuke, but also how good friends should help each other when they go astray. I had to admit that rebuke has never been a strong point of mine: I want everyone to like me and criticizing them doesn't seem like a good way to win friends. My reading kept pointing out that Christians have a responsibility to help each other avoid sin.

In this case, I was just a casual observer. Mike and I weren't close enough "friends" that he would have ever revealed his desires to me, so I could never have stopped the affair. Part of the problem with "rebuke" is that you have to be pretty close to the person. If you are close, then the "criticism" is taken with love, but if you aren't close enough, a rebuke just sounds like judgment and is usually ignored.

It was a rhetorical question, but I wondered if Mike had shared his intentions with any of the men in his Bible Study. I thought back in my life, when I was getting ready to sin. I'd always hidden it from anyone I thought wouldn't approve. When I was living with a boyfriend, I'd quit going to church because I didn't want our addresses to be the same on the church roster. People would connect that we weren't married and just living together.

I never abused drugs or alcohol, but I would drink an occasional glass of wine or beer. When I was with my Southern Baptist friends, I'd never mention it. Drinking wine or beer was something that I did with my "other", less condemning friends. Thinking through my life story, I realized that Satan worked to isolate me from people who would have helped me avoid sin. Isolation and solitary confinement are common punishments in prisons. When I was living in sin or getting ready to sin, I just found different friends to be around.

185

As I read more, I found that God forgives all sins. I knew that He had already forgiven Mike for the adultery, but it was still amazing that God could be that big to just forgive without retribution. I kept reminding myself that I can't judge God based upon what I know of humans. God has characteristics that no human can claim. I was hearing the same message each Sunday: God is a God of love, grace and mercy. The sermons would reinforce that our obedience is because we love Him, not because we are afraid of being punished.

Why was I so emotionally distraught over Mike's indiscretions? Our six meetings in the past eighteen months had been financial planning sessions or political receptions, definitely professional. It wasn't like we were close friends, but I couldn't get him out of my mind. I knew that I'd put Mike on the "ideal Christian man" pedestal. *How could I have been so wrong?* On the other hand, I was hoping that God had forgiven him because if He had, there was a chance He'd forgiven me for all my past sins, too.

❧ ❧ ❧

The sermons at St. George's were rich with Scripture and just what I needed to hear about loving God and our neighbors. There was another message that I was picking up about repentance and transformation.

One Sunday, the Reverend Malone Gilliam commented that the Episcopal Church was like a fishing net that took in all the good and bad fish, old boots, and rubber tires from the ocean floor. A church is the place where we are loved as we are, but we are expected to change. *Was it really possible that by studying the Word, worshiping together and being encouraged by others in the community that people could change their thoughts and behaviors and really begin to love God with their whole heart?*

The messages asked us to reach further in our faith: once we love God with our whole heart and fully accept God's love, we are then commanded to go out and spread the good news by loving our neighbor. Scripture paints a different story than the world does: God's love allows us to be transformed. *Was I to be part of the vessel that showed Mike God's love?*

≈ ≈ ≈

It was September and I hadn't seen Mike since the Legislative Reception in February. I'd been studying St. Paul's letters to the Corinthians all summer and was starting to have "visions" when I was waking up some mornings. Some I didn't recall at all when I woke up, but on Labor Day I awoke with a clear vision: I was writing a check. During my morning Bible study I asked God, *"Why am I writing a check?"* and by the end of my study time, the answer was clear. I read in my Bible from Corinthians 2: 5-11:

> "But if anyone has caused grief, he has not grieved me, but all of you to some extent—not to be too severe. This punishment, which was inflicted by the majority, is sufficient for such a man, so that, on the contrary, you ought rather to forgive and comfort him, lest perhaps such a one be swallowed up with too much sorrow. Therefore I urge you to reaffirm your love to him. For to this end I also wrote, that I might put you to the test, whether you are obedient in all things. Now whom you forgive anything, I also forgive. For if indeed I have forgiven anything, I have forgiven that one for your sakes in the presence of Christ, lest Satan should take advantage of us; for we are not ignorant of his devices."

The phrase that stood out to me was, "you ought rather to forgive and comfort him, lest perhaps such a one be swallowed up with too much sorrow. Therefore I urge you to reaffirm your love to him. For to this end I also wrote, that I might put you to the test, whether you are obedient in all things."

Could it be possible that this test was more about me and my reaction to my friend's sin, than the sin itself? I certainly didn't want to let *"Satan take advantage of us."*

I picked up the phone and dialed Mike's number. "When are you going to be in Nashville again? I need to talk with you."

"Actually, I have to be in Nashville to get some things from my sister this Friday, why?"

"Can I meet you for a cup of coffee? I'd like to see you. It's been since February since I saw you last and it's already September. A lot has happened in between. Have you found a job yet?"

"No, no job, but I've got a place to stay a few blocks away from where the kids go to school and they keep me busy."

"Great, I'll see you on Friday. How about 10 a.m. at the Belle Meade Starbuck's. Will that work?"

℘ ℘ ℘

It was a good reunion on Friday: "It's nice to see you again, Mike, but you look a little thin."

"Yes, I've had some trouble eating and sleeping lately."

"Well, I know you are probably in a hurry to get back to pick up the kids at school, but I want to give you something. I know how much the kids enjoy your annual Christmas trip to Rosemary Beach and I want the kids to have a good Christmas, even though life as they knew it is over. Here's a check for $10,000 to cash now so you can plan your trip to Rosemary Beach over Christmas. And here's another check for $10,000 that is dated December 1. If you don't have a job by then, I want you to cash this check too to make sure the kids have a good Christmas and you can pay their private school tuition for the next semester. These are gifts, not loans; I don't ever expect to be paid back."

"No, no, I can't take your money."

"You need money, don't you?"

There was silence, which seemed like an eternity.

"Yes, but it isn't fair for you to give me money. Didn't you just get the second mortgage on your house paid off?"

"Yes, I did just pay off the mortgage but I've been really frugal since then, socking money away into my checking account. I have $25,000 and I want you to have $20,000 of it for your family this Christmas."

"But I couldn't take a gift like this from you. I promise I'll pay you back."

"Mike, I'm giving you this as a gift, but it's your decision if you ever pay the money back. This isn't about you; it's about what God is asking me to do. I've never trusted God where money is concerned. I never hoarded it, but I was always fearful that I wouldn't have enough. I don't have any family to spend money on, and I want the kids to have a good Christmas this year. Since you aren't working, I want you to have it. It's a demonstration of how much I'm learning to trust God, not of your weakness. Please take it."

"I can't thank you enough. You are a great friend."

৯৯ ৯৯ ৯৯

It was the next week when Mike called to say he had two pre-season tickets to a Titans game and asked me to come along.

"Sounds great, I'd love to go. I've never been to a Titans game, pre-season or otherwise. Nice of you to ask."

It was fun to go to the game and Mike ran into a number of old friends, including some State Legislators and U.S. Congressmen. As we sat enjoying a beer at halftime, Mike shared that he'd been frequenting a pizza place in Johnson City and one particular server had taken a liking to him. She'd trained professionally as a chef, and Mike had always wanted to take cooking lessons. She'd offered to come over to the house where he was housesitting and cook for him.

189

"Seems pretty suspicious to me. I think she's after you. Why else would she want to come over to the house when the kids aren't there?"

"I don't know. Who would want to associate with me after all the publicity at the firm?"

"You'd be surprised. But I'm telling you not to have her come over. And definitely don't even think about sleeping with her. There is nothing good that can come of her being at the house. And if I were you, I'd start eating my pizza somewhere else."

It was later in the week that Mike called, "You were right. That pizza thing wasn't such a good idea."

"You didn't have her come over to the house, did you? I thought I told you that it was a bad idea."

"No, I didn't have her come over to the house, but last night I was running late so I stopped in to grab a piece of pizza and a salad to take home and we were the only two in the restaurant. She made a pass at me; it was clear what she had in mind. 'How about if I come over and give you a cooking lesson; I've got a special romantic dish I've been wanting to try.'"

"I told you not to go by there anymore!"

"Don't worry. I told her I wasn't interested in any romantic dishes."

"Boy, I hope you were clear. She sounds like bad news to me."

"Don't worry, I've got this one under control."

I sure hoped so. This sounded like a really bad situation and I hoped that Mike could see clearly that this was a relationship that he shouldn't start. Jennifer had filed the divorce paperwork, but nothing was finalized, and there was always hope of reconciliation. The girl in the pizza parlor was just plain wrong for him to be hanging around with. But I knew what it was like to be rejected and wanting to be loved. I'd been there too many times myself.

My LIFE group met the next evening and without naming names, I described the situation. I had lots of questions like "Why do girls go after men, being forward and aggressive to get what they want?" I shared with my group that I'd been like that too. If I saw a cute guy, I'd go after him, dropping hints and charming words until he asked me out. I felt awful that I'd used one of God's gifts–an appealing appearance– to trap men into relationships. It was just wrong. I wanted to believe that I had matured in the way I treated men, but it was hard, since the rest of the world certainly hadn't gotten the message.

One of the ladies in the LIFE group said something that stuck with me, "You know, pleasure can be used as a weapon by Satan. God intends sex to be the ultimate way that a married couple communicates. But Satan takes the intimacy that we all crave and makes it a weapon to hurt our hearts and harden them until we can no longer love."

ॐ ॐ ॐ

During my quiet time in the next week, I thought about male-female relationships and what a mess we had made of them since Adam and Eve. A Christian friend submitted to the temptation of adultery and it looked like his marriage would end in divorce. I had asked what I could do to help, "Pray for me," he said. And I said, "Of course I will, but is there anything else I can do?"

I'd made a private retreat at the Abbey of Genesee during the summer and was reviewing the notes that I kept in my journal. The words of Father John Eudes Bamberger echoed in my head:

> "We all stand in need of a kind of trust, someone whose
> values we identify with, someone who is attractive to us

and who cares for us. This friend will always feel a readiness to respond when I act in a certain way.

Friendship and love are characterized by an overwhelming caring to reduce the amount of anxiety in another person.

A spiritual friend is one who will help us to continue to perceive our world as friendly and to help us maintain an appropriate level of anxiety that ensures that we are caring (a lack of all anxiety is indifference), yet engulfing us with love so that our anxieties do not overwhelm us."

I wanted to offer that overwhelming caring by decreasing anxiety in my friend. I believe that a Christian demonstrating Christ's love for another is one of the most powerful emotions on earth.

But my friend had said, *"No, nothing else. For now, just pray for me.*

ço ço ço

The following Saturday, I was sitting drinking my morning coffee when I heard an angry voice: "I am furious with you, and I will bring my wrath down upon you!"

"But what have I done wrong?" I asked.

"I sent that girl in the pizza parlor to tempt him again. As strong a Christian as he is in other areas, I can always tempt him with a pretty young lady who comes after him. It makes him feel important when he is feeling sorry for himself, when he thinks, 'I deserve more.' And then I have him. Sometimes he resists for a long time, but in the end I always get him."

"But what does this have to do with me?" I asked, shaken.

"I was close to success in tempting him again. He was feeling low and he thought that it wouldn't matter. 'No one would find out, and my life is in ruins anyway, so why does anyone care what I do?' But then you interfered. When he told you about the girl in the pizza parlor and that he was being 'hit on', you said, 'You need to be clear that you will not have a sexual relationship with her. You can be friends but nothing more.'

"Then the girl contacted him after being hospitalized from a drug overdose and told him that she was pregnant with her boyfriend's child. When Mike told you the story, you said, 'You definitely have to make it clear that you will not have a sexual relationship with her, but that you do care about her as a child of God. You need to tell her how much God loves her, and that she needs to turn to Him.' So, he did. And now she won't even call him, let alone try to have a sexual relationship with him."

Even though the voice paused, I was silent. I felt stony cold and was too afraid to speak.

"So, you thought you spoiled my plan, that you saved him from temptation. Next, I turned to his bank accounts. To increase his anxiety level about caring for his family, I used up all the money that he had in checking and savings, and then I turned to his 401(k). I made sure that there were education bills that needed to be paid and dental work that couldn't wait. I thought I had him again, where he would turn to me in pain from not having the financial resources that he was used to. But no, you had to go and give him money. Seriously? Not as a loan, but as a gift? You even said it was one Christian helping another, like that made it less stupid.

"Now I ask you. What kind of a fool are you? To give money to a friend or even family member is ridiculous. You may never see him again. What are you going to do in your old age, when you are poor and alone, and no one cares about you? All you will have left is your money, and here you are giving it away. To answer my own question, you are a stupid fool."

Those words were the same words that Curtis had used during the divorce: "You will die poor and alone." *How could I be hearing those exact words again, after twenty months?*

I was afraid to respond to this barrage of abuse. My silence seemed to upset him more. Finally, he shouted, "Aren't you going to say anything? Don't you see how stupid you are for helping him? I don't care about the girl. She means nothing to me. I already have her in my grasp. He is the one that I am after. He has the ability to do great things for God's kingdom, but I need him to work for the glory of *my* kingdom, the underworld. In fact, I really don't even care about you. You go to a church and talk to a few people, but you aren't an influencer like he is. The only reason I care about you at all is that you are interfering with my real goal: to get him firmly in my grasp, and to have him only work for my glory, the glory of Satan, here on earth."

My blood felt like it had turned to ice as I realized that the voice belonged to Satan. He had revealed himself in his anger.

After a long pause, he continued, "Because you have chosen to interfere with my plans, I will cast tragedy upon you. I will take away your health again and even something more precious to you: I will take away your desire and ability to pray for the healing of others. You will be ineffective in your little healing prayer ministry. In fact, when you pray for others, you will make them sad instead of comforting them, and they will turn away from God because of you."

Now it was my turn to be angry. Summoning all my courage, I said, "I don't care about your threats; do what you need to do. I will continue to protect my friend from your deceitful web and the temptations that you use so well to break us. I will use all my powers to protect him from your evilness, and all of my power and authority come directly from God."

With that, he left my mind.

ᏉᎧ ᏉᎧ ᏉᎧ

That evening I sat down to read the Scripture verses for the next day and I couldn't seem to quiet my mind. I replayed Satan's promise: that he would take away my health, and that my words in our healing prayer ministry would turn people away from God. I was scheduled to be the lay healing prayer minister at the 8:45 a.m. service the next morning, and I wondered if I should ask someone to cover for me. I didn't want to take any chances that Satan would make good on his threats. But as I prayed that evening, I was more convinced that I should trust the Holy Spirit to give me the right words for healing. Instead of running like a coward, I decided to stay and fight.

$$\text{☙ ☙ ☙}$$

I was strangely calm as I sat in church the next morning. The healing prayer ministry was still new for me and I was usually anxious about what God asked me to do, but not today. I was at peace and felt strong, aware that friends would be coming forward with a newly diagnosed cancer, impending surgeries and lost jobs. We would all be seeking comfort and peace in a difficult world.

I left service immediately after taking communion and made my way to the chapel where we pray for those in need. As I pushed the chapel door open, I heard a voice, "I am here." It was uncharacteristically cold and dark in the chapel for a bright September day. Our clergy and healing prayer usher hadn't arrived yet, so I was the only one in the small room. But I knew I wasn't alone.

"I told you that I would come for you. Did you think I would forget?" he said with a snarl.

I glanced up in the direction of the voice and saw a ghoulish figure, perched on the rail above the old organ pipes high in the back of the chapel. I froze. I'd walked far enough into the chapel that the only way out was to cross back underneath the figure.

I heard a rustle and turned to the front of the chapel. Through the darkness, I saw three shapes standing in front of the altar by the communion rail, but I couldn't see the detail on their faces. A low white glow emanated from them.

The voice drew my attention back to the ledge: "I am even angrier with you that you have brought them with you. How disgusting. This disagreement is between you and me, and you brought your 'friends.' Just remember these words: 'When you least expect me, I will be back for you.'"

It was odd that I was calm, but I could feel the protection from the presence of the Holy Trinity: the Father, Son and Holy Spirit. I looked back to the ledge and stared directly into the eyes of the small figure. Speaking with authority, I said aloud, "I have work to do, and will continue to pray for my friends as God directs. Be gone, Satan, I have no time for you."

In an instant, the ghoulish figure disappeared from his perch and the chapel returned to a warm autumn glow.

As I turned back to the communion rail, I saw that the three shapes were fading. "Agatha," said a calm, peaceful voice, "remember that we are always with you. Never fear, we will protect you from the Evil One."

The chapel door opened as a priest and usher arrived, and people started streaming into the chapel for healing prayer. I was amazed that I was so calm after what had just happened, but I now knew with certainty that God is always with me and will protect me. There is nothing to fear.

I didn't mention the encounter to anyone, because I wasn't sure they would believe me. I was certain it had been Satan and that God had protected me. There are hundreds of stories in the Bible about Satan's evil deeds and his constant temptations, but this time it had happened to me. The best news was that God was there, had been there all along, and would be with me always.

℘ ℘ ℘

I needed to get a lot of things sorted out, and I wasn't so sure that I should share about the experience in the chapel when the PORCH CLUB met in a few weeks. It was too fresh in my mind, and I was still working through what it all meant. I knew it really happened, but others might think that it was too wacky.

"What about your State Representative," Jackie asked, "the one you had the hots for? What's he been up to?"

"Well. That is one thing I need your help with."

"I knew it! You are having an affair with him, aren't you?" Jackie again.

"No, absolutely not. He helped me with my finances when I was so far in debt after the divorce, and he sends me encouraging emails with Scripture verses or a meditation once in awhile. But then this past June everything blew up. His wife found out that he'd been having an affair and they are getting a divorce."

"You are kidding!" they all chimed in at once. "How did you find that out?"

"Well. He actually called me in June to ask me to pray for him and his family."

"You sound a little envious that it wasn't with you," Carol observed.

"No, not at all. He was somebody who I looked up to as a Christian and he let me down. I guess you can say I'm disappointed, but more than that, I'm confused. I want to be the kind of Christian that imitates Christ, not just one that reads and talks about Him. I'm trying to reconcile my human desire for revenge with Christ's forgiveness. It's a lot to think about."

"Are you sure you're not jealous?"

"Definitely not. I was attracted to him at first because of his powerful role in the Legislature, but I had vowed that I would never have sex again with anyone that I wasn't married to. I had that one night fling after I'd filed for a divorce, and I realized that I couldn't work for God and continue to lead my double life. But it hasn't been easy. I had made an idol out of having a man in my life, longing for a husband and children, but it was the wrong thing to do. I put them all ahead of God."

"How did you figure all this out?" Kim asked.

"First there were the guys from St. George's on the South Africa trip. They were so wonderful. Treated me like a real person, not just a sex object or a woman to chase. They cared about my faith, and it continued at church after I returned. Then I met Mike. He seemed so sophisticated and charming and a State Representative. I've always been attracted to men with power, but this was different. I wanted to change and have relationships built on our mutual love for God, not our mutual self-centeredness. After I met Mike, I met Brian, and then Matthew.

I know I told you about Brian, but I don't think I've mentioned Matthew. I met him this year on Holy Saturday, the night before Easter at St. George's. We were both holding candles at the bonfire in the courtyard and waiting for the procession to start into the church. He was wearing a nametag, and I recognized his name from the Confirmation Class. It was a huge class and we hadn't met, so I walked up and introduced myself. We talked for a few minutes and found out that he works right next to the Frist Center for Visual Arts, where I give docent tours. We have something else in common; we both have season symphony tickets for Friday nights."

"Okay—so this sounds like a romantic interest!" Carol interjected, "Tell us more!"

"No on this count too. Matthew is wonderful and has a Master's in Divinity from Trinity Evangelical College in Chicago. He is incredibly bright and very faithful. He knows a lot of Scripture and has read tons of books, both historical and contemporary. We often go to the Frist Center for an exhibition opening, have a glass of wine and talk about the sermon from the past Sunday. And he's not bad to look at. But he's gone through a painful divorce and he has three boys that he adores. It's the perfect friendship. We both enjoy each other's company and want to enrich each other's faith. He is always willing to talk and explain Scripture, as well as art. He's an artist too.

"Brian, Matthew, and the men from the South Africa trip are teaching me a new way to live, where I feel honored and valued by them. They care more about my faith than they do about a male-female relationship. They are willing to correct me when I stray."

"Back to Mike," Kim said, "Are you interested in a romance since he'll be single again?"

"No, not at all. I was attracted to him when we met because of the power and authority he had as a State Representative. I was always looking for an all-powerful, all-knowing human in my life to love me, but all humans fall short of perfection. "

"So if there is no romance with Mike, are you still friends?" Jackie asked.

"I started praying in earnest on that day in June. You know I go to church every morning, and I carry my prayer card with all the names of the people I'm praying for. I prayed for reconciliation and a repaired marriage, so I'm not sure why my prayers haven't been answered. But I also asked God what I was supposed to do to be a Christian friend to Mike and his wife. The answer came back that I needed to help them financially. Just like Mike got me through my financial crisis during the divorce, I needed to help them."

I really wondered if I should continue. I paused longer than necessary when Kim finally said, "And...."

"So in mid-September, I met Mike at the Belle Meade Starbucks and gave him two checks. One for him to cash immediately to take the kids to Rosemary Beach for Christmas and the other one to cash in December if he didn't have a job yet."

"So, how much were the checks for?" Kim asked.

"$10,000...each."

Jackie let out a whistle. "You're kidding! You gave him $20,000? How much did you have in the bank? I thought you just got the mortgage paid off. You couldn't have had much more than that in savings."

"I did get the mortgage paid off and I've been socking money away ever since. It is interesting, but with a budget, I've been living on much less money than I make and it is really freeing. Before I was always looking for something 'new' to buy:

clothes, something for the house, or a vacation. Now I don't have as many things to worry about. I haven't been on vacation at all, other than coming here to Louisville to be with all of you, and I realized that I don't have to be 'escaping' to the beach in order to be with God. When vacations became a mandatory escape from my daily life, something needed to change."

Jackie still wasn't convinced. "You know that they say you should never loan money to family or friends. So what kind of a note did he sign? When will he pay you back? Are you charging him interest?"

"I know that everyone advises against loaning money to family or friends. So I didn't. I told him the money was a gift, free and clear."

"You can't be serious," Jackie said.

"I didn't think about it for very long. I really feel that God was calling me to help him. I don't have any family to spend money on, and I wanted the kids to have a good Christmas. Besides, he doesn't have a job and may need the money to live on. It's the first time I've ever really trusted God to take care of me and provide everything that I need. The money was more about me trusting God than it was about Mike, Jennifer and their three children. For the first time, I wasn't trying to get somebody to like me by doing something nice for them and trying to buy their affection. It really was a gift. I just need you all to tell me that I've done the right thing. It's just so contrary to what the world thinks that I get confused at times. But aren't we supposed to care for our neighbors? And isn't everyone our neighbor?" There was a silence, which I interpreted as approval.

"Enough about me, who's going to talk next?"

❧ ❧ ❧

I was so thankful for the girls in the PORCH CLUB. It helped me to tell them about the transforming power I was feeling in my life. Instead of using other people for my purposes, I was starting to care more about their needs. Situations appear very different when I look at them from the other person's perspective.

I knew my commitment to not have sex outside of marriage seemed odd to the rest of the girls, but I'd made such a mess of my relationships that I had to make changes, and that is where it all would start. Having sex after a handful of dates had always stifled the relationship from going further. It was too powerful an emotion to be misused. I wanted to honor God by showing that I understood He'd reserved the pleasure of sex as the ultimate communication between married people. It is like the intimacy that we individually know with God.

I was halfway home from Louisville when my thoughts turned to the approaching holidays. I'd spent some Thanksgivings alone over the years, but this year would be different. My good friend Nicole was coordinating an International Student Ministry project and I'd volunteered to host some of the students for Thanksgiving dinner. I was learning that part of being a Christian was to not keep my faith to myself, and I was welcoming opportunities to serve others.

Jackie volunteered to drive down from Louisville and help with the dinner, and Matthew offered to co-host. It was so great to have old and new friends under the same roof to celebrate the holiday. I was even looking forward to Christmas, as there were parties planned at church and I'd already committed to serve with Dru as an usher at our church service on Christmas Eve.

෴ ෴ ෴

I checked my bank statements online the second week in December and saw that both checks I'd given Mike had been cashed. I said a prayer of thanks to God that He was teaching me how to trust Him and be obedient with the resources He had given me. I checked the weather on Christmas and was glad that it was unseasonably warm in Rosemary Beach.

16

Turning Inward

We forgive as we rediscover the person behind the offense, as we surrender our right to revenge, and as we wish good things for the person who did bad things to us, just as the Father did.

— Lewis Smedes

I've always looked forward to the calmness after Christmas, but the arrival of this New Year, 2010, brought me some new challenges as well. For some reason my hot flashes always were worse in the winter months, and this year I was miserable. I knew that the Lupron shots made the hot flashes even more severe, but I didn't have a choice. Keeping in a menopausal state was important to prevent a recurrence of breast cancer. I was grateful that my LIFE group was still meeting; I needed their support more than ever. We were all about the same age and understood how miserable hot flashes are. Not being able to sleep was the worst part. I was taking another drug for cancer prevention that caused bone density loss in my hips and back, and mild joint pain. Most days I didn't feel great, but every morning I woke up and gave thanks that I was still alive.

❧ ❧ ❧

To keep my body feeling limber, I had developed a daily stretching routine. One particularly stiff day in March, I was in the middle of my back exercises when my right eye started to water. I blinked a few times and tried to clear my vision, but it wasn't any better. I'd been living with blurry vision in my right eye for three years now, and the doctors had still not figured out why. It was like looking through cheesecloth and there was a huge "floater" that was constantly moving around; it had never watered like this, though.

What could that mean? I'd prayed every day for the first two years that my vision would be restored. There are many stories in the Bible of the lame and blind being healed, and I prayed that I would be just like them. But after two years, I'd quit praying and moved on to praying for others. I kept thinking that my vision problem might be related to the medications I was taking, but my doctors thought it was just stress from school and the lack of sleep from my nightly hot flashes.

It was a long winter with my physical woes, but I didn't miss any days of work, and was glad that I had a church family to be with every morning. It had been four years since my cancer diagnosis, and with seven doctors, I had frequent appointments and follow-up tests. In April 2010, I was waiting for the results of my annual diagnostic mammogram, when the technician called my name and ushered me into an office.

A pleasant, middle-aged woman greeted me, "Good morning. I'm Dr. Tupper, one of the Radiologists here at Centennial."

Dr. Tupper turned her computer screen around so that I could see the image while she talked. "See here in the right breast, these little points of bright light. Those weren't there before. I've compared them with all your other mammograms since 2004 and they are definitely new."

My heart sank. "What does that mean? What are they?"

"Well, we don't know for sure. I had to increase the magnification in order to see them at all, and they are too small to biopsy. There's nothing we can do but watch them for the next ninety days. I want you to do your breast self-exams and if anything changes, let Dr. Cooper know immediately. Otherwise I want you to come back in July for another diagnostic mammogram. Sometimes they can disappear on their own, or are just residual scar tissue that we didn't pick up before. But hopefully we'll be able to tell more in three months."

I couldn't believe that I was going through this again! Well, not exactly going through this again, but close enough, a test that wasn't "quite right", and this time on the right side. I retraced my original diagnosis and treatment decisions and wondered if I should have had chemotherapy. There wasn't much evidence that chemotherapy would have dramatically increased my survival potential, so I'd opted to just have surgery followed by Lupron shots with oral medication. I'd made the right decision with the information I had at the time, and you can't go back and second-guess yourself.

As I left the parking garage, I thought about who I would tell about this latest development. So many people had supported me over the past four years, and I hated to burden them all again. On the other hand, I remembered how much I felt loved and cared for when people reached out to me with thoughts and prayers. It really had made all the difference when I was sick.

I decided to tell just a few people, since there wasn't really anything anyone could do right now, except pray. I sent a quick email to my LIFE group at church, the PORCH CLUB, Brian, Matthew, and Mike. I explained briefly about the ninety-day waiting period until my next exam, and asked them to pray for me. My spirits were lifted when each person responded that they had already lifted up prayers. I thought back to the time when my arm was bandaged and Reverend Leigh Spruill had prayed for me at the communion rail. The same warm feeling came over me again that people cared about me, and that God was present and going to take care of me, too.

ᏇᏇᏇ

I was following a blog about the cancer journey of a fellow Nashvillian, Sigourney Woods Cheek. Sigourney had written *"Patient Siggy"* when she was first diagnosed with cancer, and started blogging in earnest when she had a relapse. She wrote:

"The confirmation of cancer again is just not as tough as the 'you have cancer' in the first place. As a survivor, you are prepared. As a survivor, the hospital drill is not the scary unknown. You might be cured for years, but you still go to the doctor every six months, just in case. You knock on wood when you are telling people, 'I'm in remission.' Only once are you a well person, an unsuspecting person, a discovery of a lump or bump that is surely nothing and will soon go away to the confirmation that you are a well person—no longer, never again. The planets have realigned; the orbit has tilted, bending in another direction. Reynolds Price, a novelist and teacher of writing at Duke University, lived in a wheelchair for years from an operation to remove a tumor on his spine. He writes, "When you undergo huge traumas in middle life, everybody is in league with us to deny that the old life is ended. Everybody is trying to patch us and get us back to who we were, when in fact what we need to be told is, 'You're dead. Who are you going to be tomorrow?'""

Sigourney's words described my feelings exactly when Dr. Tupper said I had tiny little spots on my right breast. This time I wasn't as terrified, but a lot had changed in three-and-a-half years. I was dead back then. Now I was a totally different person.

There wasn't much I could do for the next ninety days but pray and thank my friends for their prayers.

∽ ∽ ∽

It was barely a month later that it started to rain and didn't stop for three days. I went to church that morning and then to Pilates class, like I did every Saturday. It was raining pretty heavily and was predicted to continue all weekend, so I stopped at the grocery store to get my week's food. It was raining heavier when I got out of the store and continued relentlessly into the evening. As I drifted off to sleep, I dreamt of the 1998 flood in San Antonio. I hoped that our Nashville rains weren't a repeat.

I got up early the next morning and decided by my first cup of coffee that I wasn't going to leave my house; it was safe on top of a huge hill. It was all I could do to get Rachel, my dachshund, to go out for a quick walk. I gazed into the backyard and watched a small poplar tree fall over in slow motion. There was no wind; it just looked like the roots had so much water that it wasn't strong enough to continue standing. I checked the weather app on my phone and realized that I'd received a text message from Mbali, my friend in South Africa, "R U OK?"

"Hmmm, why wouldn't I be okay?" I hadn't spoken with Mbali since Christmas and hadn't shared any of my recent health news. I looked out the front window and saw sheets of water overflowing the storm drains in the street. I turned on the TV and saw helicopters over River Plantation, a subdivision just a few miles west. It looked like the whole area was almost completely underwater, and I had two close friends that lived there. People were being rescued with boats from their rooftops.

I texted Mbali back to tell her I was okay, but when I tried to dial one of my friends in River Plantation I couldn't get a cell signal on my phone. My landline was out, too. This looked pretty serious, so I stayed glued to the TV all day. Internet access and email were spotty, so I occupied myself with sending text

206

messages and watching it rain. By late afternoon, I received a text that the HCA Corporate Office would be closed on Monday, and I was relieved that I wouldn't have to venture out.

Early Monday morning, it looked like the rain was letting up, but I decided to stay in, safe and sound. I still had only spotty Internet connectivity and my landline phone was dead. My cell phone would work for one call and then go dead, but texting seemed to work. I wondered what was happening at St. George's, since Richland Creek was right across the road. As if my thoughts were answered, I received a mass email from Larry Trabue: The church server is down, but we need men volunteers at the church at 10 a.m. this morning. If you can help out, please come.

My LIFE group from church was scheduled to meet that evening, and periodic emails were getting through, debating whether we should cancel. I realized from the tone of the email that many people had been displaced from their homes, and we couldn't meet at the church because of water damage. One of the ladies suggested that we meet at her home that evening. We needed to be together, and we could use the time to plan how we could help our church and community. Our clergy member, Marcia King, wouldn't be able to make it as she was helping with some pastoral emergencies in the congregation.

I still had horrible memories of the flood in San Antonio in 1998, but by late afternoon the sun was shining brightly and the world looked new again. I was safe and had no water damage, and I wanted to help others.

As I was driving to Gail's house for our LIFE group meeting, my phone rang. It was from one of the girls, Beth. "I just can't come tonight, I'm too devastated," Beth said. I could tell she was choking back tears.

"What's wrong, did you have damage at your house? Are you okay?"

"We just had a little water in the basement, but I just heard that they found Bill and Frankie."

"What are you talking about? Bill and Frankie Rutledge?"

"Yes. Haven't you heard? They were washed away in the flood. It happened yesterday morning, when they tried to get out of their car to go into church for the 7:30 a.m. service. Some men from church found their car early this morning; it was in the ditch across from the church, by Richland Creek. They just found their bodies, a half-mile apart, behind the Publix store at Hill Center at Belle Meade."

"Oh, no!" I cried, "I had no idea. Are you on the way to Gail's house for our LIFE group tonight?"

"No, I'm too upset. I wouldn't be good company," Beth sniffled through her tears.

"Beth, you've got to come and join us. We all need to be together to deal with this news. At times like this, it isn't good to be alone. We need to pray together."

ᑫ᙮ ᑫ᙮ ᑫ᙮

I couldn't believe what I had just heard. Bill and Frankie Rutledge were the most wonderful couple. I'd first met Bill in January 2008, when I started going to weekday morning service at St. George's. The Eucharist was the only thing that got me started some mornings, and Bill was always there, sitting in the first pew on the right side of the chapel. Bill would arrive every morning at 5:30 a.m. to make coffee, and then he'd come to the chapel for Eucharist at 7 a.m. There were only three other people that came to church every morning, and we felt like a little family. No matter how bad I felt in the morning, physically or emotionally, I knew I'd be accepted by these four and that Bill would have coffee waiting for us after the service.

My thoughts drifted back to the second Sunday of May 2008, when I'd been "received" into the church by the Bishop. It was a special day, not just because it was my entrance into the Episcopal Church, but also because it was Mother's Day and Pentecost Sunday. A huge wind was blowing that morning, and it made me feel alive. I knew that I had made the right choice in joining the church and I was ready to go out and serve others, but wasn't exactly sure how.

There was a break between Confirmation Sunday and the start of the new Sunday School classes in June, and I was eager to keep learning about my faith in a disciplined way. Marcia King was teaching a class about a Philip Yancey book, and I'd decided to attend. Still, I was a little apprehensive about walking into a new classroom with people I didn't know. I felt silly, but the discomfort was real.

When I walked into class that first Sunday, it was just as I had feared: I didn't know anyone. Then I spied Bill from the weekday service. He spotted me in the same moment, and motioned for me to sit next to him. Bill introduced me to his wife, Frankie, and they made me feel so welcome, like I belonged in that room and in that class. They graciously introduced me to their friends at the table. The next Sunday, I walked into the room and Bill stood up and motioned for me to come over. "Come sit with us; we've saved you a seat!" was Frankie's cordial greeting. I thought, *what a great church,* and realized that it was a wonderful church because of the wonderful people. It was Bill and Frankie Rutledge who made me feel welcome at St. George's that summer.

༅ ༅ ༅

Only five of the ten women from our LIFE group gathered the night after the flood. There were so many stories to share, and I learned the extent of the damage to the church and what had happened to Bill and Frankie. St. George's had taken on eighteen inches of water throughout the first floor, and parts of the second floor had flooded from roof leaks. Although the rain had stopped, the devastation was enormous from the swollen riverbanks. We were uncertain whether the church would re-open for Sunday service. There was only one entrance, as most of the first floor was boarded up as we waited for cleaning crews and insurance estimates. Everything from choir robes to prayer books had been scooped up and was scattered throughout Nashville in hundreds of parishioners' homes. Of course, the worst news was about Bill and Frankie. They were both such delightful people, and faithful stewards of God's resources. My LIFE group was a godsend. I don't know how I would have gotten through that night without them. We toasted Bill and Frankie with multiple glasses of wine and felt blessed that we had known them.

On the long drive home alone, I asked the obvious question to God, *Why did this have to happen to them? They were so wonderful. They loved each other so much, and they loved St. George's. This doesn't make any sense at all.* I didn't make it into the house before I broke down in tears. I was too upset to talk to anyone, but I did send a message to Mike and Matthew: "Just learned two dear friends from church perished in the flood: devastated." Matthew immediately texted back: "Am so sorry for your loss. I know how much you admired Bill and Frankie. My heart weeps with you tonight."

ৎ৹ ৎ৹ ৎ৹

The rest of the week was a blur in Nashville, as displaced friends looked for places to stay, and volunteers worked at the church around-the-clock to start the cleanup process. Reverend Spruill sent a message saying it was important that the main sanctuary be ready for worship the following Sunday. I was shocked by the devastation of the church building when I arrived for worship Tuesday morning. I couldn't imagine that we'd be able to have services in five days. It wasn't just our church, but all of Nashville that was reeling from the destruction. The Symphony Center was closed downtown, and entire neighborhoods of homes and businesses were still under water.

In my prayer time that week, God made it clear that some questions we ask as humans don't have answers. I was trained in science and thought that if you looked hard enough, there was always an explanation. But this week there were no answers.

Instead of asking more questions, I turned to prayer, hoping that God would tell me what I could do to help.

Late in the week, we learned that there would be one Sunday service in the sanctuary, followed by a funeral service for Bill and Frankie. My good friend Anna and I volunteered to be "greeters" and hand out service bulletins at the one entrance. I wasn't sure that I could put on a happy face to greet people, but it was important for us to worship together as a family. Mine was a small contribution compared to what everyone else was doing, but I was coming to realize that we all have different gifts and we are all called to do different things for God.

When I stopped by the church on Saturday afternoon to see how the cleanup crews were doing, I was amazed to find furniture, kindergarten supplies, and other assorted things out on the side lawn, still drying out from the flood. Some of it wasn't salvageable and had been placed aside until it could be hauled away. I peeked inside the church door and saw dozens of people with brooms and mops, painstakingly cleaning dust from the pews and kneelers, and wiping the waterlines from the walls. *How would it ever be ready in time for the worship service and a funeral?* I stopped to visit with the staff and volunteers, and they assured me the church would be ready by the next day. Not perfect, but ready to worship God.

The volunteers were eager to share stories of the wonderful hearts of the Nashville community. There had been an article in The Tennessean on Thursday morning about the devastation at the church, as well as our loss of Bill and Frankie. Later that morning, some people showed up at the church door and asked if they could help clean. The volunteer coordinator didn't recognize them and asked their names before putting them to work. "Oh, we don't attend here. We just read in the morning paper what had happened to your church. We work in the Attorney General's office and thought you could use extra hands to get it ready for Sunday. We are here to help you."

The graciousness of the area churches was also amazing. Immanuel Baptist Church opened their building to host a reception with our Bishop, which had been planned for the following week. They not only provided the building, their ladies also helped with the cooking and hosted the reception for us. The Temple just down the road invited us to use their building for our nursery and Sunday School classes. It was a great partnership, since they didn't use their building much on Sundays. A fifth grade Sunday School class from St. Paul's in Franklin, sent a huge greeting card, signed by all the children, that read: "St. George's, we love you!"

I realized that St. George's was a special place of caring people, but that warmth and love extended throughout all of Nashville and Middle Tennessee. The community rallied to help each other recover from the flood without regard to race, creed, or social status.

୧ ୧ ୧

I couldn't understand how the world could look so different after seven days. The sun dawned brightly Sunday morning, and I was anxious to get to church for our first service since the flood. One week ago, the heavens had opened up with sheets of rain, but today was bright and sunny.

At first it was hard to keep from crying as people entering the church saw the severity of the water damage for the first time. But as more people arrived, a buzz began echoing through the room as they began to share stories. However, it was not the sound of despair, but of the desire to serve God through serving others.

Anna and I grabbed a cup of coffee at the Belle Meade Starbucks before we returned to St. George's for Bill and Frankie's funeral. The front pew where Bill and Frankie always sat was empty, except for two beautiful bouquets of white roses. Anna and I kneeled in a pew midway back on the right side of the church to say prayers until the service began. I was sitting quietly but fighting back tears. I looked up and saw Matthew, dressed in a suit, coming in the side door of the church. Without a word, he quietly made his way to where we were sitting and sat between us. It was good to have the strength of a friend to help us honor Bill and Frankie.

The funeral was beautiful, and the eulogies and sermon spoke of Bill and Frankie's love for each other and for St. George's. I heard someone say that they had left their estate to St. George's as an outpouring of their faith and stewardship. I didn't realize that they also didn't have any family to leave their estate to, and thought back to how difficult it had been for me to make out a will. Bill and Frankie were a wonderful example of how to be good stewards of their money and to recognize that everything we have in life really does belong to God. What an honorable gift from Bill and Frankie. I'd never been to an Episcopal funeral before and was amazed at how uplifted I felt, unlike any before. The back of the service bulletin read:

> The liturgy for the dead is an Easter liturgy. It finds its meaning in the resurrection. Because Jesus was raised from the dead, we, too, shall be raised. The liturgy therefore is characterized by joy, in the certainty that "neither death, nor life, nor angels, nor powers, or height, nor depth, nor anything else in all creation, will be able to separate us from the love of God, in Christ Jesus our Lord.

As I choked back tears, all I could think was, *Amen.*

ℒ ℒ ℒ

Later that week I learned that two friends needed a place to stay while their condo was being re-built, and another friend needed to store some furniture in my garage. I was so thankful that I had decided to keep the house after the divorce. This was what God had intended all along: that I would have a place to care for others. I'd never opened my home up to anyone except an occasional weekend guest, but it was time that I shared my resources with others.

Preliminary estimates said that it would take almost a year to re-build St. George's. Although a few classes were cancelled, morning services would continue in the main sanctuary while the chapel was being cleaned and reconstructed. It was a different feeling for those of us who attended each morning, but it didn't matter. I had come to understand that worship was central to my faith and that I needed the daily forgiveness I felt when I received Holy Communion. I had come to depend upon my morning ritual to help guide me through the rest of the day.

℘ ℘ ℘

In June, Mike called to ask if I had room for a female friend and business associate of his. She would be in Nashville for a weekend in July to work on a project with him. Mike thought that it would be good for me to talk with her about my faith, as she'd recently experienced a lot of personal heartache. By July, my guest bedroom would be unoccupied and I welcomed the opportunity to share my home with a stranger again.

I was glad when she agreed to go to morning worship with me. Even though the church wasn't "pretty" with the construction going on, it was *my* church and I still sought refuge there every morning. We had a good discussion, comparing notes about the religions of our youth and where we currently were in our relationship with God. I could honestly share with her, "It is an amazing place. I never fail to meet God when I am at St. George's."

When we continued our conversation that night, I learned that she'd just been through a huge romantic breakup. She was a single mom and had been dating a great guy for over a year. She thought everything was wonderful and that they were headed for marriage. Then one evening she happened to pick up his phone and recognized the number of her best friend. She immediately knew in her gut that they were an "item". He didn't deny it and said that he'd been trying to tell her for quite some time that their relationship was over.

I told her about my two failed marriages and we agreed that personal relationships with family, close friends and romantic interests are by far the hardest part of life. It was almost 4 a.m. when we got to bed, but it had been a good discussion and we agreed on one other thing: our relationship with God was the most important one, and unlike other humans, we could rely on God without fail.

While we were talking the next morning, she said, "You should be dating by now. It's been over two years since the divorce. Do you think you need to see a psychiatrist?" I was stunned. I didn't know her well enough to feel anything but judgment. If a closer friend had asked the question, I might have answered differently, but I could feel the redness rise in my cheeks and my defense barriers going up.

I asked, "Why do you think I need to see a psychiatrist?"

"Well, it isn't normal not to be in a relationship. After two years, you must be afraid of something. What is it you are afraid of?"

"I'm really not afraid of starting a new relationship, but God hasn't sent me the right person. A good Christian friend told me to 'guard my heart' a few weeks ago, and I think that is great advice. I've always done the opposite. I wanted to fall in love, picked out the guy and then determined that I would make him 'love' me. I'd cook gourmet dinners, buy him gifts, shower him with attention and praise, and of course there was always sex involved, and plenty of it.

"Now I've taken a step back, to learn a better way. There are some married women in my LIFE group and others from church that I've gotten to know. I've asked them to tell me about their long, successful marriages. I'm learning a lot, but I know that God isn't done revealing relationship wisdom to me yet. I feel like I'm sixteen again and just learning to date, but it's okay. I'm learning to have wonderful male Christian friends like Brian, Matthew and Mike, who support my faith with their friendship."

"I still think it's abnormal that you aren't dating. Mike and I talked about it when I was on the drive to Nashville. We can get the male perspective when we have lunch with him tomorrow."

That stung. I couldn't believe that I'd just heard that Mike was discussing my relationships--or lack thereof--with someone I didn't even know! Then I considered how I felt about her comments. *Was I too sensitive about not having a man in my life, or was I distressed because a stranger knew so much about my personal life?*

The weekend was over, but the words had stuck: "Maybe you need to see a psychiatrist because you don't have a man in your life." Those weren't her exact words, but they were the ones I'd heard. I knew two people who would be honest with me: a friend from work, and Father Tim. I decided to make an appointment to talk with them soon and see if they could help me sort through all of this.

ร ร ร

I had lunch with my friend from work the very next day, and it didn't take long for me to blurt out my question. "Is it wrong for me not to be dating after two years?" My friend immediately probed for more information. Had I turned down dates because I was afraid of being hurt again? Had I shunned making friends with any single men at church, for fear of involvement?

I truthfully answered "No," to all the questions and explained that after thirty-five years of dating, I thought it was time to take a "time-out" and learn what a real male-female relationship looked like. I even laughingly remarked that I knew of four Christian guys who had divorced and remarried within a few months. One had started "dating" even before the divorce was final. It seemed like some men couldn't live without a woman

216

in their life and went from one failed marriage right into the next one. I explained that I wanted to give God some space to act in my life, instead of me rushing out and "attaching" to the next eligible bachelor.

My friend listened intently, then talked for a bit about her own marriage, which was based upon mutual respect, a shared feeling of being called to do God's work (but not necessarily together), and a true desire to love and protect each other from Satan. I realized that I had never experienced that kind of love from a man, but I had also been incapable of loving in that way, too. I'd always settled for a "human" relationship where we were compatible, had a good time together, and enjoyed each other's company, but nothing spiritually intimate. I'd always gone after the guys that were charming and sophisticated. I loved the thrill of chasing them, as well as the prize of catching them; that's what dominated the relationship, but it only lasted for so long. At some point, we found out that we didn't have anything in common except a mutual desire to not be lonely, and that isn't enough to sustain a marriage.

I was encouraged when she responded, "You are thinking along the right track. A marriage isn't a person to be conquered for your own satisfaction or to fulfill your needs. It's when God has called you to become one with another person that your yoke becomes light and your union can be used to bring glory to God. Any other foundation will surely crumble. As I was leaving, I heard for the second time in as many weeks, "Remember, guard your heart, my dear."

ço ço ço

I was glad that Father Tim Jones could see me the next week. I felt like he knew me well enough to know whether I needed to see a psychiatrist about my "non-dating". I enjoyed meeting with Tim, as he always started every meeting with a prayer. This time he prayed for wisdom and clear direction for any problems. Then I gave him more details about the divorce and the rather off-putting conversation with Mike's friend. I told him that I'd felt judged by a stranger.

Father Tim was very thoughtful, asking additional questions, and then he said, "Agatha, I feel like I know you pretty well from seeing you in church each day, working with you in different ministries, and traveling to South Africa with you. You don't strike me as the 'needy type' that has to have a man in your life. Do you think that is how you really feel, or are you covering up something?"

"No, that's how I really feel. Until Mike's friend suggested that I needed professional help, I hadn't even thought about it being a problem. I've enjoyed learning about God and my relationship with Him, and I need to get that right before I embark on another intimate human relationship. I'm also learning to quit chasing men. God needs to speak to the guy first. I'd often chase them and they'd slow down enough to get caught. I don't want that kind of a relationship again, where I am the pursuer. A man needs to be the pursuer, willing to pursue God first, and then pursue the woman that God sends to him. It just doesn't work successfully the other way around."

"I'm not ruling out counseling," Tim replied, "but first I'd like you to read a book, and then come visit with me again. It's called *The Art of Forgiving*, by Lewis Smedes, and I've recommended it to many people. It will help you discern whether you've forgiven Curtis. If not, you can't pursue another relationship honestly and I could confidently recommend some counseling. I'd like you to read the book and then tell me your impressions. I want you to understand that God doesn't call everyone to be married, or even in a romantic relationship. Remember that St. Paul felt it was honorable to be single and not be distracted from serving Christ by family responsibilities.

"Our culture leads us to believe that there is something wrong with us if we aren't paired up two by two, but there is no Biblical basis for that. Often the church places too much emphasis on families and children, and doesn't do enough to honor single people and their calling. Keep reading your Bible, studying, and conversing with your good Christian friends. I think you are on a marvelous track to have healthy, holy relationships in your life, maybe for the first time ever." With that, Father Tim ended our conversation with a prayer for discernment on holy relationships.

Two weeks later, I'd finished the book and stopped Father Tim after the Sunday morning service.

"Thanks for recommending Smedes' book. It helped me to realize that I've never hated Curtis and there is nothing to forgive. We both had human faults that led to the divorce, but I don't blame him at all. I know honestly that I'd be ready to move into a serious relationship if God sends me that person. It's not that I'm afraid of another human relationship; it's just that at this point, God has called me to be single so that I can work exclusively on my relationship with Him. That may change in the future, but I'm trusting God on this one."

It had been a wild ninety days with the flood, Bill and Frankie's death and an important conversation on forgiveness, but my follow-up diagnostic mammogram was looming. I'd expected three months of quiet prayer to prepare myself in case I had cancer again, but it had been anything but quiet. I was still thankful to be alive, and this time I was putting everything in God's hands, instead of mine.

17

Cancer, Round Two

Pray with the expectation that something will happen—or why bother to pray at all?

— Tom Holladay

I needed more time to pray. God never asks us to do two things at once because He knows our limitations as humans. When my life feels out of control it's because the things I want to do get mixed in with the things that God asks me to do. I need more balance, with times of rest and times of work, just like Christ's time on earth. He was always doing the Father's will. Sometimes that was preaching, teaching or healing, and sometimes it was praying in the stillness and quiet by himself. While I was waiting for my next mammogram, I started studying the Gospels so that instead of just following Christ, I would learn how to imitate Him.

༄ ༄ ༄

I arrived at the Woman's Hospital at Centennial Medical Center fifteen minutes early to check in and fill out all the paperwork. I chuckled that the paperwork was the same whether it was a "full" diagnostic mammogram or just a "right" diagnostic mammogram. Since my left breast had been removed, my mammogram on the left side would only show a silicone implant. On the right side, I needed a mammogram to see whether I had cancer in the breast tissue. I'd been so busy for the past few months that I hadn't thought about it much, but now, as I sat in my skimpy gown, it hit me full force: there were spots last time that were too small to biopsy. *What was I to pray for?* If they hadn't grown, we still wouldn't know anything. If they are bigger it won't be good news, but maybe they could be biopsied. If I got to choose my prayer, I'd pray that they had disappeared completely.

I recognized the technician who came to get me in the waiting room. "I'm back again so soon because they found some small spots back in April," I said feebly. I searched the familiar face at the end of the test for reassurance. It seemed like she'd taken a lot more pictures than any other time, and I was trying to keep my mind from spinning.

"Stay here in the exam room for a few minutes while I check with the doctor to make sure the pictures are okay."

I expected a chirpy, "Everything looks fine this time," but instead I heard, "Dr. Tupper says that the films are fine, but now she has to read them. If you'll have a seat in the waiting room marked Diagnostic, we'll come tell you the results when they are ready."

Why does time march so slowly when something unpleasant is occurring and so quickly when it's pleasurable? There were five women in the "Diagnostic" waiting room, all making small talk about nothing. We didn't offer introductions because we were all hopeful that we'd never see each other again. Because we were sitting in the "Diagnostic Room", it meant that we were all under closer scrutiny from a previous or current problem. Everything seems otherworldly when you are waiting for cancer test results. It was taking much longer than I expected and none of the magazines in the waiting room looked interesting.

One by one the ladies were dismissed, until I was the only one left. Maybe the doctor had taken a lunch break or had an emergency interrupt her normal day. I was glad I'd taken the whole day off work since it looked like I was going to miss quite a bit of it. Finally the technician came into the room, and sounding all business she said, "Ms. Nolen, Dr. Tupper wants to go over your results in her office. Please follow me."

I knew that wasn't a good sign since the other ladies had been told on the spot that everything was "fine". Instead of my heart sinking in my throat like it did when I had first heard the word "cancer", I was calm. I was grateful that I had of lot of people praying for me, and having, or not having cancer, is something I can't control. God is much better at conducting the symphony that I call my life.

Dr. Tupper was cordial as always. "Well the news is not good," she said, "but it's not devastating either. The spots we saw in April have grown larger, but they're still not big enough to tell with the naked eye whether they are cancerous. But they are big enough to biopsy, so I'm recommending that we do a stereotactic biopsy as soon as possible. You've had one before, right?"

"No. My cancer was a surprise to everyone the first time. No biopsies, I even had a negative mammogram. What's involved in the biopsy?"

Dr. Tupper provided a thorough explanation of what I would undergo and how long it would take to get the pathology results back.

"Will I need general anesthesia? I have a favorite anesthesiologist, I can check to see when he's available."

"No, you won't need general anesthesia. We'll provide some local anesthesia and light conscious sedation. You'll be awake through the whole procedure."

The first time I had cancer, my first thought was to look at my work calendar to see when I could "squeeze" in a surgery. All that had changed, and now my health was the most important thing. This time, I immediately said, "Dr. Tupper, I'd like to get this done as soon as possible. How quickly can we get it scheduled?"

"How about tomorrow at 1 p.m.? You'll need someone to bring you and pick you up, but you shouldn't have any pain after the procedure that some ibuprofen or Tylenol won't fix."

"1 p.m. tomorrow it is. Thanks, Dr. Tupper."

As I walked back to my car, I recognized that I wasn't fretful like I had been four years ago. I was thinking, *Lord, I'm trusting You this time. If You need me to have cancer, I'm good with that. I believe that You are a loving God and that You will care for me, but You never said that following You was going to be easy. I know that You are here with me every step of the way. Thank You."*

Then I thought, *Well, that sounds a little nutty, to trust someone who you can't even see. What if I'd said it aloud?*

But there were two groups that would understand what it is like to trust the Lord and not be afraid: my LIFE group at church and the PORCH CLUB.

੭ ੭ ੭

My first stop back at work was my boss's office, to tell her I needed the next afternoon off for the biopsy. I was grateful again for her compassion. Then, as soon as I settled into my office, I dialed the number at St. George's to talk to Reverend Marcia King from my LIFE group. I was no longer ashamed of needing help and prayers. Rather than sounding weak, it seemed like the most logical thing to do. Next were two emails: one to my LIFE group and one to the PORCH CLUB.

Everyone returned encouraging and uplifting messages. Some called, others emailed or texted. It was warming to be loved and know people were praying for me. I looked on my Bible software to find the story where the paralytic was let down through the roof on a mat by his friends so that he could be healed by Jesus. It was in Mark, Chapter 2 and I read, "When Jesus saw their faith..." and Jesus healed the man so that he stood up and

223

walked home. It wasn't because of the man's faith that Jesus healed him, but instead because of the faith of his friends.

It was a particularly restful evening, knowing that friends were praying for me and that tomorrow would take care of itself. As I climbed into bed, I realized that I hadn't let Brian, Matthew or Mike know what I was facing the next day. I didn't want them to worry, or sound like I was whining, but I needed their support too. I texted them all the same message: Breast biopsy tomorrow. Please pray for me that it isn't cancer.

Immediately I got a text from Brian: Will do, prayers coming your way. What time is the procedure?

Matthew texted back a few minutes later: Yes, prayers for your health and God's will in your recovery. I texted them both back: Procedure at 1 p.m. Thanks for your prayers.

Forty-five minutes later, my phone rang. It was Mike. "Got your message but was having dinner with the kids. What does it mean? Why are you having a breast biopsy? I thought you had a mastectomy."

"I did, but only on the left side. I still have to have mammograms and breast MRIs each year on the right side. In April they saw a few spots on the mammogram, so I had to go back today for a follow-up. The spots have grown large enough to biopsy, so at 1 p.m. tomorrow, I'll have it done. The pathology should be back in about three days."

"We need to come up with a strategy; you need to have a plan."

"No. I don't need a plan. God has the plan. All I need are your prayers."

"Certainly. Prayers go without saying, but you need a plan if you have cancer again."

"No, all my effort tonight is on resting in the comfort of God's loving arms. I'm getting out of the way and letting God work."

"Call me tomorrow after you get home from the hospital. I want to know that you are okay."

Four years ago, I'd been up all night before each surgery, searching the Internet for answers. But it had been so confusing and alarming. Some posts sounded like sound medical advice and others sounded like emotional rhetoric. Dr. Cooper kept warning me about spending too much time on the Internet, but I'd wanted answers. This time was different. I decided to get plenty of sleep and trust God. I was comforted in knowing that so many friends were praying for me right then. I was in awe that I was trusting God instead of trying to figure out everything on my own.

I fell asleep with a ring of protection around me. No matter what happened the next day, God would be at my side.

೫ ೫ ೫

Exactly fifteen minutes after I arrived at the hospital, I was meeting with Dr. Tupper and signing the consent form. She was very encouraging during the procedure, and she was able to get all of the "spots" through the biopsy needle. I was surprised that I didn't have any pain. Dr. Tupper said to expect a small "knot" where the needle had entered the skin and to take a few ibuprofens. It was a short procedure and now it was just a matter of waiting for the pathology results to come back. Since it was Tuesday, Dr. Tupper thought it would be Friday before the report would be available, and Dr. Cooper would be notified first since he had ordered the mammogram.

I was back home by 4 p.m. and my only complaint was a stiff right arm from being in the same position for more than an hour. I reminded myself that it was an inconvenience, not a real problem. I settled in with a cup of tea and decided to do some reading. I needed something inspiring and chose BELIEVE, by the Reverend Desmond Tutu. As usual, God spoke through written words: "A time of crisis is not just a time of anxiety and worry. It gives a chance, an opportunity, to choose well or to choose badly." I wondered what choices I would need to make in the coming days, but I was trusting that God would guide me and take care of me no matter what.

I had such fond memories of meeting Archbishop Tutu on my first trip to South Africa in 2007. We'd met when he celebrated mass at St. George's Cathedral in Cape Town, and it had been a life-changing encounter for me. I had a copy of our group picture with him, prominently displayed on my desks at work and at home. I thought of my three trips to South Africa, and prayed that I'd be able to go again in 2010. I always felt so accepted and so loved when I was there. The people didn't care who I was, what I did, or how many academic degrees I had. I was loved because I existed.

My trust in God had grown on that first trip, too. Before that, I had worshiped a distant God who I would turn to when I couldn't handle things on my own. My South African friends taught me how to love God in the everyday, when things were bad as well as good. I remembered how they sang to Him in praise, whether they were experiencing joy or sorrow.

I flipped to another page in the book with a full-page picture of Archbishop Tutu and the quote:

"If I diminish you, I diminish myself. In my culture and tradition the highest praise that can be given to someone is, "Yu u nobuntu," an acknowledgment that he or she has this wonderful quality: ubuntu. It is a reference to their actions toward their fellow human beings; it has to do with how they regard people and how they see themselves within their intimate relationships, their familial relationships, and within the broader community. Ubuntu addresses a central tenet of Africa philosophy: the essence of what it is to be human.

The definition of this concept has two parts. The first is that the person is friendly, hospitable, generous, gentle, caring, and compassionate. In other words, someone who will use his or her strengths on behalf of others---the weak and the poor and the ill—and not take advantage of anyone. This person treats others as he or she would be treated. And because of this they express the second part of the concept, which concerns openness, large-heartedness. They share their worth. In doing so, my humanity is recognized and becomes inextricably bound to theirs.

People with Ubuntu are approachable and welcoming; their attitude is kindly and well disposed; they are not threatened by the goodness in others because their own esteem and self-worth is generated by knowing they belong to a greater whole. To recast the Cartesian proposition, "I think, therefore I am," Ubuntu would phrase it, "I am human because I belong." Put another way, "a person is a person through other people," a concept perfectly captured by the phrase "me we." No one comes into the world fully formed. We would not know how to think or walk or speak or behave unless we learned it from our fellow human beings. We need other human beings in order to be human...

But anger, resentment, a lust for revenge, greed, even the aggressive competitiveness that rules so much of our contemporary world, corrodes and jeopardizes our harmony. Ubuntu points out that those who seek to destroy and dehumanize are also victims—victims, usually of a pervading ethos, be it a political ideology, an economic system, or a distorted religious conviction. Consequently, they are as much dehumanized as those on whom they trample...

This expression of Ubuntu showed that the only way we can ever be human is together. The only way we can be free is together."

I was thankful that I had experienced Ubuntu and the forgiveness that comes with it. I vowed that I was going to live my life more intentionally as "Yu u nobuntu." My friends in South Africa and in America love me as a child of God and take care of me during times of trouble. I was at peace while I awaited the pathology results.

ço ço ço

I felt great the next morning, and as Dr. Tupper had predicted there was only a small bruise on my upper right breast where the needle had gone in. I took two Aleve and put some Vicodin in my purse, just in case I needed it at work later in the day. I spent thirty minutes reading my Bible and then headed out to church. It would be good to see my friends and start the day in restful, quiet worship. I always felt fortified when I came out of church, and today the respite from the world was a needed blessing.

My mind was quiet, listening to some music on the ride to work. I rarely answered the phone while driving, but it was my friend Jackie from the PORCH CLUB.

"How are you doing? How was the procedure, do you hurt this morning?"

"Actually, I feel great! I have a bruise to show for it, but just a little discomfort. I took two Aleve this morning about an hour ago and am still feeling good."

"Great. When does the pathology report get back? Didn't you say it would be sometime on Friday?"

"That's what Dr. Tupper said, that it would take about three days. Strangely, I'm not tense at all. I know Dr. Cooper will call me when he gets the report back."

"Well, love you much! I've been praying for you. Call me when you get the report back. And we need to plan our next get-together. How about in a couple of weeks at my place? You could use a drink and a relaxing weekend by then."

"That does sound great. As soon as I get the pathology report back, let's make some plans. Thanks, Jackie, you're a doll for calling to check on me."

"More prayers coming your way. Call me Friday."

"Will do. Thanks."

I thought again how blessed it is to have friends who know God and care for each other.

When I got to work, there were more emails and text messages from my ladies LIFE Group at church and the rest of the PORCH CLUB. Brian, Matthew and Mike had called to check on me and Reverend Marcia King even sent a prayer for healing.

I took a few moments to give thanks for my friends before starting my workday. For much of my life I'd had acquaintances and friends, but these people were different. I'd always tried to control the friendships, keeping score on the "nice things" that I'd do for someone, and always expecting something in return. It seemed like my previous relationships had been more like military engagements, where each person tries to figure out the other person's next move. It was particularly obvious with the men I had known. I was always nice in a relationship, but for the wrong reason. I was kind and caring because I wanted to be liked and admired, not because God had commanded that we should "love our neighbor".

In these past four years, God was teaching me how to really love through the example of my friends. They weren't just being nice; they actually loved God and believed that God loved them. For the first time, I believed that I could have that kind of a relationship with God where His love for me overflows and I can't help but give it away. It was clearly a freedom that I wasn't used to.

It was 4:15 p.m., and I was feeling a little tired. I decided to call it a day and was reaching for my purse when my cell phone rang. When I saw "Centennial Medical Center" on the caller ID, I figured there must be a problem with the insurance claim.

"This is Dr. Tupper's office. We'd like to talk with Agatha Nolen."

"This is she."

"Please hold the line for Dr. Tupper."

In a split second, I realized that I was talking with Dr. Tupper just a little over twenty-four hours after the procedure. Ordinarily, my mind would have jumped to the conclusion that it was bad news, but instead I was calm. "Hi, Dr. Tupper."

"Hi, Agatha. This isn't exactly proper protocol since Dr. Cooper should be the one to call you, but I know he's in surgery all afternoon and wanted to give you the good news right away. NO CANCER! And we got all the benign spots with the needle biopsy. I personally reviewed your post-procedure films and they are all gone!"

"Thank you so much, Dr. Tupper. That was so sweet of you to call me personally. This is such good news."

I hung up with a warm feeling, bathed in the love of my friends' prayers and the kindness of Dr. Tupper. I wanted to call everyone individually, but that would take awhile, so I resorted to emails: one to my LIFE GROUP, one to The PORCH CLUB and another to Brian, Matthew and Mike.

"GREAT NEWS! NO CANCER! The Doctor just called with FINAL Pathology report. YEA!"

Immediately, the return emails came in with short prayers of thanksgiving and congratulations. I was learning how to be thankful to God for the good things in life, too.

��� ��� ���

It was time to plan the next meeting of The PORCH CLUB. Everyone was in agreement that a celebration was in order, for my health and the marvelous things going on in our lives. Three short weeks later, I was on the road to Louisville. This meeting was going to be really low-key, with wine, dinner and movies. We had been meeting for five years and been through a lot together. We all needed time to rest and just be.

18

Accepting God's Love

The way forward, out of despair is to discern the idols of our hearts and our culture. But that will not be enough. The only way to free ourselves from the destructive influence of counterfeit gods is to turn back to the true one. The living God, who revealed himself both at Mount Sinai and on the Cross, is the only Lord, who, if you find him, can truly fulfill you, and if you fail him, can truly forgive you.

– Tim Keller

"I can't wait to get there and see you all. We have so much to talk about: the past, the present and the future," I said to Jackie when I called to tell her that I was within one hour of Louisville.

"Well, hurry and get here," Jackie replied, chuckling. "I just picked up Carol and Kim at the airport and we've already poured our second glass of wine."

"I should be there in about forty-five minutes. Can't wait to see you!"

ॐ ॐ ॐ

After hugs all around, I poured a glass of wine, gathered some cheese and crackers, and settled into the overstuffed chair in Jackie's living room. "I want to talk last this time. I want to hear what's going on in your lives first."

Kim shared that her kids were doing great in school and a friend of her son's had come to live with them. Kim had the gift of hospitality and I was learning a lot from her. She'd moved back to Jacksonville and lived close to the beach. We all voted that the next meeting of the PORCH CLUB was definitely at her house!

Carol shared how grateful she was that she had gotten her mother back to Wisconsin. Her mother had come to live with them when they moved to Nashville in 2004, but then Carol had found a great job not too far from where she'd grown up in Wisconsin. They'd all moved there six months ago. Although it was sad that her mother had died four months after arriving back in Wisconsin, it was heartwarming to know that they'd had some time to catch up with old friends and spend quality time with family. Jackie remarked how God had an amazing way of working things out, if we would just let Him.

"But Carol, what about your job?" I asked. "Didn't you take the job at the hospital so you could get your mom back to Wisconsin? What is going to happen now?"

"Yes, we went back for Mom, but I like Wisconsin, too, and I have a really great job as director of cardiovascular services. Bill hasn't found a job yet, but we aren't in too much of a hurry. With the winter coming up, he's looking forward to doing some fishing and hunting, so all is good."

"I just wish we all lived closer," Kim remarked.

"I know, but after we go to Kim's place next spring, everyone should come to visit me in Wisconsin. Or maybe we need to do an extra meeting in the winter. Wisconsin is really pretty in the wintertime."

Jackie spoke next, filling us in on her new consulting job. She'd be traveling a lot, but it was interesting work, consulting for hospitals and physician office groups. Her Mom and Dad were getting up there in age, but still doing well, and faithfully attending the Catholic Church where Jackie grew up. Not much new on the boyfriend front, but Jackie was patient. She wasn't ready to jump right into another marriage so soon after her divorce. There were lots of men out there and she was meeting more through her job.

It was my turn to catch everyone up. Some days it felt like life was still traveling pretty fast with me being cancer-free for four years and divorced for two. Other days, it felt like life stood still. *Where should I begin?*

Before I had a chance to speak, Jackie started my story for me. "It's been over two years since your divorce, hasn't it? How come you aren't dating anyone, or are you holding out on us? Don't tell me you never want to get married again."

"No, it's not that I don't ever want to marry again, but I've had two failed marriages, and I've figured out that the common denominator, unfortunately, is ME! My cancer in 2006 started me on some soul searching about me as a person and the life I was living. I need to know who I am before I get into another relationship."

"But it's not healthy to not be in a relationship. Are you sure you aren't afraid of getting hurt again, or maybe you haven't forgiven your husband yet?"

"You sound just like Mike and his friend from last summer!" I recounted the story of their suggestion that I needed "psychiatric help".

Carol remarked, "You know, it was right of you to go to see your clergy friend, and your other Christian friend, to help you through it. We would have helped you, too, if you had shared that with us. That's what friends are for."

"I know, but they were both close and very helpful in sorting it all out. I'm not in a relationship now for the right reasons. I have to be true to myself before I start a new relationship. Father Tim gave me sound advice: "The most important thing is to wait on God. If you are to marry again, He'll bring you the right guy and you'll know it. There isn't a timetable that we can see on relationships. Just keep sticking close to Him and enjoy your relationship with Him. Don't worry about what other people say or think."

Kim asked, "Is there more to the story? Why did he tell you not to worry about what other people think?"

"I'm still working through a lot of this. Really, let's have fun this weekend and not dwell on a lot of sadness in the past. It can wait until another time."

Carol said, "Since the cancer, I've heard you say dozens of times that there is no time like the present. We never know when our next breath will be our last. We are here to listen to each other."

"It's a pretty long story; are you sure?"

"Yes, we're sure," Kim, Carol, and Jackie said in unison.

"Well, here goes. I haven't shared about my childhood with anyone in a long time. I realize that I'd buried it in my memory, but I'd never really worked through it. You are such good friends to be willing to listen.

"We've got all weekend. That's what we get together for. Go ahead," Carol said.

"This is still really hard for me, but I'm learning to embrace it. It is the life that God intended for me, and everything I've experienced is part of the story.

"Let's start when I was seven years old, right after my brother died. My parents would argue in the evening after I'd gone to bed. A few times, I went downstairs to see what was wrong and they told me to go back to bed. As I got older, the fighting would happen in front of me. Mom and Dad would start arguing over the smallest thing, and without warning, it would turn physical. I never heard Dad apologize and Mom would just retreat to another room, praying to saints I'd never heard of.

"I was terribly confused. Even after all those prayers, life never changed. My father never beat me, but it would be in those drunken rages that he would become sullen and critical of everything and everybody. Mom would react by yelling back. That's where I learned about the affair my father had when my

234

mother was pregnant with my brother. I also heard about the six abortions my mother had between my brother and me. When I asked her about it later, she said, "I finally put my foot down and refused to have another abortion and I'm so glad. You are all I have in the world."

With my brother gone, I was raised as an only child. I'd sneak into my room and shut the door so I couldn't hear the yelling. I'd study or read books; I really liked biographies. I had friends at school, but I never dared invite them over to play. My father's drinking was unpredictable, even in the middle of the day. The scariest part was when my father would stand over my mother and threaten to harm or kill her. I'd try to distract him, to get him to talk about the baseball game on TV, the weather, or anything to break the cycle. I learned at an early age to manipulate people."

"How awful!" Carol exclaimed. "I had no idea your childhood was like that."

"I vowed that I'd never put up with what my mother did. She told me over and over, "Never depend on a man; they'll only disappoint you. Go to college and get a good education and learn to take care of yourself. You can make it alone in the world."

"So you grew up independent?" Carol asked.

"Probably too independent. I vowed that if my father ever hit me like he did my mother, I wouldn't put up with it. So when I was seventeen and he hit me over a boy I was seeing, I left home. It was four weeks before my high school graduation, and I went to live with the Chief of Police and his wife until I could find an apartment of my own. My mother was devastated, but I wasn't budging. Just like she had taught me, I was determined to take care of myself.

"Well, that tells us about your upbringing," Carol said. "No wonder you've had difficulty with relationships. I'm sorry that you had to grow up with that."

"Thanks. But that really isn't the worst part. Promise that you won't judge me? There are things in my life that I've never shared with anyone."

"Of course we won't judge you. We are your friends. Tell us your story," Kim said.

"Well, here goes. I stayed with the Chief of Police and his wife for three months. Then I got a job at Peterson Drug as a pharmacy technician and moved in with a girlfriend to start my freshman year of college at SUNY Geneseo. We met some older guys from town who had jobs and seemed pretty sophisticated. My roommate and I double-dated for a while, but it didn't last long. By the end of the first semester I was dateless again.

One day right before Christmas, I was working at the drugstore, and a customer came in to pay on his account. We struck up a conversation and he seemed very nice. He'd often come into the store late around closing time and offer to buy me a cup of coffee. I didn't have a car and I welcomed the ride, especially when it was cold and snowing. I knew that he was married, but it seemed pretty innocent. He was just trying to help a struggling college student.

I was closing up the store one evening in January when he asked if he could come up for a glass of wine after he dropped me off. We started kissing and making out. It was so good to feel a warm embrace again. Somehow it seemed okay since I was single and he was the married one. I'd stopped going to church when I'd left home the year before, so I wasn't thinking a lot about God or sin, or even whether what we were doing was right. I was pretty focused on myself, my loneliness and figuring out what would make me happy. It was on Valentine's Day that we had sex at my apartment. It was romantic, with candlelight, and everything I'd ever dreamed of."

"Okay. So you had an affair with a married man. You were young and impressionable, but your sins are forgiven. Surely you still aren't feeling guilty after all these years? You were eighteen!" exclaimed Kim.

"We had an affair for the next eighteen months. He was older and very sophisticated and so much fun. We'd meet twice a week on his days off, either at my apartment or his house. During the summer, we'd pack a picnic lunch and go for a ride on his

236

motorcycle through the wine country in the Finger Lakes. We'd make love outdoors in the afternoon and still be back into town by the time his wife got home from work."

"Didn't you get tired of being his mistress and being a second-class citizen all that time?" Carol asked.

"Not really, I didn't look at it that way. I was focusing on my college studies and my eventual career as a pharmacist. My mother had instilled in me to 'take care of myself' and that was what I was doing. Everyone needed to look out for themself. I didn't look at the relationship as anything but a fun time with an older guy who was good-looking."

"So. What happened?" Kim asked. "Why did it end?"

"That's the part that has taken me a long time to understand. We were still having sex twice a week throughout my sophomore year, but he knew that I'd be leaving the end of August to go to pharmacy school in Oklahoma. We'd never discussed marriage, children, church, or anything really important, only that we were 'in love' and enjoyed our afternoons together.

We'd said our goodbyes and my parents drove me out to Oklahoma the third week of August. The second week of school, he called my dorm--this was 1974, before cell phones and computers. He said that he missed me and wanted to see me again. I was surprised, really taken aback. I'd thought that when I left him in New York that would be the end of things. It was sad but not devastating; after all he was still married and had a wife to go home to. And I had college, my career and my whole life ahead of me. He was sending me an airline ticket; *would I meet him for the weekend when he was on a business trip*? Next thing I knew, I was headed to the airport in Oklahoma City for a flight to Charleston, South Carolina."

"Why did you go?" Carol asked, "If you thought the affair was over, why continue it?"

"I really don't know. The whole idea of sneaking around to have an affair with an older married man was mysterious and intriguing. I got caught up in the excitement of the deception."

"Sorry I interrupted your story," Carol said. "Go on. What happened when you got to Charleston?"

"Well, what do you think?" I said with a laugh. He picked me up at the airport that evening and we went straight to the motel. We didn't leave the room until the next morning. The whole weekend was spent strolling on the beach, hand in hand, without a care in the world. In fact, he told me that he was thinking about going back to school and might be moving to Charleston. He still hadn't decided yet, but thought he needed to make a change. We had a romantic dinner on the beach Saturday night and made love under a cabana by the outdoor pool. It was a dreamy weekend."

"Did you see him again after that?" Jackie asked.

"Not so fast. I'm not done yet describing my Charleston weekend. I think this is the most important part. So we got up Sunday morning, had breakfast, and made love one more time. I had a 2 p.m. flight back to Oklahoma, so we didn't have much time before we had to head to the airport. He grabbed me in his arms and kissed me once more and said that he wanted to go for a walk on the beach and talk."

I paused to catch my breath as the vision of that walk on the beach popped into my head.

"Don't keep us in suspense!" Jackie exclaimed. "What happened on the beach?"

"Well, he turned to me and kissed me tenderly. And then he said that he was planning to go back to New York and tell his wife that he wanted a divorce so he could marry me."

"What?" everyone screamed in unison.

"Well, my reaction was a little different. I was stunned. As I mentioned, we had never talked about children, church, or anything important in life. Not what our dreams were, not what we wanted to do or where we wanted to live for the rest of our lives. For almost two years, we had been having an affair, a cheap, tawdry affair that involved his sneaking around on his wife. I didn't know what to say, so I didn't say anything for a good five minutes. I was trying to process his declaration of love and that he was getting a divorce to marry me."

Finally, I said, "You don't want to do that. We're both young and we have our careers ahead of us. And you still have Diane. She really does love you."

"But I don't love her anymore. I love you."

"But you can't divorce her. I'm not ready to get married to you or anyone. We had sex and lots of it, but sex doesn't make a long-term relationship. The weekend was fun, but I just can't see you anymore. Our lives need to go on."

"Wow, did you ever see him again after that?" Kim asked.

"Strangely enough, yes. For a few months he kept calling and sending letters, but then they finally stopped. I had a college boyfriend that I brought home at Christmas, so I didn't see him during break. I was hopeful that he'd forgotten about me and moved on."

"But I take it he hadn't?" Carol asked.

"No. Later in the spring I got a call from him; he told me he was going to be a vendor at a pharmacy meeting I was attending in Atlanta, and wanted to know if I'd have lunch with him."

"Surely you said no, right?" Jackie asked. "It was over."

"I guess I should have, but I was curious and thought that an innocent lunch wouldn't hurt. So I met him for lunch at a Japanese restaurant around the corner from the convention center. I greeted him warmly and he kissed me on the cheek. He started the conversation by asking if I'd reconsider his offer of marriage, and I politely said no, I thought we should move on. He then went on to tell me how he had started another affair with a student at the college in New York; he even blamed me for his promiscuity. He said that he couldn't ever love his wife again, so if I wouldn't marry him, he'd just continue to have one affair after another.

"I didn't know what to say, but I was uncomfortable taking the blame for his lifestyle. I hastily finished lunch and told him I thought it best if we stopped communicating with each other. We never saw each other again."

"Wow! It does seem like a bit of a mess. But why are you telling us this story now; it was so long ago and it was over back then, wasn't it? Or are you still carrying a torch for him and wish that you'd married him?" Carol asked.

"No, not at all. I recognized that it wasn't a 'real' relationship. I was young and insecure and constantly worried if I was pleasing him. His wife could have passed for a Playboy model; she was beautiful. But I realized many years later how awful it must have been for her to love him and not be loved in return. She had done nothing wrong; I was just willing and available and didn't consider it to be a sin on my part. It was twisted logic, but I'd vowed that I'd never withhold sex so that it wouldn't be an arguable point in a relationship."

"So here it is 2010 and this happened in what, 1974? Why is this still important to you?" asked Jackie.

"Well, in 2006, when I was making the deal with God in my room that night, I thought about my past sins, and this one was always on the top of the list. It didn't matter how many times I went to confession, I never felt that it was forgiven."

Everyone was looking puzzled. "I told you all that story, about my pathology report and God asking me if I was willing to die for Him. I did tell you all that story, right?"

"Oh that; yes, you did tell us that." Jackie confirmed.

"Well, in 2006, when I said I was willing to die for Jesus, I asked myself, what exactly did that mean? What exactly was going to 'die' so that I could serve Christ? It was my old self that had to die before I could become a true servant. That image has been slowly coming into focus with studying Scripture, going to this wonderful Episcopal Church and with the help of my friends, like all of you.

In looking back on my early dating relationships, I realized that what I wanted was affection, but I wasn't capable of giving my heart to another person. I tried to please my father, but always just missed the mark. As I got older, I realized that I liked boys and they were attracted to me. But I didn't feel loved and was acting out of the fear of never knowing love. In 2006, I realized that it wasn't just a matter of intellectually recognizing my insecurities; I had to learn to accept and embrace God's love. I'm not there yet, but I'm on the road. I've been chasing God all these years, and He's been right there, chasing me. It was amazing that I was so blinded by Satan's misuse of sex and affection that I couldn't see God.

Carol asked, "You have to accept God's forgiveness. That is where healing starts."

Jackie chimed in, "It was so long ago and you were young."

"Yes, we've all made mistakes, but God has forgiven us all," Kim added.

"I'm grateful for your friendship. It's late. Let's get some sleep. We've got all day tomorrow to swap more stories. Good night, everyone."

"Goodnight," everyone chimed in.

℘ ℘ ℘

We all slept in the next morning. As usual, Jackie was the first one up and started breakfast for everyone-- her signature mimosas, scrambled eggs, toast and sausage. We headed out to the back porch with our after-breakfast mimosas and settled into soft lounge chairs to take in the morning sun.

Kim spoke first. "I've thought about what you said last night and I am glad you shared the story with us. You obviously trust us and we won't harm you with the information. Are you up for a few questions this morning?"

"Sure," I replied.

Kim said, "It sounds like he was the pursuer, hanging around the store and giving you a ride home for many months before he kissed you the first time. He was the aggressive one, right?"

"It would be unfair to blame him for the affair. I guess you could say he was aggressive, but so was I. I craved affection and once I'd given my heart away, I'd dreamed of kissing him long before it happened. I never got a kiss or a hug from my father. I dated some guys in high school and we kissed and made out, but we were all kids. Once I got into college, I wanted a real grown-up relationship. He was eight years older than me, had a job and was very sophisticated. His wife worked too, but he was the main breadwinner. I was infatuated with him. I guess you could say we were both willing partners."

Kim asked another question. "Why do you think you didn't fall in love with him after sleeping with him for eighteen months? That's a long time to be with someone without making any plans for a future together."

"That is a great question. I guess I still thought that a nice, church-going boy would fall in love with me, sweep me off my feet and we'd get married and raise a family. I knew it was wrong to be sleeping with a married man and I didn't expect anything more. It was exciting and glamorous, with an element of espionage. We had to park our cars on little dirt roads so we wouldn't be seen leaving town together. And of course anytime we were asked by anyone if we were an "item", we denied it. But it added to the intrigue. We had a secret between the two of us that no one else shared. Isn't that one of the reasons affairs are so exciting?"

"You still haven't answered my question. You slept with the guy for eighteen months and never wanted to marry him. How come?"

"I guess it was always in the back of my mind that if he was cheating on his current wife with me, he'd cheat on me with somebody else. Why would I want to marry someone I couldn't trust? We all have this romantic ideal that we are going to fall in love with someone and together we're going to overcome every obstacle in our life.

"So what happens if the person of our dreams comes along and we are married to someone else? It's love. So what if we come from different backgrounds? It's love. What if we belong to different political parties? It's love. So what if we have totally different commitments to our faith (or none)? It's love. Neither one of us were churchgoers, although we'd both been raised in a church. Sometimes we allow ourselves to be blinded by 'love' so we can ignore the reality of our incompatibility. I always knew that it was just an affair, nothing more."

It was Carol's turn for questions. "If the affair was 'nothing', why are you still talking about it thirty-five years later?"

"Matthew gave me a book to read–it helped me to understand that as a child, I was constantly looking for affection. My mother was very supportive and kind, but what I really wanted was the approval of my father. When my brother died, I decided that I was going to be the perfect daughter *and* son for my father. And then when I heard my mother talk about all the abortions that she'd had, I tried even harder. I never knew if my father really wanted me or if he was even glad I was born, so I tried to please him in every way."

"Oh no," Carol exclaimed, "You're not going to tell us that you had sex with your father, are you?"

"Oh heavens, NO!" I shouted. "I didn't mean that at all. What I meant was that I was always trying to be 'good' so my father wouldn't get upset like he did with my mother. I thought that if I could just be perfect, our family would be peaceful and Dad would love me."

Kim said, "Remember the book I mentioned, *Moral Politics*?"

"Is that the one with the two types of people? What were they again? One was STRICT FATHER."

"Yes, Carol. It's the book that shows the differences between the STRICT FATHER and the NURTURING PARENT.

Well, Lakoff says that the biblical interpretation of the STRICT FATHER is a person who has a need for self-discipline and self-denial. Reward and punishment is based on moral accounting—reward for following the rules and punishment for breaking them. It's possible your Dad was the STRICT FATHER type—withholding affection or even approval unless you earned it. Your father would never forgive you without making you work for it. In his eyes, if he just forgave you for any wrongdoing, it would be an incentive to be immoral. Is there a chance that you fell for this guy because he gave you approval without you having to earn it?"

I was quiet, listening intently. That was a whole lot to absorb in just a few minutes. But what Kim said made sense. I'd never felt unconditional love from my father. I couldn't decide if I was more confused, or if this conversation was actually helping. Then I remembered something Kim had once said about the NURTURING PARENT: only through receiving nurturance do children learn to nurture others.

"I'd always thought I was a nurturer," I said. "I took care of my mother when Dad was yelling at her, and was always the one who was throwing parties for others, or taking food to church socials. But you've made me think about my motivation. Was I caring for people because I loved them, or because I wanted them to like me? My motivations behind my 'nurturing spirit' may have been all wrong.

"I didn't feel loved, so I couldn't love; I was trying to buy friendships, and with romantic relationships I'd start by sleeping with the guy after a few dates, just to please him. But I never thought of it that way, because in the early 70s, my behavior just looked like a liberated female, playing the field like a guy. But this perspective paints a totally different picture. I wasn't having an affair because I felt loved and wanted to love someone else, I was actually taking advantage of him, trying to prove that I was more lovely, more attractive, more intelligent, more 'something' than his wife. It was a game of one-upmanship; I was trying all along to earn his love."

"That's a good point about motivation," Carol interjected. "So often our reasons for behavior aren't clear. You sound like you are still an encourager, but now your motivation is different."

"I spent forty years trying to earn love, but now I'm encouraged by a God who loves me and I want to please Him by loving others. I carry a small card with a Scripture verse,

'Therefore encourage one another and build one another up, just as you are doing.' It reminds me to be a NURTURING PARENT, because I first feel loved by God."

I continued, "Being an 'encourager' doesn't mean saying, 'everything is going to be alright.' Christ has promised that when we follow him, our life will not be easy. Instead, being an encourager is about building up another person's faith and trust in God. Tim Keller in *Counterfeit Gods* says that we may be able to suppress an idol, but then another one just takes its place. Until we've replaced all the idols in our life with God, we will never find rest. Just like replacing our idols, I need the collective voice of my Christian friends to drown out the voice of Satan that plays that endless tape in my head."

I reached for my iPad and said, "I'm writing this story for a blog post. Let me read it to you."

Satan's voice: "You're not pretty enough."
My Christian friends: "You are made in God's image; you are beautiful."

Satan's voice: "You'll never give up the sin in your life. You might as well give up trying and have a good time."
My Christian friends: "God takes us back over and over and over again through the grace and mercy of Jesus Christ. We learn from our mistakes; we don't have to be shackled by them forever."

Satan's voice: "You are getting too old to be a success. Life has passed you by."
My Christian friends: "You are following what God has asked you to do and that pleases God. Don't worry what others are accomplishing in the world or even for God, God's plan for you is YOUR PLAN!"

Satan's voice: "You shouldn't hang around or talk to non-Christians. They are beneath you."

My Christian friends: "Everyone is a child of God and made in His image. You are no better than anyone else. For all you know, that stranger might be Christ."

No one said a word. I wondered if I'd said something wrong when Carol said, "What did you just say about a blog?"

"Well, there you have it! I accidentally spilled the beans. I was going to tell you all before we left to go home that I'm starting a blog in a few weeks. A good friend from church is in the publishing industry and has recommended that I start one to see if there is any interest in my stories and to improve my writing skills. All authors have a blog on the Internet, so I'm creating one, too. I bet The PORCH CLUB will star in many of the stories."

"What?" they all exclaimed at once. Jackie added, "The PORCH CLUB is going to be famous on the Internet? Perfect!"

"All kidding aside, we have great sermons at St. George's and since I go to service every morning, I hear seven every week. I'd like for people who can't attend our church services to hear the inspired words, too. I plan to write posts on the sermon messages that talk about relationships and share some stories about how Scripture and daily meditations are changing my life. I'm still a work in progress, but maybe other people would be interested in coming with me on this journey."

"You, go girl! And The PORCH CLUB will be famous!" Carol said emphatically. "So when are you going to start posting on your blog?"

"I'm still about a month away. I've got a friend from Boston helping me with the programming, since I don't know anything about website design. I'm trying to launch it in September so that I can post stories when I'm in South Africa."

"You're going back to South Africa? How many trips is this for you?" Carol asked.

"This is number four. I need to be refreshed by the Spirit there. One of the blog stories I'm working on is about my first trip in 2007 and how I learned about forgiveness. It was a message that stuck, because I started going to daily church service when I joined St. George's in 2008 and celebrating the Eucharist is the most important part for me. One of my first blog posts will be about Holy Communion.

"How exciting!" Jackie said, smiling, "And we'd be glad to help with the editing."

"How about one more story?"

"Sure, we've got the whole day in the sun," Kim said.

"Some of these thoughts were swirling in my head when I heard a great sermon at St. George's by the Reverend Malone Gilliam, *"Simil Justus et Peccator"* or "Righteous and at the Same Time a Sinner." Let me read a portion of it. I've titled it: 'Sin Management'.

> I spent over forty years in sin management, trying to overcome the evil that lies close at hand. I thought if I just tried harder, I would become a righteous person. I was raised in a denomination of rules that held me captive. I'd miss church one Sunday and think, 'why bother going again?' I'd already sinned, again. Honor thy father and mother is a tough one for an eight-year-old, sometimes even for a thirty-year-old. I'd sin, I'd confess, and be resolute in my conviction to not sin again. But, I would sin, again. I'd be racked with guilt that I wasn't strong enough to overcome my desires and my flaws.

"Reverend Malone explained Romans 7 with a statement from Martin Luther: *'Simil Justus et Peccator'* or 'Righteous and at the same time a Sinner.' The Bible teaches us to focus not on ourselves and our sins, but instead to focus on Jesus Christ. In Colossians 3:1-2, we learn: If then you have been raised with Christ, seek the things that are above, where Christ is, seated at the right hand of God. Set your mind on things that are above, not on things that are on earth.

Paul reminds us in Romans 8:1-11 that God has done what the law, weakened by the flesh, could never do. By sending his own Son, he condemned sin in the flesh and justified us. Jesus has already defeated sin; if we don't accept this we are attempting to decrease Jesus' grace. In 2 Corinthians 12:9-10, we learn, 'But he said to me, 'My grace is sufficient for you, for my power is made perfect in weakness.''

I've finally learned the unforced rhythm of grace. I am a sinner, and will continue to be a sinner, but at the same time I am redeemed by the grace and mercy of my Lord and Savior, Jesus Christ. The more I know myself, the more I understand that the 'whole life of believers should be repentance.' I've stopped trying to 'manage my sins', deluding myself that I have the strength to overcome them."

There was silence, like they were still trying to absorb the words. Then Carol said, "Wow! Your blog is going to be great if you keep these stories coming. You sound like you are still on a journey, like you haven't arrived yet."

Kim said, "Agatha, you can relate to the story of the blind man who Jesus healed. After Jesus put saliva on his eyes, he got some of his vision back, but 'people looked like trees'. It wasn't until a second application of healing that his sight was fully restored. Healing is a slow process, but exciting at the same time.

Carol said, "Totally agreed, Kim, and it's exciting to be on this journey with you, Agatha. But, it's getting late. How about we grill some steaks for dinner?"

ℭ ℭ ℭ

On the drive home, I replayed our conversations, filled with gratitude for my friends. A weight had been lifted from my shoulders when I shared the story of my childhood and college affair. I'd always been embarrassed by my father's uncontrolled anger, and his resentment towards my mother. It had been a slow journey, but in the past four years, I had learned much about not judging others, even in the most horrible of situations.

Looking back, I'd judged my father for being an alcoholic and often being without work. I'd judged my mother for not loving my father, and for having all those abortions. I'd judged myself to be unworthy of God's love. Now I could see clearly that it wasn't my job at all to judge other people, God would do the judging. My job was to love everyone.

I was seeing things through the other person's eyes. If I could just go back in time and ask my father, *"How did you feel when your only son died? Was it hard when he was born with physical problems? How did it feel to be unemployed and needing to take care of a family?"* To my mother, I wanted to ask, *"How did you feel when my brother was born and you realized that he was never going to grow up healthy? How did you feel about the abortions; do you know that God still loves you?"*

஽ ஽ ஽

After I'd returned home and started a load of wash, I picked up the notepad that I kept at my bedside: Next New York trip: When you see Mom and Dad again, apologize for judging them. You had no idea what they were going through. It isn't your place to judge others."

19

Stand Up For Justice, Freedom, and Love

You are the indispensable agent of change. You should not be daunted by the magnitude of the task before you. Your contribution can inspire others, embolden others who are timid, to stand up for the truth in the midst of a welter of distortion, propaganda, and deceit; stand up for human rights where these are being violated with impunity; stand up for justice, freedom, and love where they are trampled underfoot by injustice, oppression, hatred, and harsh cruelty; stand up for human dignity and decency at times when these are in desperately short supply.

– Archbishop Desmond Tutu

I was looking forward to my fourth trip to South Africa. Each trip was unique. With a new Nikon camera, my plan was to take photographs and capture the stories of the people of South Africa for my blog. The long plane ride always gave me plenty of time to think, and I recalled a time when I felt the Spirit of Africa long before I had ever traveled there.

My work as a weekend docent for the Frist Center for Visual Arts is unpaid, but it gives me a free art education, as the traveling exhibitions change every three to four months. Anyone who is in the galleries at 1:30 p.m. can take a docent-guided tour, and it's interesting that each group sees and hears different things.

It was a rainy, cold Saturday in February 2006, and I was stationed at the Visitor Information Gallery by 1:15 p.m. Fifteen minutes later, two lovely African-American girls entered the gallery.

"Are you interested in a tour today? I'm starting one right now."

"Is it just the two of us?" one of the girls asked. "We don't want you to have to do a tour for just us. We can walk through the galleries on our own."

"Absolutely not," was my response. "Sometimes I have forty people and sometimes just two. I really enjoy giving tours and it would be my pleasure to share this exhibition with you. Is this your first time at the Frist? Did you come specifically to see the downstairs show, *African Art, African Voices: Long Steps Never Broke a Back*?"

"No, we've never been to the Frist Center before. There was an ad in our school newspaper about the exhibit."

"I'm glad you're here. What school do you go to?"

"Meharry Medical College, we're both second year medical students."

"Wonderful and welcome! Are you new to Nashville?"

"Yes, I'm from Atlanta," said one girl.

"Yes, I'm new here too. I'm from Boston," said the other.

"It's a pleasure to meet you. We'll have about a forty-five-minute tour, and please interrupt me at anytime to ask questions."

"Are you sure with just the two of us?"

"Yes, it's my pleasure!"

It started out like every other tour, with me giving a little information about the Frist Center and then heading into the exhibition. I usually give an overview as we enter each of the galleries, then I select a few pieces that we look at in depth.

Instead of giving a lecture, we encourage our visitors to "see" the art objects for themselves by asking them questions about color, texture and emotions. The girls were delightful, interacting with my questions and interrupting me when they had questions of their own.

We entered the fourth gallery, which was filled with objects collected from Cameroon and Nigeria. The most impressive piece was a mask and gown that were over seven feet tall and displayed as if it were still occupied by Basinjom (literally, "God's medicine"). We'd learned in our training that the role of witchcraft had expanded during the time of British intrusions in Cameroon, when the natives relied on witchcraft to resist the new government. The Basinjom comes to earth and becomes a detective in masquerade. The gowned figure would appear with an entourage of musicians and gun carriers and search for places of sin and misfortune. No one in a village could escape the examination of the Basinjom.

Our training indicated that the native's witchcraft addressed a central tension around the question of personal achievement. How much status should accrue to a single person? If special abilities were employed to promote oneself and trample others, the community agreed that the deceit had to be detected and exposed. The Basinjom could detect deception and point out the sinner.

I enjoyed telling the story from the early 1900s and the imposing gown and mask made that story come alive. Brilliantly colored feathers ordained the mask, with four-foot porcupine quills attached to the sleeves of the robe. Raffia, cowry shells, eggshells, metal and cat skin ordained the body of the cloth robe. A rattle was in the raised right hand to claim that a sinner had been found. We could see our own reflections in the mirrors attached to both cuffs. I'd asked previous tours: *Could we be the sinners that the Basinjom is hunting?*

I stopped to the right of the Basinjom and turned around to begin my story, but the two girls were staring at me, wide-eyed.

"We have to leave this gallery, now!" one girl said loudly.

252

"What's wrong; are you not feeling well?"

The other girl chimed in, "No, there are Spirits that live in that gown and mask. We can't tell if they are friendly or harmful. We have to leave now."

With that, the girls quickly exited to the next gallery, always keeping the gown and mask in front of them, never turning their backs to it.

My mind raced as we continued our tour, and I tried to get back on track. We went through the remainder of the exhibition and I could see that they once again were relaxed and enjoying the objects in the final gallery.

"Thanks for coming to the Frist Center today. I hope you'll come back again. I do have a question, though. Can I ask you what was so unsettling in the fourth gallery? What did you see?"

Both girls started to shake their heads and one said, "It wasn't what we saw, but what we felt. The spirits in that gown and mask were circling the room as if searching for something."

"You must have heard the story, then, about the Basinjom?" I asked.

"No, we don't know any story, but we know what we felt!"

"Have you traveled to Africa?"

"No, but we'd like to go someday. As part of our medical school training at Meharry, we go overseas to do some international work. We're both hoping we get assigned somewhere in Africa."

I thought about my encounter with those two delightful girls at the Frist Center. Even without having been to Africa they'd felt the spirits that can identify the sinner among men. As I was dozing off to sleep for the last eight hours of the flight, I wondered if I would experience that spirit, too.

℘ ℘ ℘

My friend from Kagiso, Mbali, had recently been in the hospital, so although I would see her on the trip, I would be staying with another friend, Dipuo. I felt like everyone was my "best friend" in South Africa. They all accepted me without judgment. I keenly observed them, asking how they had developed such an outward focus. *Did it have to do with the leadership of Nelson Mandela and Archbishop Tutu?* America was known as the land of riches and South Africa was known as the land of forgiveness. I knew which one would more likely get me through the eye of the needle.

I still wasn't sure what my "purpose" was on this trip. I'd waited until the last minute to sign up and almost hadn't come, after praying for months, and no "reason" had been revealed. I couldn't do any gardening or lift anything heavy, so my physical contributions on mission trips were limited. An old herniated disc had left my back weak, and I was still having joint pain from the Femara I was taking to prevent a recurrence of breast cancer. I loved to cook with the ladies and then feed the children on Tuesday afternoon, but that was only one day of the trip. Dyer had said, "Just show up, God will use you where He needs you," but it was Matthew who had the answer. "Why not write about the people we meet? With photographs, you can tell their story."

☙ ☙ ☙

I was excited but apprehensive when I got off the plane; after all, I wasn't a professional photographer or journalist. It was good that Matthew was on the trip. He is an artist, working in oils and acrylics, and was encouraging my photography. He had a keen, observant eye, and I was hoping to learn from him. I chuckled, "Maybe I just want another chance to visit my friends in South Africa." Whatever my purpose, I was here now. After a quick dinner, we climbed into bed so we'd be ready to start our work early the next day.

There were two projects we'd be working on: tending to the sustainable garden, and refurbishing a house. I wanted to make sure that I got photographs in both locations, so I started out with the house-building crew. On the trip to the house, members from St. Thomas Church told us the story of the family they were trying to help. Up until February of this year, a mother and her sister had been taking care of six children, ages three to seventeen. The mother had died of AIDS in the spring and her sister had assumed responsibility for the family. But then she too had died during the summer, leaving the seventeen-year-old girl, Mashadi, to look after all her brothers and sisters.

What a horrible situation! I couldn't imagine what it would be like to be seventeen and have all that responsibility. I'd left home at that age, and lived apart from my parents for almost two years, but I didn't have five brothers and sisters to care for! I also had the benefit of a high school education and a Regent's Scholarship to pay for my tuition in college. I imagined that living on your own in South Africa was quite different from living on your own in America.

A dirty, three-year-old boy who was sitting on the ground greeted us at the house. He held a paper sack in his hand, and screamed as one of the ladies from St. Thomas took the sack away. She told us that it held two pieces of bread and some candy. In Tswana, she asked him where his sister was, but there wasn't any response. She said that it wasn't unusual for a child so young to be alone during the day, especially as in this case, with his older brothers and sisters enrolled at various schools. One of the fathers came to take one of the girls to school in a neighboring town, and the rest of the children walked almost two miles to school and back every day.

I didn't know what to say. I was glad to hear the children were all attending school, but how could you leave a three-year-old by himself all day long? I remarked that the people here have to make difficult choices that are unheard of in America. I was beginning to see Africa through their eyes instead of mine. *Could I capture their story and post it on my blog so others would understand why we have to travel to South Africa and try to help?*

Two men took measurements in the house so that they could go to the store and buy the lumber and paint for the next days' work.

I was upset when we all drove off. I didn't have much time for despair, though, since we were next headed to the school, where another crew would work in the garden. I was troubled that we'd discovered a three-year-old alone, and we weren't doing anything, but I had to trust the people from St. Thomas Church who lived here. I was learning that our way of life in America doesn't always translate in foreign countries.

ഇ ഇ ഇ

We pulled into the school parking lot and a marching band with cheerleaders greeted us at the entrance. There was a sea of 800 black and yellow uniforms as the students poured out of their classrooms to line the streets and sing the national anthem of South Africa for us.

A light tea and reception followed, with a visit from the Minister of Education in the Gauteng Province. He was very gracious and explained how schools were funded and how students are evaluated in South Africa, which has a standardized education program throughout the country. But it wasn't time to begin work just yet. Everyone piled back into the two buses and went to another school, where we'd be working on a second garden. Another reception followed. We soon realized that it was 2 p.m. and we hadn't done a single stroke of "mission" work. I had to laugh, because some of the newcomers on the trip were getting anxious that they hadn't accomplished anything yet.

"But we have," I explained. "Our friends from South Africa care more about relationships. They want to honor those friendships, both old and new. Relationships take time. In South Africa we learn that it is worth the investment, far more than what we do for them in the garden or building a house. Here, it is the relationship between people that counts the most."

It was already 3 p.m., but I decided to join the group heading back to the house. I wanted to get to know the seventeen-year-old, interview her, and take some pictures of her and her family. I only knew two phrases in Tswana, so I was hopeful that she'd studied some English in school and we could communicate in my native language.

On the way the way back to the house, one of the ladies from the church said, "Let me give you a little more information on the family we're trying to help. You know about the six siblings, but there is a seventh, a bad boy, who is staying at the house too. His name is Buti. We don't know if we have the whole story, but there are rumors that he has abused the three-year-old, and maybe even Mashadi.

"The six-year-old girl's father is the one who comes and takes his daughter to school. The father has a part-time job in Midrand, but his girlfriend doesn't work and is in bars most of the time. Buti is her son and she made him come to live at the house after Mashadi's aunt died in the summer. He takes the food that we leave for the family and gives it to the neighbors. He may be selling drugs with the boys he hangs around with. He never goes to school, but he always 'disappears' whenever we pull up. Mashadi won't tell us much about him, but we just know he is bad news. His mother has no use for him; she's always drunk, no matter what time of day it is."

I was stunned. What a complex situation for a seventeen-year-old to sort out. I was glad that the parishioners of St. Thomas had stepped in to help.

I asked, "How did St. Thomas learn of this family? What's the original connection?"

"The mother had AIDS," Dipuo volunteered, "and we had heard from a neighbor that she was struggling to work. We started bringing her food and medication, but by the end of the spring she was unable to work any longer. We sent out our

257

friends from a local hospice to make sure that she was cared for and comforted in her last days."

Dipuo paused as if to relive that time. "We kept bringing food to the house and supporting her sister, who didn't have a job. Then we found out she had too had AIDS, as well as tuberculosis. She passed away quickly, at the end of July."

"And how is the teenage girl doing? It must be awful to lose your mother and aunt within just a few months. Where is the father? No where to be found?"

"Actually, the six children all have different fathers. I'd mentioned that the six-year-old's father stays in touch and pays for her schooling, but now we have to contend with his girlfriend and her degenerate son."

"But doesn't the family qualify to get foster care or have the government take care of them, since they are all under eighteen? How do they expect them to make it on their own?"

"I appreciate your concern, but there are thousands and thousands of families just like this one. The parents have died of AIDS and the children are orphaned. In many cases, they are all split up and adopted by distant relatives or even strangers. In this case, the eldest daughter is trying to keep them all together, but she can't work and go to school at the same time.

"Even with government help and St. Thomas bringing them food and medicine, it's an unsustainable situation. Someone needs to be around all the time to care for the youngest boy. That's a full-time job. It's unfortunate that Mashadi can't even go to worship with us at St. Thomas. Sunday is when she can watch Aubakwe and does all the cleaning and wash for the week."

"Aubakwe?"

"The three-year-old you met this morning."

I was trying to absorb all this information, but it wasn't easy. I was learning that while America and South Africa shared some similarities, they were, in many ways, worlds apart.

I was anxious to talk to Mashadi but didn't have any idea how to go about it. I was afraid of appearing too forward. I didn't want to pry into her personal business and I imagined that sharing private information with a stranger was culturally incorrect. But we were there to help the family and rebuild their house, and I wanted to be able to capture Mashadi's story for everyone back home.

ഇ ഇ ഇ

We returned to the area ready to work, but it was too late in the day to get much done. The parishioners from St. Thomas had already arrived and unloaded some lumber and paint cans. The next morning we would get an early start and have a full day of "mission work". The house had only three rooms: a sitting room/kitchen and two bedrooms that were hardly eight-by-eight feet each. It wouldn't take much to redo the inside, but we had grandiose plans for a small but sustainable garden that would give them a food supply. What they didn't use they could sell or trade with their neighbors for other things they needed. But for the next two days, the focus would be on the house.

I spoke with Mashadi briefly, asking whether she was willing to talk to me so I could write her story and take pictures of her, her family and her home. She knew enough English to graciously accept the invitation, and seemed appreciative for all we were doing. I said goodbye and that I'd be back early in the morning to get a fresh start.

ഇ ഇ ഇ

The next day, we did start bright and early. Once the painters were set up with their tasks I sat with Mashadi on the front lawn and asked her questions about her life, concentrating on the last six months when she'd lost her mother and aunt. She confirmed most of the story I'd heard, although sometimes communication came to a halt when we couldn't find a word that we both understood. When I asked her about school, she said it was hard because she would miss so much time trying to take care of the family. She brightened when I asked about her favorite subject: "English! I like to write."

"Really! That's wonderful! Can I see some of your writing?"

Mashadi didn't answer right away. I thought that I had misunderstood her or somehow embarrassed her. "I'm sorry. Did I say something wrong?"

"No, you didn't do anything wrong, but I can't leave my writing in the house because it will get stolen when I'm at school. I leave it at my girlfriend's house."

I was speechless. I couldn't imagine not being able to keep something as simple as a notebook in my home, for fear that it would be stolen. All I could think to say was, "I'm sorry. Maybe when we come back at the end of the week, we can go to your friend's house so you can show me."

Mashadi gave me a smile and said that she would very much like to show me her writing.

I was enjoying playing the role of "photojournalist" and I was always renewed and energized when I was working alongside the people of St. Thomas. I talked with Mashadi for over an hour, and then went outside to take photos of the house and neighborhood. I didn't dare venture outside the yard alone, but I took shots of the dusty road and houses next door that would add to the story I was trying to capture. As I walked along one side of the building, I noticed a boy squatting below a window with a winter cap pulled over his head, drawing with a stick in the sand. I said "Hello" as I approached, but he immediately averted his eyes. I knew instantly who he was.

"Buti? Are you Buti?"

He raised his eyes to stare at me. "How do you know my name?"

"I've been talking with Mashadi about the family." I remembered how uncomfortable I'd been when I heard the story about Buti that morning. I didn't know if I was reacting to the content, or that the story had been retold, almost like gossip. I wondered if Buti knew what people were saying about him.

"Why are you outside here by yourself?"

"When the people come from the church, I usually leave with my friends. I wanted to see what was going on today with you people from America. I don't go in the house when the church people are here."

"Does Mashadi not want you in the house?" My heart was racing, as I was asking questions that really seemed inappropriate to be asking a stranger. It was a different culture and although I had been here several times, I wasn't aware of all the boundaries. "Do you go to school? What are you studying?"

"No, my mother doesn't have enough money to send me to school. I hang around with my friends and do odd jobs when people need something. I'm glad I have a place here with Mashadi."

"Did you used to go to school? When did you stop?"

"Last year. My mother said there wasn't enough money anymore, so I just quit going."

"When you went to school, what did you study? What was your favorite subject?"

"Math and science. I want to be an engineer and work on bridges."

"Really? My favorite subjects were math and science, too. They are very important subjects. Do you want to go back to school?"

"Yes, I liked school. But I don't see how that can ever happen again."

I paused and looked deeply into his eyes, hoping they would tell me if the story I'd heard earlier in the day was true or not. But I didn't see any answers, just resigned sadness.

"Do you want to help us paint the house?"

"Yes, I would like that."

I surveyed the ragged boy and felt his isolation, like he was an unwelcome guest. But he was eager when I asked if he wanted to help with the work. I didn't want to get involved, but I was moved to walk back into the house.

"Mashadi, is it okay with you if Buti comes in here and helps paint?"

All eyes were on Mashadi and me.

"Yes, Ma'am. That would be good. Buti should help us rebuild the house. After all, he lives here with us."

I marched outside and repeated her words to Buti. "You should be helping us. Follow me and we will get you a paintbrush." Buti scrambled to his feet and trailed close behind me as I re-entered the house. I introduced him to all the men from St. Thomas and our crew from St. George's, and then made sure that he had a paintbrush in his hand and some supervision. I took more pictures of the work inside the house, including Buti painting in the children's room. I was thirsty and walked outside to get a bottle of water from a large cooler that had been dropped off with the morning paint. As I gulped the refreshing water, a woman approached me. I recognized her as one of the workers from St. Thomas.

"You shouldn't have done that."

"Done what? " I asked. I was thinking that she meant the bottled water wasn't for me.

"Talked to that boy. He is nothing but trouble. We're trying to get him evicted from the house. We hear about the terrible things he is doing with the family and his friends. We're sure he is stealing the food that we leave for the family and selling it. We want him out of the house. Don't be nice to him."

"If he's evicted, where will he go? I heard that rumor about him too, but I also heard that his mother is a drunk and is in bars every day starting at 9 a.m. Buti told me his mother won't pay for him to go to school. What will become of him?"

"That is not our problem. He is from a different jurisdiction. They need to be taking care of him, not us. We have started court papers to make sure he can't stay here any longer."

"Oh, my," was all I could say.

I took a few more photos and then it was time to go. We'd had a full day and I was anxious to get on the Internet and see if I could post a blog story on my new website. I'd promised to share the trip with my friends back at St. George's, and I thought it would be better if I wrote the stories when they were fresh in my mind, with my emotions still engaged. But first, there was one more question I needed to ask Mashadi.

Walking back into the house, I was relieved that Mashadi was by herself in the boys' bedroom: "Mashadi, are you afraid of Buti? Do you want him out of your house?"

Mashadi stared at the floor.

"You don't have to answer me if you don't want to, Mashadi. I do care about you."

"Thank you, Ma'am, you are very kind. No, I'm not afraid of Buti; in fact, it is good that he is here at night. It keeps the other men from coming around."

I looked straight into her soulful brown eyes, and saw a look of resignation, but also one of wisdom beyond her years. That look, that instant recognition, would be all I could think about on the bus trip back to Soweto.

မ္မ မ္မ မ္မ

I was thrilled when my iPhone immediately responded to my attempt to get online. I posted my story, and then joined the others for a restful dinner and a brief reflection led by Reverend Leigh Spruill. We were a large group of twenty-six, and the first night we encouraged the "new pilgrims" to speak, telling us what their eyes, ears and hearts had felt in this new land. There were the inevitable stories about the incredible poverty, but there were also many about the joy of the people. There were comments about how the work of St. Thomas glorified God. We were all amazed at how positive everyone was, even in the face of relentless poverty, illness and death. I tried hard not to think about Buti and what an awful life he was destined for, virtually abandoned by his mother, not going to school, and hanging around with the wrong friends. I hated to think that he had no hope of a better future. But I was reluctant to speak because I was confused. *I knew that I was supposed to love Buti as a child of God, but what if he was doing the terrible things they said?* I seemed to be facing this conflict rather frequently of late.

When the reflection ended, a few people in the group wanted to go up the street to a little bar that we frequented each year, but I was tired and wanted to charge the battery in my camera to make sure that I was ready for the next day. We had a rule that no one ever walked alone on our mission trips, and as Leigh Spruill was also heading back for the night, I asked if I could walk back with him.

As we walked in the darkness together, Leigh asked, "I know you've been here before, but has this trip been different from the others? Has the newness of the poverty worn off now that you've been here four times?"

"That's a good question. On my first trip, I felt an incredible love for the people, but a sadness of how they live. That first day, I was overwhelmed with the poverty and numb with despair. My thoughts were paralyzed when I couldn't get the picture of those children in Soul City out of my mind. I remember the first night that I started to cry during our evening devotion saying, 'But it's hopeless. No matter what we do when we are here, there is too much that needs to be done. We can never make a difference.'

"Larry Trabue consoled me that night, saying, 'God doesn't ask you to eliminate all the poverty in South Africa. It would be an impossible task for one person, even if you were Bill Gates. But God does ask you to listen to His voice and do what He asks you to do. It may mean when you get back to Nashville that God asks you to send a note of encouragement to someone, or perhaps to read a book to a senior adult in a nursing home. Remember, you don't have to do 'great' things in the world's eye by seeking fame and notoriety. Instead, God asks us all to do small things every day. What's important is listening for God's voice and obeying Him, even if the task seems small. If it is what God wants you to do, it is huge in God's eyes.'"

"A great piece of advice, particularly for your first trip, when you were overwhelmed by the conditions here. So, is this trip striking you differently?" Leigh asked again.

I started to answer but had to swallow hard as tears welled up in my eyes. I was tired from the day and struggling with my emotions.

"What's wrong? What are you feeling?" Leigh asked.

"I'm crying for Buti, the seventeen-year-old boy at the house. Did you meet him?"

"I don't think so. Is he the one that we heard the stories about, the father's girlfriend's son?"

"Yes, he's the one. You were painting in the front room and he was helping in the other room. I'm crying because of the way everyone was judging him and treating him. I had been interviewing Mashadi for my blog and when I walked outside, I saw him sitting in the dirt. At first he wouldn't look me in the eye, but when I said his name, his eyes met mine. I asked him why he wasn't helping fix up the house and he said, 'I'm not wanted'. It was the way that he said the word, 'wanted'. He didn't just mean he wasn't needed to help paint; he was saying he wasn't wanted as a person, that he's an outcast.

"I knew immediately he was the boy we'd heard about. But everyone was ignoring him, like he didn't exist. They'd walk right by him and not even acknowledge him with any word, let alone a kind word. His mother is an alcoholic, he doesn't have any place to live and he has no money for food. What an awful life for a young boy. I'm upset because I don't know how to feel.

"Here we are, Christians, and we are treating him poorly. I know he shouldn't do the things he's been accused of, but isn't he just trying to survive? He told me he wants to go back to school, that his favorite subjects are math and science, and he wants to be an engineer. I'm all for helping Mashadi and her family, but can't we help him too? He's a child of God, just like we are. And we are sinners, just like he is. How do we measure the difference in the sins? Is there no difference? I guess my tears are for everyone tonight, Mashadi, Buti and us. We are all sinners."

"Yes, we are all sinners. It's okay to cry for those who are being hurt by the world. And you've raised some great questions. Why do we choose to single out the people that we are going to love and care for? After all, Jesus said love thy neighbor and he meant everyone."

"Thanks for listening, Leigh. I'll keep everyone in my prayers tonight. Good night." The tears were dripping silently as I placed the key in the gate of my house. "Thanks for walking me home."

I couldn't sleep. *How could a seventeen-year-old with no parents and no education hope to survive?* I was wrestling with the fate of both Mashadi and Buti, looking for answers when there were none.

ᘒ ᘒ ᘒ

For the next two days I took more photographs and wrote more stories. My favorite part, though, was still cooking with the ladies and feeding the children after school on Tuesday. The children were all adorable, and it was a wonderful feeling to be able to provide them with a nutritious meal.

On Wednesday, we boarded a plane for Cape Town, where we would visit Robben Island and Table Mountain, and shop at the open-air market. Each year we'd bring back jewelry and other handmade items to sell at St. George's, the proceeds of which went back to the Feeding Scheme program.

I always enjoyed our time in Cape Town, as it was a break from the emotional intensity of Kliptown and Soul City. Cape Town gave us a chance to experience the beauty of the country and to take a deep breath, reflect on our time as pilgrims to a foreign land, and listen for God's voice. I had realized on the first trip that my life was too outcome-oriented. I'd rarely stop to ask God for direction in my life. Instead, I would plow ahead; trying to accomplish things that I thought would please God, but never asking His opinion. It was here in Cape Town that I'd learned to build in periodic time for reflection first so that God has the opportunity to speak to me, and to be heard without competition.

Early on Friday morning, we boarded our bus and headed to the cathedral where Archbishop Desmond Tutu celebrated mass whenever he was in town. As I did on every trip to South Africa, I felt his overpowering presence and his love for everyone. It would be great if we got to meet him again.

We knew we were in luck when we arrived fifteen minutes early and the church was already packed. There was always a larger-than-normal turnout for services when he celebrated.

As always, Tutu's words were inspiring, and at the end of the services, he graciously stood for pictures with endless groups, including ours. Archbishop Tutu's daughter, Theresa, mentioned that her father would be having breakfast in Café George underneath the cathedral immediately after picture taking and we could speak with him there.

We were delighted to spend a few moments over coffee with him, and I was even more excited when he autographed a South African Prayer Book and a copy of his book, *BELIEVE*. It was no wonder that I always came back from these trips so excited about my faith.

We spent our last few hours in Cape Town in the market, and I spied a discount bookstore. I immediately thought about Mashadi and Buti. It was great that we were helping them rebuild their house, but I wanted to give them something personal that they could keep and that would remind them of our love. I bought a pretty writing journal and a small book of devotionals for Mashadi, and a book on astronomy for Buti.

We then boarded the plane back to Johannesburg to stay our last night with the parish families. I couldn't wait to get back so I could take photos of the finished house and give Mashadi and Buti their gifts.

ை ை ை

We heard the good news as soon as we arrived: St. Thomas had made arrangements for a full-time caregiver for Mashadi and her family. This meant Mashadi would be able to go to school every day! It seemed like prayers were being answered. I didn't dare ask what that meant for Buti.

We drove straight to the house from the airport, but it didn't look like the same place we'd left days before. The house had a new coat of paint, two sets of bunk beds, all new bed linens and towels, and a "washing machine" that attached to the kitchen faucet. St. Thomas had also arranged for the electricity to be hooked up to the line in the street.

St. Thomas parishioners had set out food on the front lawn, and I took photos of the house and of everyone eating and talking together in celebration. Then I went back to grab the gifts from the van and approached Mashadi first: "Mashadi, these are for you; gifts from me."

Mashadi gingerly opened the devotional book and journal.

"See, the pages are blank—it's for you to write your poetry in. It's small enough to carry in your backpack each day so no one can take it from you."

The gratitude in her eyes spoke volumes. I opened the devotional book and showed her the inscription: "To Mashadi, with love. From Agatha—St. George's—America."

"Mashadi, I hope when you are back in school full-time and your caregiver has gotten settled in that you will consider going to church. Everyone at St. Thomas is warm and wonderful; I'm sure you would feel welcome there."

"Thank you so much, Ma'am."

"Mashadi, is Buti still here?"

"Yes, Ma'am. He's around back, playing with the younger boys."

I walked to the back of the yard with the book wrapped in the paper sack from the discount bookstore.

I spoke his name, but he barely looked at me. I said again, "Buti, it's me, Agatha, from America."

268

This time he raised his head and his eyes showed that he recognized me. "Hello."

There was no smile, but his eyes stayed focused on me.

"Buti. I want you to have this, from me, to you. It is a book about the science of the stars. It is so that you will study and become an engineer some day. Will you promise me that you will go back to school and study hard so that you can leave here?"

"I would like that very much, Ma'am. Thank you for the book."

"You are very welcome." I opened the book and showed Buti the inscription: "To Buti, with love- from Agatha—St. George's—America."

"Can you read that, Buti? Do you understand what it means?"

"Yes. Ma'am. Thank you."

I walked away wondering what would become of Mashadi and Buti in this land of unknowns.

ॐ ॐ ॐ

All at once, I was extremely tired. My emotions from the past seven days had finally caught up with me. I curled up in the window seat on the bus and closed my eyes. As I was reflecting on the day, I thought, *That's all you could do, but that is all God asked you to do today. It is most important that you listened and obeyed.*

Fortunately, I slept well that night, because I would need all my energy for the two church services and an 11 p.m. flight back to the United States the next day.

I hastily packed the next morning and thanked my hosts, Dipuo and Bizzah Matsobane, for opening their home to me. Bizzah had been imprisoned at Robben Island at the same time as Mandela, but he rarely talked about it. He was the most gracious and forgiving man; how could that be possible after all that he had been through? Dipuo and Bizzah had given me the answer the night before, as we were getting ready for bed: "With God, all

269

things are possible." For them, it was that simple. I hoped to one day find that degree of simplicity in my life.

It was a glorious day, which made me sad that we were leaving in less than fourteen hours. I loaded all my camera equipment and suitcases into the car for the ride to St. Thomas for Sunday service. I was hoping to get to church a little early so I could photograph the entrance procession.

I stopped at the entrance to find the best position for photos, but then decided to go inside and find my friends, Mbali and Lorraine. I joined them in the second row in the seat they'd saved for me. We all embraced, and I remarked how good it was to be worshiping with friends again in South Africa.

As I turned to greet another friend, I recognized Mashadi and Buti seated quietly in the row behind me! I stepped out to give each of them a warm embrace, and told them how happy I was to see them. *Had they walked to church?* For a fleeting instant, I wondered what the congregation would think about me giving Buti a hug. I figured it was acceptable in their culture for an older woman to embrace a boy young enough to be her son, but I suspected that everyone in the congregation knew who he was and had heard the rumors about him. In the next moment, I realized that I didn't care what anyone thought. I was glad to see them both, and weren't we all sinners, anyway?

I went outside to take photos of the procession and then returned to take my seat. I felt Mashadi's hand on my shoulder as I sat down, "I have something for you, after church service."

Mashadi had something for me? Whatever could it be? She and her family had virtually nothing for themselves, let alone anything to give away.

I was soon lost in the singing and dancing of the church service. Father Victor gave a sermon on the story of the blind beggar, and emphasized that the beggar became the hero of the story because he had faith. I always scribble a few notes during a sermon. Today, I jotted down Father Victor's five characteristics of faith: eagerness, assertiveness, hopefulness, impetuosity, and courage. He concluded, "Like Bartimaeus, we all have wounds, terrible burdens, agonizing situations. Some blindside us unexpectedly in the dark. Others are grinding, nagging at us over seemingly endless years. Today's lesson is to rise up and take courage, for Jesus listens all the time to us and our concerns."

I'd gone from a few tears to crying a river. Fortunately, Larry always carried a handkerchief for just that reason. Father Victor's sermon was personal because of my vision problems for the past three years. I hadn't talked much about it, but I still couldn't see anything from my right eye, except blurry shapes. When Father Victor told the story of a blind man having faith and being healed, it gave me hope too.

The service continued as everyone went forward to put a monetary contribution in a large wicker basket. I'd completely forgotten that there was a second "offertory" that day. The people of St. George's had made a special "store run" the day before to buy clothes, books, and toys for Mashadi and her family. After the collection was blessed, the service proceeded, with members from St. George's going to the altar rail and placing unwrapped gifts in an ever-growing pile. At the conclusion, Larry stood up and motioned for Mashadi and her brothers and sisters to come forward so that we could present them with the gifts.

Of course, that was why Mashadi and Buti were at church that morning! I surmised that one of the parishioners had gone to pick them up and bring them there. I was pleased that the whole congregation would meet the family, and that Mashadi and Buti had participated in the service at church.

Once again, I counted my blessings that I had become a part of St. George's and had the opportunity to travel to South Africa and meet these wonderful and generous people. These friends lived thousands of miles away, but were truly brothers and sisters in Christ, and now I counted Mashadi and Buti among them.

After the service and a short reception, we helped load the gifts into a van, which would drive Mashadi and Buti back to their house. As we put the last items into the van, Mashadi said, "I have something for you."

"Mashadi, you are a wonderful person. I hope that you will do well in school and study hard in your English literature classes. May God bless you!"

"But I have something I want to give you. I started reading the book you gave me. Last night I decided to write a poem for you."

"A poem for me?" There I was, starting to tear up all over again.

"Yes, this is for you. I will remember you forever."

With that, Mashadi handed me two pieces of ruled 8-1/2 x 11" paper with colored hearts and flowers outlining meticulously printed words.

"Ma'am, here is your poem. It is titled:

Don't Look Away

As he raises his hand
In his mind
Nothing but anger
Deeply creates
A revival of revile

Tears flow down her cheeks
Like a stream, Nile River
Like a lamb, dying is the inner soul
Like a Cyclist, joining a Circle
Of Speechless noise
A mountain of wheels
As UBABA raises his hand

UMamA u nagheghtla his integrity
With her Smile, with her happiness
The need for help in her eyes

Her help was ten digits away
A phone call away

A call that separates non-humans from human
Creates a Society for each party
A freedom-fighter, a Community liberator
Who eliminates degradation among the future generation
To a brighter nation
After all it's just one step
A Step of Courage
To make a call, Don't look away.

As I finished reading, I had to stop to wipe away my tears. I gave her a quick hug, and then Mashadi was gone.

I heard my name being called and realized that everyone had already boarded our vans to St. Monnica's parish in Midrand, where Father Xolani had transferred since leaving St. Thomas. We had been invited to participate in his church's 60th anniversary celebration. It was an hour's trip, and all I could think about was whether I would ever see Mashadi again.

ৎ৹ ৎ৹ ৎ৹

A grand procession opened the service at St. Monnica's and it was another holy celebration. This was a more formal liturgy than the one that we had just left at St. Thomas in Kagiso, but spirit-filled nonetheless. We were given front row seats and recognized as "friends from America" during the service. We were happy to be called "friends" by such joyous and loving people. It was another lesson that I didn't want to forget: I vowed to intentionally look for the joy in my life. Here in South Africa, it was obvious that their joy came from knowing and trusting God, no matter what happens. *Could I learn to live my life in America that way, too?*

273

There were many inspiring speakers, including a beautiful young college student, who spoke with a clear and unhesitating voice from the pulpit. Her name was Lindiwe Zulu and she read a poem she had written entitled, *STRANGER*.

We finished lunch, then joined the crowd who were observing the planting of trees to honor St. Monnica's pastors, past and present. I recognized Lindiwe from her bright blue scarf and told her how much I had enjoyed her poem.

"You have a very deep faith. I've just started a blog on the Internet about faith and how important it is to put God first. It is so hard with human relationships. It seems that you have incredible wisdom for a young lady. May I have your permission to use your poem on my blog? I'll be sure to give you credit. In fact, I'd like to have some more information about you to post with the story. Do you have time to talk now?"

"Actually, I have only a few minutes before I need to be home, but I will give you my email address and telephone number. If you send me an email or text me, I'll send you some information. And thank you. I would like it if you would use my poem on your blog. We should stay in touch."

"Thanks so much! In fact, I'll send an email right now and you can write me back when you have a few minutes. It was such a pleasure meeting you. Have a good semester at school."

"I would love to come to the States for a visit. I hope we get to meet again."

I had met two wonderful young ladies who were much wiser than their years. They were from very different backgrounds, but both loved and trusted God, and were able to put their feelings and emotions about life and their faith into beautiful poetic words. We were packing up the vans to drive to the airport when my phone chimed that I'd just received an email. It was from Lindiwe. As promised, it was her poem and more information about her life.

STRANGER

A thousand miles in the shoes of a stranger
In search of self in strange new places

Without this mask, you'll find I'm faceless
Saved, 'cause I was told He'd change this

Lost my question in a sea of answers…

There's a me I'm looking for, and I'm wondering if you've met her
Think I hear her laughing when I paint her face in mirrors
And I think I hear her asking why I'm always trying to trick her
Trick her into thinking someone out there's going to fix her
When I haven't even tried for one day to let her be her

And sometimes I think it's maybe 'cause it cuts me deep when she hurts
Or maybe 'cause the ones I feel, I feel they wouldn't feel her
And I've lived so long believing that I'd never have to free her

But when You called, I knew that only she would have to answer
Answer for the many lies and trespasses against her
For the life she never lived and the love I never gave her

But on the day You saved her, the tears flowed because you made her
Made her like You've never made a precious thing before her
With Your own hands, You formed her
And with the blood that flowed, redeemed her
In that moment, it took all the faith I had to claim I am her
In the words of a misplaced letter, I'll never be able to send her.

With the attached poem, Lindiwe sent her interpretation: "The poem entitled 'Stranger' is about the inner battle between who we truly are and who the world says we should be. It is the perpetual war within us, between who God has created us to be and the identity we have adopted from our past and our circumstances. I believe that anyone who has deeply questioned the authenticity of their identity will be able to relate to this piece."

What a beautiful girl, and how expressive she is with words.

It was time to board the plane for the trip back home. It was always bittersweet to leave my friends, but this time I had photographs and stories to share. I knew that their examples of forgiveness, reconciliation, grace and mercy were transforming me. It wasn't a transformation that happened in one blinding second; instead, it was a slow turning around, and a gradual understanding that I could lead a better life. My better life wasn't one with more material things; rather, it was a life with more meaning. As I drifted off to sleep on the plane, I knew I had an obligation to share what I'd learned with others. *But how was God going to use me?*

20

Divorce Pending

Remember that when we give up a destructive relationship, we will feel a loss. Many times people try to leave a destructive relationship and do not adequately face the loss, only to find themselves going back to the same relationship, or to another one just as destructive. Loss involves sadness. To have something new, however, we must first lose the old.

– Dr. Henry Cloud and Dr. John Townsend

Christmas 2010 was joyous, partying with close friends and serving as an usher with Dru for the third Christmas Eve in a row. A huge snowfall on Christmas Eve turned Nashville into a twinkling winter wonderland. The happiness of the holidays jettisoned me into the new year, when I received more good news. My research proposal on healthcare information technology had been approved, and I could start my dissertation project at school when the semester started mid-January. The last phase of my graduate career was about to begin, and I was excited to be studying the hottest topic in healthcare policy under healthcare reform.

❧ ❧ ❧

It was clear that God had said, "Wait" for a reason. In the past, I would have demanded that He tell me what the reason was, but I was getting more accustomed to trusting Him with everything. I finally believed that He loved me and wanted the best for me, so I didn't need to know His every thought. A verse from the Book of Malachi came to mind about not wearying God with our words. I was grateful that I was learning to be silent with God and just let Him love me. God was taking more opportunities to teach me about patience. I'd thought about dropping out of graduate school twice, but in both cases, after much prayer, it was obvious that God wanted me to finish the degree. A selfish part of me had wanted to prove I could finish. But after some reflection, I had reframed that thought. It's important to not be a quitter when you are doing God's work, but if you are doing something that is not God's will, it is good to stop.

I knew I would need to be disciplined in order to work full-time, complete my research, and maintain some balance in my life. I decided to get up at 5 a.m. each morning for thirty minutes of quiet time and Bible reading; at 5:30, I'd take Rachel for a walk; and at 6:45, I'd leave for the 7 a.m. service. After work, I'd come home, have dinner, and then start typing up my research until 10 p.m. The rest of the evening was for reading. Some nights I'd take a break from my routine to write a blog story; writing helped me keep my day steeped in the Lord. I'd given up watching some of my favorite sitcoms, but after a few weeks, I didn't miss TV at all.

It was a relief that I wasn't dating anyone, because I already had enough on my plate. My friend Brian said, "Churches really should honor single people more. If I had a wife and children to take care of, I'd never have the time to serve the Lord in all the ways He's asking me to do. St. Paul was right when he said that being single is a calling, just like being married is."

During my prayer time, I would hear God saying, "Don't worry about dating, you aren't ready yet. You will start dating when you finish your degree. But don't jump at the first guy you go out with. Guard your heart and stay faithful to Me. You may never remarry, but if you do, I will tell you when it is the right guy and that you are the right girl for him. Trust Me in all things. Dating and marriage are two of the most important things in your life, but trust Me in all things."

What did He say? I'd be dating after I finished my degree? Sounds like something to look forward to. But what did God mean that I "wasn't ready"? I guess I would have to trust God, since no details were forthcoming. And here again, I was being told to guard my heart.

Just because I wasn't thinking about dating didn't mean my friends weren't thinking about fixing me up. A girlfriend from work asked if I'd attend a formal dinner party with John, a friend of hers from Huntsville. He was going to be in Nashville for the event and needed a date. I wasn't so sure it was a good idea, but she'd said that he had been the best man at her wedding and they had all remained close friends. I remembered that God had said that I wasn't going to date until after my degree was finished, but this wasn't a "date", it was a favor. Besides, it might be a fun evening.

I told my friend I would go, and was surprised when John showed up unexpectedly in Nashville a few weeks before the dinner party.

"Just so I can get to know you better, I'd like to take you to dinner."

He'd called at my work number. I have a bad habit of saying "Yes" when I mean, "I don't know." I hated to disappoint anyone. I knew that my wanting to be liked was a weakness and it had gotten me into all sorts of trouble before. But, it had happened again. "Sure, I'm free for dinner tonight. Didn't realize that you would be in town. Isn't the dinner party next month?"

"Yes. But I found out I had some business to take care of in Nashville, and thought we could have a nice quiet dinner before the big party."

279

All I could think of was how tired I was from a long week at work, and that I just wanted to go home and put my feet up. But God also kept telling me "it isn't always about me"; I had to give some in relationships, too. "Yes, 7 p.m. would be fine. Where are we going for dinner so I know how to dress?"

"How about F. Scott's on Crestmoor?"

"Perfect, it's one of my favorite places. Thanks."

It was a nice evening. I always enjoyed eating at F. Scott's and the fruity, Oregon Illahe Pinot Noir Reserve was perfectly paired with my dinner of sesame seed-encrusted grilled salmon. It was a delightful evening, and I found myself looking forward to the dinner party in a few weeks. I was also looking forward to shopping for something to wear. I still enjoyed getting dressed up occasionally; it brought back fond memories of my time as Miss Geneseo 1970, when I was the Fire Queen and wore long formal gowns to ride in the parades all that summer.

Over dessert and coffee, I said, "Denise tells me that you were the best man at her wedding over twenty years ago. You were all in college together, right?"

"That's right, I was their best man and Jeffrey was the best man at my wedding too."

"How long have you been divorced? Denise didn't tell me many details about you, just that you sell medical devices and have been living in Huntsville for most of your life."

"Well, Denise probably didn't mention the divorce because it's not final yet. It's been dragging on for two years. We've been apart the whole time but she won't compromise at all. She wants more alimony than I'm willing to give her. Our lawyers keep fighting it out and postponing the hearings. I don't know when it will be final. And she's crazy! She's taking me to the cleaners. I should have never married her."

My heart was in my throat. Just when I was enjoying an evening out with an "intriguing stranger", I learned I was on a "date" with a married man. One of my friends in San Antonio had the same thing happen, but it had been two months of "dating" before he admitted that he was still married. My friend immediately broke it off, but she'd asked me rhetorically, "Do you know the other name for 'divorce pending'? MARRIED! Stay away if you know what is good for you. Nothing good comes from dating an 'almost divorced' man."

I felt like I was in the clutches of impending doom again. We hadn't done anything wrong; we were just having dinner. But he obviously considered it a date, even though he wasn't divorced yet. *How do I find these guys? And how come Denise didn't tell me?*

John took me home and kissed me on the cheek at the front door. It was a sweet kiss, but I reminded myself that he was still very married. The words, "Guard your heart" kept playing over and over again in my head. Wasn't it wrong for a married man to get involved with someone else when he was still married? It seemed like all the rules were different these days. So many people were living together without getting married, and if he said that he was getting out of the marriage, that it was a mere formality until the papers were signed, wasn't that good enough? He said that he'd never take his wife back.

I couldn't sleep that night. I had a lot to learn about relationships and how to make them successful, but I was confident that God wouldn't send a married man for me to date. It just wasn't right, but what to do next? *Should I still go to the dinner party with him?* It would be fun and it was here in Nashville, so no one in Huntsville, where his wife still lived, would ever know. *But what if there were pictures in The Sunday Tennessean?* It was a high profile party and there were sure to be reporters there. *How would his wife feel if she saw a picture of the two of us on the Internet?*

After much soul searching, I decided to call him on Monday and tell him that I couldn't go to the dinner party with him. I didn't want to sound judgmental, just to say that I didn't feel comfortable because he wasn't divorced yet. I had a right to draw a boundary, and I'd decided three years ago that I was through "dating" married men. I had a lot of church friends who were married, but they were brothers in Christ, not "dates".

Monday morning rolled around, and I picked up the phone three times and dialed his number, only to hang up before the call went through. How hard can it be to turn down a date? Why did I feel like I was disappointing him? After all, he was the one who was married. It was the right thing to do.

It was late in the afternoon when I got the email. It was short and to the point: Perhaps it is best that we don't attend the gala. I had a nice time at dinner with you and enjoyed meeting you. John.

I couldn't believe my eyes. I re-read the email before it sank in. I had been dumped after one dinner. But then I realized that I was off the hook. In the past, my first thought would have been, *I wonder what he didn't like about me? Was I too forward? Did I not dress well enough? Was I not smart enough?* But this time there were no voices in my head telling me that I wasn't good enough to be the 'chosen one'. Instead, I felt nothing but relief. I had turned it all over to God in my prayer time, and I was sure He had intervened. I didn't hear His voice, but I knew that His answer would have been, "Agatha, you've got to trust me. He isn't the man for you. Be patient and content with what I ask you to do to serve me. If you are to marry, I'll send you the right man."

It seemed like the more I prayed, the more I understood how God wanted me to act. My prayers these days started with, "God, help me to put You first in my life. I want You to be first, above all other things, including an intimate relationship, a family and a children-filled home. Please, let me love You first."

༄ ༄ ༄

The next month was a whirlwind, with full-time work and full-time research. I was still starting each day in church at 7 a.m., even though I'd occasionally sleep past my 5 a.m. wake-up call and have to squeeze in a few minutes of devotional time during the day. At first I was angry when I missed my Bible study time in the morning, but then I realized that it wasn't good enough to just go through the motions. I needed to be engaged when I was reading Scripture.

On some mornings, sleep was more important. Instead of being disappointed with myself for occasionally sleeping in, I felt renewed that I was walking close to God, and keeping Him first in my life, not with ritual and discipline, but instead as a friend who really understood me and my needs. I was growing accustomed to being content with a daily rhythm, even though it wasn't the same every day! It was a real mark of spiritual maturity for someone like me, who was used to controlling everything in my life.

I'd reduced my volunteer work at the Frist Center while I was finishing my research at school, but I was still attending member events. It was at a Circle Member reception that my new world of faith collided with my old world once again. I was in the second gallery of the February 2011 opening reception for *"Vishnu: Hinduism's Blue-Skinned Savior"* when I ran into an art collector from Franklin that I'd met before.

"You're a docent here, right?" he asked. "Are you planning to give any tours of the *Vishnu* exhibition?"

I don't know why I started to blush, but I still hated to disappoint people. Instead of my usual white lies, I thought I'd lead with the truth this time, "Actually, no I haven't planned any tours. I'm in graduate school and busy working on my research. It's all-consuming right now."

Gee, it was refreshing to tell the truth.

"Well, I was wondering. My wife and I are going through an amiable divorce. It's not final yet, but should be within the next six months or so. Would you like to go have lunch sometime?"

"That sounds great! I'd love to hear about your art collection!"

I could not believe the words had come from my mouth. Why had I said yes? There it was again; when I got uncomfortable, my fallback position was to please, even when a "yes" was the wrong answer. I stood speechless, silently condemning myself. *Was it because he was cute, or maybe because he was wealthy? Why had I just accepted a lunch invitation that was obviously a "date" with another "divorce pending"? What was I thinking?*

"Well, I'll call you sometime. I read your blog and enjoy your writing. I've got your email and telephone number from the site."

"See you around."

I was so disappointed in myself, again. *Why had I just led him on?* The right answer would have been, "No, I can't go out with you because you are still married." The words sounded so harsh and I knew that judgment belongs to God. I needed more practice in saying "No" to a stranger in a loving, non-judgmental way.

I was still bothered when I got home. I knew that I could trust Matthew to keep a confidence and that he'd be fair and honest with me. I called him and explained what had happened.

"Well, you were wrong to say you'd go out with him after he told you that he is still married. When he calls, why don't you tell him that you'd like to have lunch with him, but to call you after the divorce is final? It's not good to start a new relationship when you haven't closed the old one yet. I definitely think that you shouldn't go out with him until he's resolved everything. He needs to guard his heart too and falling in love again too soon is the wrong thing to do."

"Thanks, Matthew. As usual, I don't know what I would do without your friendship. Sometimes I just need reinforcement when the world tells me to do one thing and God is telling me to do another."

I'd dodged another bullet. *Why are human relationships so hard?* It was obviously a difficult question with no easy answer.

◌ ◌ ◌

The PORCH CLUB couldn't get together that spring, with my research tying me down to Nashville and Carol relocating to take a new job. We had conference calls in between our bi-annual meetings, and the next one was lively, with me recounting my two "divorce pending" invitations. It was in March that Jackie shared the news that she had gotten engaged and was planning a summer 2011 wedding. It would be the perfect time for the next PORCH CLUB meeting, and hopefully, my research would be almost finished by then.

Although graduate school was keeping me busy, I was still writing two or three blog stories a week. I had also added two new sections, one for my photography, and the other for prayers from the Book of Common Prayer in New Zealand, South Africa and the United States. The South African prayer book, which Archbishop Tutu signed, was coming in handy. God's beauty was everywhere and all I had to do was look. I wanted to capture it through words and photography to share God's kingdom with others.

By June of 2011, I'd written over a hundred stories on my blog topic: *Putting God First and the Holy Relationships that Flow from Our First Love*. I had eight posts that I thought would make a good study series at St. George's, as they were geared to single people, from young adulthood to middle age. I approached our young female priest, Sarah Kerr, about the possibility of co-leading a six-week series in the spring of 2012. Sarah was single too, and we went for coffee one day to talk about the possibility of offering a class called "Holy Desires". The name was patterned after the quote from St. Augustine in the 5th century: "The whole life of a Good Christian is a *holy desire*".

"Thanks for meeting with me about the program, Sarah. It would be wonderful if some of my stories could be used to help others enhance their relationships. We have the Marriage Course at church, but we don't really have a lot of programming for singles."

"So, are you thinking about presenting this six-week series in the fall?"

"No, that's not realistic for me. I'm still in school and working on my research. I hope to finish school in the summer, but it might be the fall before all my work is complete. I was hoping to teach at church during spring 2012, if you're willing to co-facilitate with me. My blog focuses on topics like prayer and solitude, submission, forgiveness, insecurities, fears, and false idols. Why don't I leave you with some of the materials and we can meet again in a few weeks?"

"Sounds good. But while we have a few minutes, tell me more about yourself. Are you dating anyone?"

I told Sarah about the divorce, breast cancer treatments and my experience on my first trip to South Africa in 2007, noting that the mission trip was how I ended up joining St. George's. Sarah revealed that a foreign mission trip she had gone on when she was fifteen had a profound impact on her faith, too.

I then told Sarah about the dating discussion I'd had with Father Tim two years before, and my more recent "divorce-pending" invitations.

"It sounds like you are making wise decisions about your relationships and working on putting God foremost. That's the most important thing: keeping your loves in the right order. If God wants you to marry again, He will bring the right man to you. Don't jump at the first guy that pays attention to you. Seek God's wisdom first."

"Yes, but it is so hard these days. People are living together and almost everyone I know seems to be in a monogamous relationship. Still, I do want to be sure about my relationship with God first. I've learned that He won't ever leave me or disappoint me. The security in our relationship with God can't be matched in human relationships."

"Right. Don't worry so much about what the rest of the world does. I haven't been kissed romantically in over three years. I dated a guy when I was in seminary and then we broke up. No serious relationship since then, except of course with God. I'm trusting God, too, that if He wants me to be married, He'll bring the right man to me. I keep praying, not for a man in my life but that I will do God's will, whatever that may be."

"Wow! Those are great words of wisdom. It must be really hard getting a date when you are a female priest! I'll bet you intimidate a lot of guys, even those who are pretty faithful."

"I don't know about intimidation, but every Christian is given different spiritual gifts, and I'd like to think that we are all here to minister to each other, regardless of ordination. It's when we know that it is our responsibility to help others grow in their faith that real love starts to develop."

"Thanks for meeting with me, Sarah. I'd like to plan on presenting the classes next spring. Thanks also for the reassurance about dating. I want to walk with God, and I know that I have to trust Him in every aspect of my life."

It was an affirming conversation, and it was only a matter of time before I got to use the wisdom that Sarah had shared.

21

My First Real Date

We should resist over-spiritualizing the steps He expects us to take to make choices.

– Joshua Harris

I was working hard to finish my research before it became obsolete. I'd dragged out the work on my master's degree for nine years and had to repeat my research project, and I certainly didn't want that to happen again.

I handed in my 278-page dissertation the first week of June, hoping that I could schedule my defense and graduate in the summer. Dr. Stanley warned me that I might have to wait until the fall, depending upon Committee availability, but he'd let me know what date worked for everyone. I was looking forward to closing the school chapter of my life so I could move on.

I was thrilled when Dr. Stanley called to tell me my defense was set for the end of July, and I decided to celebrate that evening with some salmon. I was caught completely off-guard when the gentleman in front of me at Kroger's fish counter said, "Hi! I really like the fish here. Have you tried the mahi-mahi?"

"No, I'm going for some salmon tonight. I'm doing a little celebrating and salmon is my treat."

"Really, maybe I could help you celebrate. Are you married?"

Seriously? Did he just ask me about mahi-mahi and marriage in consecutive sentences?

"No. I'm not married."

"Would you go to dinner with me sometime? I was just kidding about coming over for dinner tonight, but I'd like to see you."

"Sure."

"How do I get a hold of you?"

"Here's my personal card. It has my email address and cell number on it." It wasn't until later that night when I remembered that God had said that I'd start dating again when I finished my degree. Technically, I wouldn't be finished for at least four more weeks; I may even have to redo some parts, which would mean enrolling again in the fall. I wondered if this was the guy that God had intended for me all along, and I'd misunderstood the timing. Maybe God had changed His mind and I'd start dating, "slightly before" I finished my degree.

Nothing happened that night: no call, no email, although I was checking every fifteen minutes. Maybe he is married, although he wasn't wearing a wedding ring at the fish counter. I finished my salmon dinner and checked my phone once more before I went to bed. For three-and-a-half years since the divorce, I hadn't dated anyone; I was patiently waiting on God to tell me when and who.

I found myself intrigued by this man. He wasn't someone I'd known for ten years, or had met at church or work. Instead, it had been a random meeting at the fish counter of the local grocery store.

I was reading in bed when my phone buzzed a text message: Hi. This is Brandon from the fish market. I'd like to take you to dinner sometime, but I'm leaving for a fishing trip with my son tomorrow for a week. Can I call you when I get back?

I texted back: Sure. Have fun on your vacation. Safe travels!

289

Why was I so excited about a text message? He hadn't really asked me out yet, and my emotions were already leap-frogging to what I was going to wear. My desire to be in a relationship and have a family was kicking in again. You'd think I would have learned my lesson over the past thirty years. I fell asleep vowing that I wouldn't make an idol out of a romance ever again.

ॐ ॐ ॐ

It was a few weeks before we could get together, due to Brandon's vacation and his out-of-town travel for work. We finally matched schedules and made plans to have dinner on the Sunday evening before my dissertation defense.

I was all about practicing my "flexibility" skill, so I wasn't concerned about where we were going, or even what time. I figured we'd eventually connect on the details. We had texted and talked over the three weeks, so I knew the date was still on. Saturday evening he called around 9 p.m. and we had a nice talk for about an hour. I was really looking forward to meeting a new person, learning about their faith and relaxing in conversation.

Early Sunday afternoon I received a text: Pick you up at 4:30.

Ouch. That wouldn't work. I was hitting golf balls after church with Mike and his younger son, and that would run into late afternoon. I immediately texted back: I can't be ready until 6:30. Will that work?

How about 6 p.m.? If you aren't ready, I can wait in your living room.

I texted back: 6 p.m. will be okay.

Wow, a woman that is flexible and can compromise. I like you already, and I like red lipstick.

Gee, what did the text about red lipstick mean?

He arrived promptly at 6 p.m. and I was ready. He started towards me with his arms outstretched.

"What are you doing?" I asked.

290

"I want to give you a hug."

I was confused, but managed to say, "I just met you."

"I'll warn you that I'm affectionate."

I let the comment slide as I locked my front door and we headed out for the evening.

He was polite, opening the car door for me and making sure I was settled in before closing the door. I still didn't know where we were going, but I was practicing being flexible.

"You're gorgeous," he said, as he got into the driver's seat. "Really, gorgeous."

"Oh, thanks," I said, waving away the compliment. I was dressed in a sleeveless dark green blouse and a khaki skirt, a casual dinner outfit.

We chatted about where we lived (within two miles of each other) and how long we'd been in Nashville. We talked about his work, how he had previously been the CEO of his own company, but now was an engineer for an information technology firm and often traveled out of town. He said he was trying to take life more slowly as he got older; he was trying to appreciate the finer things in life.

"So how old are you?" I asked.

"Guess."

"Well, how about forty-eight?"

"Close," he said, "forty-eight on my next birthday."

"Which is...when?"

"December 14."

"You are kidding," I replied, "Mine is the 13th of December! How funny."

"And how old are you?"

"I won't make you guess. I'm fifty-six; I'll be fifty-seven in December."

"Wow! No problem, my last girlfriend was older than me too, but age doesn't equal beauty."

I let that comment slide, too.

We talked a little about my work, but more about my blog and the book I was writing. It was hard for me, but I'd been trying to concentrate on listening more and talking less.

"So, let me guess, you like to boss men around at work, but then you want them to take charge in your personal life, right?" he said with a laugh.

I wasn't sure why he'd gotten that idea, or if he was only joking, so cautiously I said, "No, I believe that I am called to work, and God directs my gifts there, but I also believe that the Bible teaches us about the appropriate roles for men and women in dating and marriage. The man has to be the spiritual leader of the family. I am trying to learn how to be a Proverbs 31 woman."

"Wonderful. Sounds like you're a Christian. I was the youth director at a church for over fifteen years, so I know my way around the church and the Bible."

This was going well, I thought. I definitely wanted to hear more about his church involvement. "Where do you go to church now? Do you still work with youth?"

"Not exactly. I've had this job for four years and I travel a lot. I haven't exactly found a church home. My son is fourteen and lives with me, so that is the 'youth influencing' that I'm concentrating on right now."

On the one hand, I was glad that he was raising a son, but it was hard to understand how that could happen without a church community. I couldn't imagine not being involved at St. George's. I was trying not to be judgmental. I thought back to the time early in my career, when I wasn't as dedicated a churchgoer either. For the three years after college, I'd worked every other weekend and commuted on the opposite weekend to see an out-of-town boyfriend.

When I stopped to think about it, I'd been pretty scarce at church during that period in my life, too. But that was when I was twenty-eight. I'd grown up a lot since then and now realized the importance of being part of a church community. But I had to keep reminding myself: it's not up to me to judge other people.

Until I really know someone and their situation, I can't have a meaningful conversation about their faith and their choices.

Over our dinner, we talked about things that we liked to do in the Nashville area and found out that we both enjoyed all kinds of music.

It was time to leave and I was again impressed that he held the door for me at the restaurant and opened the car door. Chivalry was a lost art these days, and I had to admit that it made me feel special.

We were pulling onto Interstate I-40 East for the short trip back to Bellevue when he started asking more personal questions: "Do you like flowers? What kind? Are you the type of girl that likes to be romanced?"

My radar started to go up, and I was a little uncomfortable with the familiarity. I knew that I hadn't dated in a while, but I really liked to get to know people a little more before we started talking about personal stuff. Suave and sophisticated men had swayed me before, and I didn't want my heart to stray into dangerous territory too soon.

I took a deep breath and tried to relax. I was just getting comfortable again when he reached over and put his hand under my hair, starting to massage the back of my neck.

I flinched and said, "What are you doing?"

"I'm massaging the back of your neck. I'm a touchy-feely person. Once you get to know me better, you'll find out that I'm a hugger; I like physical contact."

With that, I moved my head to the right to disengage his hand. "It seems to me that what you are trying to do is manipulate me with touch and physical affection. It's the trap that people fall into these days. They confuse physical touch with intimacy. You are playing on my emotions that I'll like you because humans crave physical contact." I was looking straight at him to gauge his reaction.

"Wow. I didn't expect that at all. You are gorgeous and dressed in a short skirt. I'm going to ask my questions again. You're the type that bosses men around at work, but then plays hard to get in relationships, right? I mentioned that older gal from Memphis I just broke up with. I did the same thing on our first date; put my hand under her hair and started massaging her neck. Within thirty minutes she was all over me! She couldn't wait to get me home and take my clothes off. I've found a lot of you working women are like that. Playing hard to get, but then being physically aggressive and making all the moves. With her, all I had to do is sit back and enjoy it."

In one short instant, it was obvious that this was not the guy God had in mind for me to spend a lifetime with. I didn't need to stop and pray about it. I finally said, "Gee, seems ideal for you. Why did you break up with her?"

"She just wasn't my type, and after eighteen months she said she was getting tired of driving to Nashville to see me. With my travel and my son, I like to stay home on the weekends, so she'd drive here. But, you know, she just wasn't a churchgoer and I thought it best to end it before anyone got hurt."

I was silent; I didn't know what to say next, but I started praying that I would get home safely.

I was glad for a few minutes of silence, but then he spoke again, "I know that this is going to sound strange but what I'm about to say is true and from the bottom of my heart. I knew it the first time we met at the fish counter at Kroger."

He paused, so I asked, "Knew what?"

"Are you ready for this? I'm baring my soul here. When I heard you talking about your faith and church, it took me back to a happier time. I believe that you are the woman that I have been praying about since my divorce. I know that God will bless me with a virtuous woman, and I believe you are the one. I'd like to court you, starting tonight."

I hadn't heard the word "court", as it applies to relationships, in thirty-five years; I wasn't even sure what it meant in 2011. *Did "courting" mean "hooking up" (having sex) on the first date?* That wasn't going to happen in my lifetime again. I'd been convicted with my Scripture reading that God designed sex only for people married to each other and anything else was wrong. I knew that wasn't a contemporary concept, but I'd read more about how as Christians we can't be conformed to the world. Now I was really confused. Was Brandon the guy that wanted to be "attacked" on a first date, or was he a sincere churchgoer that would honor and cherish a woman? I plunged ahead, "What do you mean, 'court'?"

"Well, wine you and dine you while being the perfect gentleman. We'll get to know each other over a short period of time and pray about getting married. I believe that it is God's will."

"I'm not ready to date anyone exclusively," I managed to sputter, reminding myself that I hadn't been on a real date in over twenty years and it was unlikely that my first date would start an exclusive relationship.

"That's okay. I'm willing to wait for you. I'll be traveling on business for the next three weeks, so you won't hear from me for a while. Are you okay with that?"

"Certainly. Why don't you call me when you return?" There it was again! I couldn't help but try to be "nice", hoping everyone would like me. I wanted to trust him, but this 100% about-face was too much to believe. I knew that it was important to be praying about a relationship, but after the first date? I was fighting hard between feeling manipulated and still wanting to be "nice".

I knew what the problem was. I hadn't dated in so long that I didn't trust myself. In the past I would have been the aggressive one, texting him after the date to tell him what a great time I'd had. "Can't wait to see you again" would be the message. I would let my heart get way ahead of reality. It was time that I acted like the woman that God had intended me to be, and not the one that society had raised.

Brandon opened the car door for me when we got to my house. As we approached the front door, he said, "From what you've said, I guess I don't get a good night kiss, right?"

"Right. That was a first date."

"Okay. So how about a hug—you know a 'butt out' embrace."

It was a short hug.

"I'll call you when I get back into town three weeks from now. Sleep tight, my love."

I shut off the porch light and thought, *so is this what dating is like in the year 2011? We've come a long way, but I'm not sure it's in the right direction.* I was glad I was headed to Louisville for Jackie's wedding the next weekend. It was going to be a beautiful event and it was Jackie's day, but maybe I could highjack fifteen minutes to talk with The PORCH CLUB about my "first date".

৯০ ৯০ ৯০

It was a full four days of parties; Jackie was a gorgeous bride and the reception was too much fun. I was truly happy that she was remarrying, and I was firmly convinced that God was taking care of me in the relationship department as well.

We were all getting manicures and pedicures, drinking wine and eating pizza the day before the wedding, when I said, "Can I ask you all a question? I'm confused about today's dating rules. I had my first 'date' this past weekend and I have some serious questions."

"Woo Hoo!" Carol called out. "A real date? You've always said that Brian and Matthew are just 'good friends', so this must be someone new. Tell us more."

I gave a blow-by-blow account of my first date, ending with, "What do you think I should do when he calls me in three weeks?"

Jackie offered a concise, "Dump him. He sounds like a loser."

Kim said, "Well, not so hasty. Everyone God brings to us is in our life for a reason. Maybe it isn't that you are supposed to marry him, but he's in your life for some other purpose. Relax and rest in the relationship. God will show you where it is going."

296

Carol added, "Didn't you say that God told you not to leap at the first guy that you date? Sounds like you already have His answer."

That made me chuckle. Only Carol would remember that. "Thanks, my wonderful PORCH CLUB. You are right, Kim, I should just rest and relax in the relationship. I'm going to trust this one to God! For the first time in my life, I'm not going to compromise my principles in the relationship, but I'm also not going to try to engineer it in the direction I think it should go. Life is meant to be lived, and relationships are a part of it. I'm glad that I'm trusting myself again to not make an idol of affection, to not be desperate to get married again (whether it's to the right man or not), and for valuing my relationship with God above all else. Thanks again, girls. Now let's get Jackie married off!"

൭ ൭ ൭

It was good that I wouldn't hear from Brandon for a few weeks. I was busy at school and needed a cooling off period. So I was surprised when I got a text the following Tuesday at 10 a.m.: *Hi, Sunshine, how's your day?*

Just fine, thank you, I texted back.

I'll be back in town on Saturday and I'm coming to take you to breakfast, I'll be there at 8 a.m. to get you: was the return text.

That won't work. I go to church every day, including Saturday. Besides, I thought you were out of town for three weeks, I texted back.

His next text didn't address my question. *Sunday, then. I'll pick you up at 8 a.m. on Sunday.*

You know I go to church at 8:45 on Sunday. That won't work either.

I know you're just playing hard to get. I thought about sending flowers, will that do it?

I was confused; I also didn't particularly like communicating by text, but while at work, I limited phone calls to emergencies. I texted back: *I have to work. Why don't you call me next week instead?*

Starting at noon, my phone kept buzzing, signaling that another text message was arriving. One after another, texts about how he was thinking about me, he couldn't wait to see me again, and had to have breakfast on Saturday. After the tenth message, I decided that enough was enough, but I wanted a second opinion. I called Matthew and asked if he'd look at the text messages and give me an honest assessment. Was this a bad relationship that I should stop now?

Matthew replied just minutes after I had forwarded him Brandon's texts: *Alarm, Alarm, Alarm. Stop the relationship now. Text me when it's over.*

Matthew was right. I didn't need to pray about this relationship, I needed to end it.

So I texted Brandon back: *This relationship is over. I don't want to see you again.*

Am I being too forward?

I didn't bother to reply, but I was glad that God was protecting me by not letting my heart get carried away with the first guy that asked me out. God had told me to wait until I was out of school and I wasn't finished yet. But I had to wonder if the right answer to my "first date" invitation should have been "No," in the first place.

℘ ℘ ℘

I'd plunged into a wild two weeks of "dating". I hoped it wasn't indicative of today's normal dating scene, but I decided to set it aside and not dwell on it. It was time to concentrate on my schoolwork, defend my research, and hopefully, graduate.

22

My Family

*There is probably no Christian to whom God has not given the
uplifting and blissful experience of genuine Christian community
at least once in her or his life. But in this world such experiences
remain nothing but a gracious extra beyond the daily break of
Christian community life. We are bound together by faith, not by
experience.*

– Dietrich Bonhoeffer

I put Brandon out of my mind and concentrated on my studies. A
Bible verse came to mind: "If anyone will not welcome you or
listen to your words, shake the dust off your feet when you leave
that home or town."

I was content to "shake the dust off my feet" and abandon
the dating idea for a while. I was sure God had a purpose for my
"first date", but only He knew what it was.

I was actually looking forward to defending my
dissertation, as the topic was hot: information technology in
healthcare. I knew I'd be quizzed about my research, but anything
I'd learned in my coursework over the past five years was fair

game too. I had devoted the last two weeks to preparing and was glad when the scheduled day finally arrived.

The day dawned brightly but I was concerned when my right eye started to water as I jumped out of my morning shower. I kept blinking, and each time I blinked, my vision was a little less blurry and my eye watered more. All I could think was, *God don't do this to me today! I've prayed for years that you'd restore my vision and I've had others in our healing prayer ministry praying too. But nothing's worked. The pain has gone away, but my vision hasn't returned. God, I'm ashamed to admit it, but I've moved on. I thought it was my cross to bear so I'd quit praying for my healing, and began praying for other people to be healed. Please don't change my vision today! My dissertation defense is at 11 a.m. this morning! But of course, you already know that. Anyway, please be with me as I do this presentation and answer the committee's questions. If it is your will, please make this be the last step for me and allow my graduation in two weeks during this summer semester.*

With that, I got dressed, grabbed my flashdrive with the slides and headed off to school to rehearse my presentation one more time before 11 a.m. On the way out the door, I grabbed a box of Kleenex, just in case my eye wouldn't stop watering.

On the drive in, I was still pondering why I was in school. I'd originally enrolled because I was trying to be a good wife by encouraging and supporting Curtis. When I was diagnosed with breast cancer, the homework and reading became a diversion; I didn't have to think about being sick all the time. I'd always enjoyed school and was glad that I'd made it this far and I prayed that today would be the last step.

It was 11 a.m. and I was ready. I walked in to face my committee and was pleasantly surprised that my outside reader was able to attend in person. Dr. Jonathan Perlin from HCA chaired the National Health Information Technology Committee and was an expert in my research areas of health information technology and patient safety. I was sure that if he approved my research, the committee would all sign off and I'd be graduating in a few short weeks.

I was calm, but as I talked and blinked, the vision in my right eye continued to clear. My committee members only asked a few questions and then Dr. Rodney Stanley asked me to step out of the room so that everyone could discuss my presentation and my responses to their questions. It was a short fifteen minutes later when Dr. Stanley, my Committee Chairman, invited me back into the room with, "Dr. Nolen, congratulations! It is a unanimous decision of your committee to award you the degree of Ph.D. I'll hand carry your paperwork over to the Graduate School this afternoon so that you can participate in commencement on August 13. I know it's only a few weeks away, but there is no point in delaying as you've fulfilled all the requirements. Congratulations again!"

I couldn't believe it! I'd be graduating in a few weeks and only had some minor formatting to correct on my dissertation. I wish Mom were still alive to share this moment with me, as she was the one who had pushed me to get my master's degree. I still had the picture of Mom and me on my graduation day, back in 1986.

I sent a quick email to my LIFE Group, the PORCH CLUB, Brian, Matthew and Mike telling them the good news. Emails started rolling in, and Matthew called within minutes to share my joy.

Mike called the next day and asked, "When's the commencement ceremony?"

"Well, the official one is August 13, but I'm scheduled to volunteer at a PGA golf tournament in Atlanta that weekend. I'm not planning to attend commencement; they can mail me my diploma."

"No, this is a big deal. You should go to the commencement ceremony; you'll only get a Ph.D. once. You've earned it!"

"I'd consider it, but you know I don't have any family to attend. You can't come; you're taking your new girlfriend to Rosemary Beach that week, aren't you?"

"Yes, we're going to Rosemary Beach that weekend so I can't make it, but surely somebody you know is in town. What about Matthew? I'll bet he'd be delighted to attend."

"Well, we'll see. I've already bought my plane ticket for Atlanta and I hate to back out when I've made a promise to do something. Thanks for the congratulations."

"Let me know what you decide. After I get back from Rosemary Beach maybe we could go out for a drink or dinner to celebrate. Or, pick a date in the fall when Matthew and I can cook and throw a party for you."

Friends shared in my excitement, but I'd already resolved that there wasn't really any point in attending the commencement ceremony itself. I was the only one from the Ph.D. in Public Administration class graduating in the summer, so none of my classmates would be there. I didn't want to go by myself, and I'd planned to relax and meet some interesting people at the golf tournament in Atlanta.

The following Sunday, I sat down at a round table next to Reverend Marcia King for breakfast before the Sunday School class started. Marcia was in my LIFE Group and had called immediately when she'd received my email that I'd passed my defense. Now she announced to the whole table that I'd completed my Ph.D. and would be graduating in a few weeks. She asked, "So, when is the commencement ceremony?"

"Well, commencement is on August 13, but I'm not going. I'd already planned to volunteer at the PGA Men's Golf Tournament in Atlanta that weekend, and I've already bought my airline ticket."

"But you have to go through commencement and walk across the stage! It's a once in a lifetime experience. You can volunteer to work at a golf tournament anytime. You've got to go!"

I paused, swallowed hard, and finally said, "Marcia, I'd really like to go, but I won't know anyone else at graduation and since I don't have any family, there won't be anyone there to cheer for me. There is no point in me going to the commencement ceremony; they'll mail me my diploma."

"I know you don't have any 'blood relatives', but we're your family here at St. George's! I'll go to your commencement and we'll get a group together. Don't ever forget that we're your family now."

I started to tear up. "Really? Oh my. That would be wonderful, thanks so much. I'll let you know what time."

෧ ෧ ෧

Seven people from my "church family" attended my commencement ceremony. They represented countless others who had been encouraging me in my faith for the past three years. They'd prayed for me in good times and bad, and it was glorious to get to celebrate one of the good times with them. Even more special, my LIFE group gave me a celebratory brunch after the ceremony. I could feel God's overwhelming love through the love of these wonderful friends.

Late that evening, I was reflecting on how blessed I was to have found the people at St. George's. I rifled through my bookcases until I found the book, *Life Together* by Dietrich Bonhoeffer. Bonhoeffer wrote, "God has placed us in common life with other Christians and we learn what it means to have, 'Brothers and sisters…in the Lord (Phil. 1:14).' One is a brother or sister to another only through Jesus Christ. Each has been redeemed by Christ, absolved from sin, and called to faith and eternal life. The community consists solely in what Jesus Christ has done for us and to us. The fact that we are brothers and sisters only through Jesus Christ is of immeasurable significance. I have community with others and will continue to have it only through Jesus Christ."

Bonhoeffer continues, "The more genuine and the deeper our community becomes, the more everything else between us will recede, and the more clearly and purely will Jesus Christ and

303

his work become the one and only thing that is alive between us. We have one another only through Christ, but through Christ we really do have one another. We have one another completely and for all eternity."

I prayed that I would keep this wisdom forever, that I was "good enough", that God loved me, and that I would be able to love others in the same way He loved me. The people of St. George's had shown me what God's love looks like every day. What wonderful examples to remind me how to live out God's words!

৬৯ ৬৯ ৬৯

With graduation over, I was free to devote my attention to my first trip to the Holy Land. During my prayer time, I became more convicted about our healing prayer ministry. I'd been part of the prayer team since the fall of 2008, and was often scheduled for the 8:45 a.m. service on Sundays. I was feeling more than a nudge that this was something that God was calling me to do, not just something that I wanted to do.

I met with Reverend Leigh one Friday afternoon in September to tell him about the visions I'd been having of many people coming forward for healing prayer, and not everyone desiring healing prayer was a member at St. George's. I was heartened to hear that Leigh had also felt a call from the Holy Spirit to expand the ministry and add a monthly evening healing service. I told him that I wanted to continue to pray for others and serve in whatever capacity I was needed for the ministry.

Before the September evening healing service, Leigh asked the healing prayer ministry team to assemble to share any needs or stories with each other. I hadn't planned to share, but as Leigh asked for volunteers, I felt my hand going up into the air.

"Some of you, but not all of you, know that I just finished my Ph.D. degree. Many of you have been praying for my success at school and I want to thank you for your prayers and encouragement. I'd like to share another story with you, too. I was diagnosed with breast cancer in 2006 and had an injury to my right eye during my cancer treatment, which caused blurry vision. That was in May 2007, and although the pain subsided after the first few months, I haven't been able to see clearly since then.

"It has gone on for so long that I decided it was my 'cross to bear', as my mother would have said, sort of like the thorn in Paul's side that he talks about in his letter to the Corinthians. I had even stopped praying for healing, as I felt I needed to move on to praying about other things, and for other people. But after four-and-a-half years, my eye started watering on the morning of my dissertation defense. That was a few weeks ago, and it has gotten better and better ever since. I still don't have perfect 20/20 vision, but I don't feel like I'm looking through cheesecloth anymore. The improvement has to be a miracle, since the doctors could never find a reason that I couldn't see!"

I was scheduled to read the Epistle that night, and I realized how good it was to be able to see clearly again. Some people might have called it an "unlikely event", but I was comfortable with calling it a "miracle", as I know how much I'd suffered and for how long. I vowed that night that I would volunteer at each monthly evening healing service and encourage others to attend. It was just like the early church, where Jesus did many miracles and "the crowds were amazed". On my monthly call with The PORCH CLUB, I'd shared the story of my renewed vision and my vow to devote my energies to our healing prayer ministry. The PORCH CLUB understood, because they had all experienced "miracles" in their lives, too.

ಆ ಆ ಆ

The trip to the Holy Land was inspiring and reinforced my faith, but there were so many sites to see and so little time. I blogged each day and offered to be the "official" photographer for the trip, delighted to see Israel through my camera lens. With over one thousand photographs, I had plenty to do over the Thanksgiving holiday. It was wonderful to relive our visits to healing places, such as where Jesus raised Lazarus from the dead, and the pool at Bethsaida where the lame man was healed.

One spot stuck out in my mind: the place at Caesarea Maritima where St. Paul was imprisoned. When we were there, Leigh Spruill had given us a challenge. "So, when you get home, are you going to be like St. Paul, who couldn't wait to share the good news with others, or will you be like Governor Felix, who heard Paul's preaching about righteousness, self-control and judgment, but never did anything about what he heard?"

It was another long plane ride back home from the Holy Land, but it was clear that God was asking me to write and take photographs, sharing His beautiful world with others. I was also convicted that God would use me to bring words of comfort to people who are in need of healing. I was trusting that God would bless me with the resources and skills that I needed, to do what He asked me to do.

23

Healing

The whole life of a Good Christian is a holy desire.

– St. Augustine

Sarah Kerr and I spent the plane ride back to Nashville talking about our upcoming class, "Holy Desires: Creating Redemptive Relationships". As we were going over the class materials on my iPad, I said, "You know, Sarah, your words from last summer really helped me. You'd mentioned that you hadn't been kissed in three years, and well, neither had I. But you reminded me that I needed to stay focused on my relationship with God, and that it was the most important thing. I realize that no human is capable of love like that. We can make wise choices in a marriage relationship, but we'll never achieve the perfect love that we receive from God. This trip to the Holy Land made me think how I can show God that I love Him, too. God is calling me to be more involved in our healing prayer ministry and I'd like you to pray for discernment for me."

"Of course I will! Aren't you scheduled to serve in the November evening healing service?" Sarah asked.

"Yes, and I've volunteered to serve in the special December healing prayer service, "Silent Night", in a few weeks. It is such a wonderful service to have right before Christmas, particularly for people who have lost loved ones during the year. I noticed last year that a lot of people who attended weren't even members of St. George's. I hope a lot of people from the community come again this year. I'm going to invite some friends, too."

"Thanks for being a member of the ministry team. I'll pray that God shows you how best to use your gifts in healing prayer."

℘ ℘ ℘

It was another great Christmas, serving with Dru at the Christmas Eve service. I felt my focus shifting too. I was no longer sad that I didn't have any family. In fact, my church family was my family! I had noticed another change as well. In praying for others, my needs seemed very small in comparison. Maybe this was why God commanded us to love our neighbors, so that we would center our attention on them instead of being so self-centered and focusing only on ourselves. I was looking forward to a new year, with no school and a renewed interest in serving God.

℘ ℘ ℘

The message arrived on January 13, 2012, just as I was going to bed. It came through the email address posted on my blog, and the subject line said, "HOWDY!" All I could see on my phone was the first line of the email, but something made me read it that night, rather than waiting until morning.

Hi Agatha,

You don't know me because I don't go to church at St. George's, but I've been reading your blog for a number of months, ever since a friend sent me the link. You'd invited everyone to come to your church for the SILENT NIGHT service and I thought, "Why not? I've had a lot of things happen to me this year and it would be good to hear some quiet music." So I went and sat in your church. It wasn't until they asked anyone who was interested in healing prayer to come forward that I saw your nametag and recognized you from the photo on your blog.

There was a long line of people already in line for you and the female priest, but I felt compelled to go forward. I am dropping this note to you to tell you how much I appreciate your blog, but also to thank you for your prayers for me that night. I awoke tonight from a deep sleep and the darkness has lifted.

The oppression has lasted seven years. I suffered greatly to know for myself the Power of Darkness, which I totally underestimated. However, even in sin, Christ in me could withstand multitudes and anything the enemy threw at me as a result of my curiosity to know, even when I already knew better. So you can get an idea of the intensity, I will let you know there is an unnatural crack in the plaster on the ceiling of my bedroom. That happened one night when something very, very large landed on my house and came into my room. Really the stuff of nightmares, but it all has purpose. I never gave over, and Christ was with me and did not allow death, but did allow me to suffer because I willfully walked outside his Glory.

I grew up in the Church, went to Christian Schools, and was taught Spiritual Warfare at the age of 17 by a former Witch who had become a Christian. Suffice it to say, everything I was taught then is just as relevant today, but now I have hope, purpose, and am being restored through the Grace and Power of Christ. Pagans used to let me know they could see a ring of fire around me in the spirit. The fire is back in my eyes and God will soon again surround me with His Holy Fire. I've been waiting for this season all my life.

God has had mercy on me because I have asked for those He loves to pray, specifically for me. God has heard the prayers you offered up for me (I am prompted by His spirit to tell you). Please continue to lift me up. You can imagine the ripple it causes when one of Christ's followers almost slips off the ledge of eternity, then repents and comes back to the Father. The enemy is not happy with me at all. I did learn from that perspective it has very little to do with us and everything to do with fighting God Almighty.

The bolder I get to Testify, with love and discretion, the more intense the Battle will become. However, this time around it is all about making the biggest dent in life for the Kingdom of God while I still walk on this earth. And it will be in Spirit and Truth. You are a Prophetess (I'm certain you already know this). God is pouring out his Spirit upon the face of the earth in preparation for the change that will be here before we know it. I don't have to go into detail here, it's pretty obvious to most Christians right now.

Thanks for letting me freestyle some thoughts. Your blog is right on time for me. It's like a Divine Signature. LOL I just scrolled down and saw the verse from Corinthians. Indeed, God is in control!

Blessing and Peace through Christ.

I thought back a few weeks and tried to picture the people we prayed for that night. It didn't matter who it was, they had been relieved of their burden when we prayed for them. The verse from 1 Corinthians 10:13 was the one that I had posted on my blog: "No temptation has overtaken you that is not common to man. God is faithful, and He will not let you be tempted beyond your ability, but with the temptation He will also provide the way of escape, that you may be able to endure it."

I had a connection with someone who I didn't know: we both knew that God is faithful and that He heals us.

After I'd read the email three more times, I understood that I was called to devote my spiritual gifts to sharing my experiences of healing, and to pray for others to be healed.

24

Words, Photos, and Prayer

There is a stage in the spiritual life in which we find God in ourselves—this presence is a created effect of His love. It is a gift of His, to us.

— Thomas Merton

Two of my photographs were selected for the Art Salon, which opened the 2012 C3:Christ:Church:Culture Conference. It was the perfect evening with wine, food and jazz as a backdrop for the art. I was pleased that people were stopping to ask questions about the photographs and I was eager to share my renewed passion. I'd already talked with a dozen people when a gentleman stopped and commented, "These are great photographs! How did you get the idea for them?"

I introduced myself and read his nametag: Colin, from Charlotte, North Carolina.

"Actually, I'm a little embarrassed to tell you that I had just bought this new Nikon camera and was headed out to take pictures of fireworks on the 3rd of July last year. I'd never tried to take any fireworks photos, but I'd read online and I knew that I needed to use the BULB setting on my camera to leave the shutter open an extended period of time. I was practicing with the setting and decided to take a series of photographs of this six-foot wooden crucifix that I have hanging in my stairwell. I bought it when I lived in San Antonio, and moved it to Nashville when I came here in 2003. It's really a lovely piece of art, but I was curious to see how it would photograph under different light exposures.

"As I said, that wasn't my intent. I admit that I was just trying to learn the shutter setting on my camera and this six-foot tall crucifix hanging in my stairwell was a good object for a comparative series. I was in awe when I saw the eight photographs on my computer after I downloaded them. I allowed in more light for each successive exposure, leaving the shutter open first for one second and working my way through longer exposures. I had no idea what the pictures would be like until I popped the disk into my computer. These two photos were in the middle of the eight; the first with a clearly defined crucified Christ, and then the second with only Christ's head, hands and heart barely visible.

"I remember staring in awe at the two photos side by side. Varying the amount of light coming into the camera lens resulted in a transition from the reality that my eyes see, to the perception that my heart feels. Our faith is the same. When we allow Christ's light to come into our life, our faith moves to a new dimension with the Holy Spirit. When we are abrupt and impatient, we have little time for spiritual disciplines like Scripture reading and prayer, but when we sit quietly and patiently, we leave our 'shutter' open for extended timeframes. That is when we are drenched in the light of Christ, and clearly feel His Spirit in our life. When we neglect our faith, we see only what our eyes see, but when we are bathed in Christ's light, we see what our hearts feel, the Spirit of Christ.

"I'm definitely an amateur photographer, but like Ansel Adams says, 'Sometimes I do get to places just when God's ready to have someone click the shutter.'"

Colin laughed heartily and said, "Hey, can you grab a cup of coffee, or a glass of wine after the salon tonight? I'd like to hear more about those fireworks photographs, too."

"Sure, we're closing the art show around 9 p.m. I'll look for you."

୧୭ ୧୭ ୧୭

Colin stopped by my photographs at exactly 9 p.m., and we headed to J. Alexander's on White Bridge Road. We ordered wine and began to share stories about our lives. Colin was a music minister in a small Episcopal Church outside of Charlotte, where he had moved from California three years ago. He'd been divorced almost four years and his three children all went to colleges on the East Coast. He'd grown up in the Carolinas, so the Southeast was really his home, and he was glad to be nearer to his kids.

I never know how much detail to go into when I meet someone new. When you've lived for over fifty years, some things that seemed so important when they happened end up fading into distant memories. I hated to share negative events in my life, but rattling on about only the good things seemed like self-centered bragging.

Matthew said that I needed an "elevator speech" for my blog: a three-minute introduction that would tell people just enough to get them interested and read more. I chuckled as I started to share my story with Colin: this is me, in three minutes or less.

"I grew up in Upstate New York, went to college in Oklahoma, spent ten years in San Antonio and moved to Nashville in 2003. My life was pretty predictable, with work and taking care of my family, and then everything changed in an instant. In 2006, I was diagnosed with breast cancer."

I saw the look on Colin's face when I said 'cancer', but I decided to plunge forward with my story.

313

"I'd spent the year before being angry with God. The day I received the diagnosis, I was pretty frantic and felt like I had nowhere to turn. As I was falling asleep that evening, I was visited by a presence that I believe was Christ. He asked me a question, 'Was I willing to die for Him?'. I said yes, and my life has been forever changed.

"Since then I've joined St. George's, go to church every morning, and travel to South Africa on mission trips. Because of the healing in my life, I'm drawn to our healing prayer ministry. God has asked me to share glimpses of His kingdom through a blog where I post stories, photographs, and prayers. I hope that my blog posts will encourage others and give them hope. I've been transformed since my cancer diagnosis. Even my view of God has changed. I used to fear His punishment, but now I see Him as a loving God, and I want to live my life so that it pleases Him. Well, that's the short version of my story."

I paused. I couldn't believe I had just told a stranger about my life and faith in less than three minutes. *What if he thought I was crazy, particularly about having a conversation with Christ?*

I searched his eyes to judge his reaction, but he responded without hesitation. "Thank you for sharing your story with me. I've had times in my life when God felt distant. But then sometimes, I feel like he is in the same room with me. It's important that we tell our stories and see how we fit in God's story, too."

I immediately relaxed and said, "Thanks for understanding. I know that it's odd to talk about a visit from Christ within the first twenty minutes of meeting someone, but it was a turning point for me. I mark it as the moment when my new life began."

"I feel like I know a lot about you already," Colin said, "We have many things in common. I leave in six weeks to spend a year in Cape Town. I'll be helping an organization there establish music ministries for youth in the Anglican churches. I've only been to South Africa once, when I went on a mission trip between college semesters, but I fell in love with the country and the people. I've always wanted to go back when this opportunity came up for me to help there."

"Really? That is a coincidence. I'll be there next March on my fifth trip. Archbishop Desmond Tutu is my hero. I've met him twice at the cathedral in Cape Town, and the last time I was there he signed two books for me. What he did under apartheid and with the Truth and Reconciliation Commission has really inspired me. Forgiveness and reconciliation are the keys to all relationships, and I learned about them in South Africa. What about you, who's your hero?"

Colin said, "That's easy; it's Mother Teresa. After my experience in Africa when I was in college, I came back to the States and then read about Mother Teresa's selfless love in caring for the poor in India. I wanted to be able to detach myself from worldly possessions and serve the poor, too.

"I grew up with a stern father who I was always trying to please, but I was never quite good enough. He wanted me to go to medical school like my older brother, but I love music. So I disappointed him when I changed my major from chemistry to music in my junior year and applied for a scholarship to Julliard. I planned to be a concert pianist, but then I realized how much I love to teach. I'm sure it was another disappointment for Dad, since musicians and teachers don't make the kind of money that doctors do.

"After graduation, I found a faculty appointment at a small university, but it wasn't enough. I'll admit it wasn't just about pleasing my Dad, though. I got trapped into thinking that I deserved more out of life, too. In many ways I was a good person, but not for the right reasons. It was my divorce that was the turning point for me. I had to give up my former life and live for God's glory instead of mine. I'm still learning. In fact, I'll be learning forever."

I took a deep breath. Colin had snatched the words from inside my head and spoken them back to me. I finally volunteered, "I'm writing a book. It's just a rough outline right now, but the title of the book is *Chasing My Father*. As I've been writing, I've been thinking about my view of God. I learned to pray at an early age, but God was distant, and a disciplinarian.

"For twenty-five years, I tried to get my head wrapped around Jesus. It was a futile attempt on my part, as I realized that I would never understand everything in the Bible and became discouraged. In 2009, I heard a sermon by Reverend Leigh Spruill, when he talked about our efforts to please God. At the end, he said 'Quit trying so hard', and then he just walked away from the pulpit.

"I was stunned. He'd said the words directly to me. I was trying too hard in too many ways: to please my father, even though he had already passed away; to please the people in my life; and to please the invisible judge that I heard in my head. I thought that if I tried harder, prayed harder, and hung around with better people, God would like me more, and my life would be easier.

"It took me months to process those four short words, 'Quit trying so hard', but I grew to understand that Christ died for us and washed away all those sins and imperfections in our lives. We don't have to earn God's love because it is freely given. He will never abandon us and his love is perfect in our lives."

"I like that, 'quit trying so hard'. They are certainly words to live by," Colin said thoughtfully.

"I hate to change the subject, but I want to thank you for taking the time to stop and talk to me about my photographs tonight," I said.

"They are really very good. Did you major in art in college?"

"No, but I do enjoy art. I've just taken up photography again and I have a friend, Matthew who is an artist and has helped me a lot. One evening we were discussing creativity and he told me about a researcher named Brené Brown. She says that we numb ourselves with overwork, buying things, overeating, or addictions, and in many cases it's an attempt to cover up our fears of being found out. Dr. Brown said, "the thing that most hinders our creativity is our inability to be vulnerable.

"I'm not sure I understand it all yet, but the more I've been able to open up and accept God's love, grace and mercy, the more I'm starting to see God's beauty all around me. It's no longer about me feeling that if I take a bad photograph I'll be ridiculed; it's all part of living. There is tremendous freedom in being vulnerable and it also gives me the freedom to be creative. My creativity is no longer something to be judged by the world, because I'm doing it for God's glory. I'm still learning about vulnerability, but one evening Matthew said, 'Stop studying so many books. Go out and shoot pictures. God will show you what he wants you to do.' I can feel God's pleasure when I'm taking photographs and writing."

I didn't want the evening to end, but it was getting late. "I'm sorry I've used up all the conversation with my story. It's getting late and we should go. The conference starts at 7:30 a.m. tomorrow."

Colin walked me to my car and kissed me sweetly on the cheek, "Good night. See you tomorrow."

"Yes. Pleased to meet you, Colin."

ربى ربى ربى

I saw Colin briefly in conference workshops and at lunch over the next two days. At the end of the last session, he found me in the hallway collecting conference evaluations.

"I really enjoyed meeting you and am sorry that we didn't get to talk more. Can I call you when I get home to North Carolina? I'd like to see you again."

"Sure. I'd love to hear more about you and your trip to South Africa."

With that, Colin was gone.

ربى ربى ربى

It was a week later when we first talked again. He wanted to come for a visit but his schedule was too busy. We managed to talk at least every other day for a few minutes, and shared more and more of our past histories, our dreams, and our desires. I knew that this wasn't just an ordinary man that I had met, but one who was willing to devote his life to pleasing God.

Colin sent a dozen red roses on his last day in the United States, along with a card: I'll be thinking about you and have another dozen red roses waiting for you when you visit me in Cape Town next March. Blessings, Colin.

This was so different from my previous relationships. I wasn't trying to manipulate him into liking me, or desperate for him to fall in love with me. I liked Colin a lot and enjoyed our conversations, but I was content to let God act. What path our relationship traveled would be God's will and not mine.

ೲ ೲ ೲ

There was time for one more PORCH CLUB meeting before my 40th high school reunion in New York in July. I couldn't wait to tell the girls about Colin.

25

The PORCH CLUB Meets Again

Father, if you are willing, take this cup from me; yet not my will, but yours be done.

– Luke 22:42

It was the 12th bi-annual meeting of the PORCH CLUB, this time at Kim's house in Jacksonville, Florida. The first week of May was perfect for gorgeous sunsets and hot days, when we could relax on the beach and swap stories.

We had so much to get caught up on; it was hard to know where to start. Carol shared stories of her job interviews and how she decided to take a job in Tulsa. Carol's husband liked to hunt and fish, so the areas around Tulsa would be ideal. Kim was traveling a lot as the corporate director of HIM for a large hospital system, and her children were doing well in school. Kim's daughter was graduating with a master's degree in just a few weeks. Kim traveled frequently to Kentucky to see her parents, but just hearing Kim talk about Florida, you can tell that she is a beach person at heart.

Jackie was coming up on one year of wedded bliss. She was doing a lot of traveling for her consulting job, and was still enjoying both her work and married life. Her daughter had just enrolled in a graduate program in Philadelphia and Jackie had just returned from settling her in at her new school. Kim and Jackie were sure proud of their offspring, as well they should be.

Jackie prompted, "Well, you're the only one that's still single. Tell us about your love life."

"Well, you remember Matthew from church, don't you? Jackie, you met him at Thanksgiving a few years ago when we had the six international students for dinner."

"Sure. I remember Matthew, very engaging and really good-looking."

"Well, he met this girl last year and got engaged right before Christmas. They got married in April at her farm in Strawberry Plains, Tennessee. I was thrilled because I got to serve wine during the Eucharist at their wedding ceremony. Reverend Malone Gilliam traveled with us and did the ceremony outdoors, and it such an honor for me to participate. Jennifer is just wonderful!"

Carol asked, "I'm sorry. Aren't you just a little bit jealous? You spoke of Matthew often. Although you always said that you were 'just friends', I suspected that there was more to the relationship."

"I wasn't jealous at all. I would have been in the past, but now I want the best for others, instead of just thinking about me all the time. I was thrilled when Matthew told me that he and Jennifer were engaged. I've learned that it is just as important to have friends in your life. Matthew is a great friend and has taught me a lot. Our friendship has always been based on mutual trust and affection. We both felt called to help each other with our faith in different ways.

"He taught me how easy it is to relax around a guy who loves the Lord first and doesn't have a 'secret agenda' in a relationship. In the past I'd always taken advantage of guys when I met them. Trying to get them to like me in a romantic way, or I didn't want much to do with them. I used to thrive on sexual tension and if I couldn't use it to manipulate a man, I was uncomfortable. Matthew and Brian both showed me that it is possible to be friends in Christ, honoring each other and bolstering each other's strengths instead of competing or running each other down. They are wonderful examples because they are very compassionate and really care about people.

"It was relaxing to have Brian and Matthew as friends and it allowed me to 'quit trying so hard', and let God work in my life. I've shared with you about the healing prayer ministry that I've been involved in since 2008. It's been almost four years now and I've been privileged to pray for a lot of people and have them pray for me.

"What I've learned in just the last year is that when I pray for other people, I quit focusing on 'poor little me' and what is going on in my life, and instead I focus on the needs of others. Sometimes when I pray for people it spurs me into other actions. I've given money to people in need, gone for coffee when people have a story that needs to be told, and just listened and cried with people who have faced the death of a loved one. It is hard to be miserable when you are focused on serving others.

"The other thing that happens when I am a healing prayer minister is that I focus my attention on getting out of the way and letting the Holy Spirit speak. I picture the Holy Spirit coming down to use me for prayer and to communicate the words that are needed in someone else's life. It is amazing, but the Holy Spirit drowns out all the voices from Satan and his legions that used to be ever present in my head.

"It took me a long time of going to church every day, listening to great sermons, and lots of prayer before I really believed that God loves me. I know that sounds crazy because we all grow up singing, 'Jesus loves me, this I know, 'cause the Bible tells me so.' In my case, they were just words on a piece of paper until a few years ago. When I started really believing that someone so wonderful as Jesus could love me, a sinner, it has made all the difference in my life.

"The third thing I've experienced through healing prayer is actual healing in my life and in the lives of others. It is amazing the stories from St. George's of physical, emotional and spiritual healing. I've regained eyesight in my right eye, and it was just a few years ago when I had severe back pain that required physical therapy. I had dozens of people praying for me and now my back is much better.

"It warms my heart to know that people are calling on their relationship with God to try to help me. I know that I told you all of what happened two summers ago with my breast biopsy. You, my LIFE group and many friends were all praying for me. Although I am grateful that the spots were all benign, the most amazing thing was how peaceful and calm I was through the whole ordeal, totally different from when I was first diagnosed with cancer. It was because people were praying for me that I was willing to accept God's will in my life. If He needs me to have cancer again, I'm okay. You three are a part of that human chain that surrounds me with prayers and love. I am forever grateful for your friendship and your prayers."

Carol said, "We will always be there for each other. No matter what happens, we can count on our friendship and faith to see us through."

Jackie said, "Didn't you tell us on your first trip to South Africa that someone asked you if you were a priest? Have you ever considered it? You certainly sound like you have the heart for it now."

"That's a nice thought and I've asked God that very question. The answer keeps coming back to me: 'No. I need you to sit in the pews and welcome visitors. Every baptized person is a 'minister'; you don't have to go to seminary to carry out God's plan. You are doing exactly what I've asked you to do, and I am well pleased.'"

"Okay," Kim said, "now back to the romantic interests. What's going on with Brian?"

"Okay, guys. Again, we are just good friends. I value his friendship and am inspired to learn from him, but that's all. No romance there."

Carol chimed in, "You seem very committed to your blog tagline of always putting God first and then letting the relationships flow from that first love. So, let's see, your divorce was in 2008 and this is 2012. Four years and no romantic interests at all?"

"Well," I started to stammer a little and there was a bit of a blush in my cheeks. "I want to tell you a story about a friend of mine and then one more story about me.

"Okay, okay... sounds good; let's hear it!" Kim said.

"Remember I told you about Sarah Kerr, the young female priest that came to St. George's two years ago, right after the flood? She's just wonderful, beautiful and Spirit-filled. Well we taught a class together this spring called *Holy Desires*. I think I sent you all an email with copies of the handouts."

"Yes, I remember that," Kim replied, "You said that you had good attendance and the class went well."

"Yes, it did. But that isn't the story. I talked with Sarah when we were planning the class, and she told me that she'd last dated a guy in seminary, but hadn't dated anyone else in over three years. I even remarked that it must be hard for a female priest to get a date. Well, she told me to be patient and wait for God to send the right guy, that chasing guys because they were 'shy' just wasn't the right thing to do. She said that if a guy had a heart for God and was in constant dialogue with him, God would tell him which girl was the right one. God doesn't need help from the female species to help the process along.

"Here's the story: A wonderful guy who attends St. George's heard Sarah preach and thought she was great. He studied her from afar for quite some time but never felt he could ask her out, since she was a priest. After a year, with some encouragement from trusted family and friends who believed they would be a good match, he asked her out, and the rest is history! Their first "date" lasted three hours over a cup of coffee, and within four months they were engaged! They both truly believe that God created them to be each other's life partner. They've just set the date and will be married in September. I am so thrilled for her! She is just wonderful and he is a great guy too.

"I guess I always chased guys and thought that if I hung around long enough I'd wear them down and they'd marry me. That's truly not what God has in mind. Sarah and Dan are the perfect example of how beautiful it is when they each have a relationship with God, and then they ask for God's direction in their relationship. I can't wait to dance at their wedding!"

"That is a wonderful story and I'm glad for your friends that God put them together," Kim said, smiling, "But you said there was a story about you."

"Well, I've met a man who sees God just the way I do."

"What?" Jackie complained. "We had to listen to all this to get to the juicy part of the story? Who's the guy?"

"Well, he's a wonderful man I met at the C3 Conference in Nashville back in early March. He's from North Carolina and a music minister. You know how much I love music."

"Great! So, you've been commuting back and forth? Where in North Carolina does he live?"

"No, I haven't been commuting. I knew up front that it was going to be a long distance relationship. He left three weeks ago for South Africa; he's helping to establish some youth music programs in the Anglican churches in Cape Town. He'll be there at least a year, maybe longer."

"Now, that's a real long distance relationship! But isn't Cape Town one of the places that you visit when you go on your mission trips with your church?"

"Yes, we do spend three or four days there. I'm going next March and I've already made plans to see Colin," I said, my eyes twinkling.

"What? You are already talking about seeing him a year from now? Tell us more. Is it serious?"

"Well, we met at the conference when he came up to talk with me about my photography. We had a glass of wine later that night and it was amazing that we have so much in common. Not necessarily our backgrounds, but how we view God and our responsibilities to serve others by loving our neighbors. You know that we've talked about the concept of different personality types, the STRICT FATHER versus the NURTURING PARENT? Well, I've had a lot of friends over the years and as I think back, each one falls into one of those two categories, both men and women.

"I would say that Matthew and Brian have been my two closest male friends who are the NURTURING PARENT type. I realized that I am at ease when I am with them. They are never condemning or critical. Even when they question me about a behavior or comment, they do it in a discerning way, like someone who wants to me to think through things, not just to condemn, disgrace or belittle me.

"I feel that way when I read about Jesus. In the Gospel of John, I like the story about the woman at the well who is the adulterer. Jesus walks up and first asks her for a glass of water. Now, Jesus knows full well what she's been up to, and all the men she's slept with. It would have been easy for Jesus to say, 'Woman, you are wicked and have used your beauty to entice men into sin. You've hurt a lot of people along the way, and you should be ashamed of yourself. You need to try harder to be a better person and then your life will be better'."

Kim said, "Wait a second. I don't remember that in the Gospel of John; in fact, I don't remember it anywhere in the Bible."

I replied, "Exactly. You won't find it because that isn't the way it happened. Jesus didn't say, 'You are wicked and despicable and my Father hates you.' Instead, he says, 'I am the living water. Let me show you a better way.' Jesus invites her to share in a better life with him.

"I think that Jesus would be classified as a NURTURING PARENT. He wasn't just meek and mild, saying, 'Don't worry, everything will just work out', and he never belittled anyone who was reaching out in faith to him."

"Okay, does this somehow relate to meeting Colin?" Carol reminded me.

"Oh. Sorry. We had a glass of wine that night and we talked until late into the evening. I am sure that he is a NURTURING PARENT type too. When I asked him who his mentor is, he replied, 'Mother Teresa'. That's something for an Episcopalian to look up to a Catholic who hasn't even been made a saint yet! I asked him why, and he answered: 'Mother Teresa is all about serving others, putting your wants, and even your needs, on the back burner when God asks you to do something. Mother Teresa would look at the dirt and grime in someone's life and love them anyway. She is an incredible example to us of always giving to help others.'"

"And a guy said this?" Jackie asked.

"Yes, unprompted. I never once got the feeling that he was just saying words to impress me. Remember my story about my first date? This was totally different."

"So, I want to hear more about Colin," Jackie said.

"Well, he's tall and handsome. We've talked every week on SKYPE since he got to Cape Town. I admire him so much for giving up all his comforts here in the States to go where God has asked him to go. He had a good job with a small church outside of Charlotte, but he's working as a volunteer missionary now. During his last SKYPE call he told me that he was amazed at how little it takes to make him content. As long as he has his faith and trusts God, he is very comfortable with few 'creature comforts'. And, he misses me."

"So, what happens next?" It was Carol's turn to prompt the story.

"Well, when we are on SKYPE, he always closes our conversation with prayer, praying that God will show us where our relationship is going. Perhaps we will remain as good friends who help each other in life to stay close to God. Perhaps it is a different relationship that may lead to marriage. But we pray together that God will show him the answer to the relationship and then he will share that with me.

"Of course, I pray to God to show me about the relationship, too, but I'm not getting too far ahead of myself this time. Colin needs to take the lead. It's between Colin and God first, just like with Sarah's future husband. So we pray together on every call. I'm comfortable that I have a wonderful new friend and am content to have the relationship stay there. We all need good friends to help us through life.

"Colin always prays for us to be protected from our temptations. I've shared my past with him, so he prays that angels will surround me and keep me from being tempted in romantic or sexual relationships with men. Colin (and God, for that matter!) knows that it has been a huge part of my life and that I need constant protection.

"For Colin, we pray that he will be protected from pride. He's shared that he gets angry and prideful when people confront him. He's a real people-pleaser, too, and has a hard time saying no. He thinks saying no means a failure on his part, so he's gotten involved in things in the past that he shouldn't have. We pray for protection for Colin when he is around people who provoke him to anger, or those who he wants to please. I'm glad to offer up prayers for him just as he is for me. The other thing that I admire is his willingness to teach me and share his relationship with God."

"What do you mean by, '...share his relationship with God'?"

"He reads his Bible and attends church regularly. Three or four times a week, I'll get an email or text message with a Bible verse, a note of encouragement, or sometimes a YouTube music video that has inspired him. Then when we talk over the computer, he can't wait to share a new revelation. I really need someone to teach me, and it's part of being the spiritual leader of a family. I want a guy that not only prays about decisions in the relationship, but also teaches me more about loving God.

"Ladies, there is one other thing that I want to share because it is so different with Colin. It is really the first time in a romantic relationship that I have felt that I should be obedient and submissive. Now, now, I don't want you to think that I am a doormat and just fall for anything Colin says. But the Bible does instruct us that the man is the spiritual leader of the family. I've made that mistake too many times thinking that my faith was so strong that 'he' didn't need to have a strong faith. Wrong! Colin is committed to following God's will, but we agree that one person needs to lead and one needs to follow in a relationship. So this is the first time that I've met a man that I willingly yield to his authority and not try to take command of his life."

My eyes started to twinkle again as I continued. "There is one exception. I speak up when he is not acting like Jesus. I do so lovingly and I'm not trying to condemn, but as Christians we are here to help each other. This freedom has helped me, too. When Colin tries to gently correct me, I don't get defensive with him and get my hackles up. Instead I know that he is coming from a place of love for God, and for me. Criticism isn't as harsh when it is done with love. I asked him to read one of my blogs so he would understand where I was coming from; it's the story of Abigail in 1 Samuel 25:

Obedience to God, not Man

The word of God teaches us that wives should submit to the authority of their husbands, just as husbands should submit to Christ. Much has been written and more discussed how this plays out day-to-day. Is there ever a time when wives shouldn't be obedient to their husbands? This is one of the hardest questions we face as Christian women.

In 1 Samuel 25 we meet *Abigail, the wife of Nabal*. She was intelligent, discerning and beautiful and a foil for her husband, whose name means, "fool". King David and his men protected the flocks of Nabal, but Nabal wasn't appropriately appreciative, in fact he rebuffed David's men when they came for a visit. Abigail saw what happened and knew that her husband and the entire household would be killed when word got back to David. Abigail took it upon herself to prepare a peace offering and to make amends.

John MacArthur says "knowing the Lord's choice of David, Abigail recognized the consequences...by her actions, she chose to obey God rather than man, as a wife may sometimes need to do." In Acts 5:29 we hear Peter and the apostles answering the high priest's accusations: "We must obey God rather than men."

Abigail disobeyed her husband when his actions were not motivated by God, but by his own humanness.

How should modern women respond if faced with a similar situation? *They should ask for God's guidance.* Not a time for blind obedience, but a dialogue with God about His will.

Blessings that you will first consult with God in all your words and actions and trust Him for guidance.

"Well, what did Colin say about the story?" Carol asked.

"He said that it all started with a man being obedient to God."

Kim agreed, "I think it is helpful when you can start a relationship with some common understanding, like this one on being obedient."

329

"So, there you have it. I don't know where this relationship with Colin is going, but I am content to let God be in control. I trust Him completely."

Jackie said, "I've got one more question; this is a tough one. So, now you've found someone that you are attracted to; you see God the same way, and your relationship seems to be moving along really well. What happens when he wants to have sex? You've told us over and over again, and even written on your blog how much you've changed and that you are reserving sex for marriage only. Would that still be true if you were engaged? Wouldn't you have sex then? What if it wasn't any good and you were disappointed? Don't you need to find that out before you get married?"

I had to laugh. "This is too funny! You are one of at least a half dozen people who have asked me that question, almost all women! *'Don't you need to know if you are compatible sexually before you decide to get married?'* is the sixty-four-million-dollar question in today's society. Our society really does have an unhealthy fascination on sex. Don't get me wrong: sex and intimacy are important in a marriage, but they aren't the only things. I'm even working on a story for my blog, "Lies that Satan told me about sex"; it seems to be a popular topic these day."

Kim said, "Give us the short version."

"I didn't realize at first that it was really Satan talking. When I turned eighteen in 1972, it was a 'liberating' time for women. I was just starting college and almost every girl I knew was on the Pill, and many of us were having affairs with married men. But it was Satan that filled my head with things like:

If you don't have sex with him, he'll think you're 'frigid' and quit going out with you.

Women need to be as liberated as men have always been; women should enjoy sex without having to commit to a long-term relationship.

330

When you are single and have sex with a married man, it is his sin and not yours.

If you don't want sex all the time, your spouse will have an affair, or leave you for a woman who does.

All men care about is sex, they don't really want a woman they can relate to on an intellectual, emotional, or spiritual level."

I continued, "When you start hearing those voices in your head, it clouds how you act in relationships. I'd go after the 'bad boy' type, like a married man, thinking that his wife didn't love him and that if he fell for me, he would be reformed and be a 'nice guy'. There is a part of every woman that is a 'rescuer'. We just know that with our love, our guy will be transformed and faithful.

"As women in the 1970s we were told that we have a lot more power than we actually do. I don't have the power to transform anyone; that is the job of the Holy Spirit. I can love people as my neighbor, but I don't have to give my heart away to men who are going to be bad for me and harm my relationship with God. At the same time, I need to be the kind of woman that won't harm his relationship with God, either.

"Back to your original question on testing out your sexual compatibility before you are married, here's my answer: 'I'm trusting God completely in my whole life, including the most intimate parts. God would not speak to a man and then to me about marriage unless it was His will. And if it is His will, I'm going to trust that he will work out the sex part too. If I am faithful to God in my sex life as a single person, then I will be faithful to God and a spouse as a married person. The short answer: I trust God completely.''

Kim said, "You've described a wonderful faith-filled relationship, but it's not what the world lives by."

Carol chimed in, "That's for sure. Just look at TV, movies and popular books. It's all about how we can have more 'sex' in our lives."

Jackie added, "But the way the world lives isn't the answer. The divorce rate has never been higher, even among Christians. What would it be like if everyone honored relationships the way that Agatha is describing?"

I knew it was a rhetorical question that didn't have an answer, but I was glad that we'd had the discussion.

"Thanks for listening about Colin. I'll keep you posted on where God leads us."

26

Resting In Him

Only in God is my soul at rest; from Him comes my salvation.

– Psalm 62: 1

I was excited to be flying back to Upstate New York for my 40th high school reunion. Some of my best friends from high school who I hadn't seen in thirty years were going to be there. It had been fun to reconnect with them on FACEBOOK over the past few years, but I really wanted to see them in person.

I'd adopted a new travel philosophy; instead of planning each minute of a trip, I had decided to concentrate on the necessities, and then let the details unfold on their own. To start, I'd scheduled three days of cooking lessons at the New York Wine and Culinary Center, and was staying at a bed and breakfast on Canandaigua Lake. The following week, I'd be making a silent retreat at the Abbey of the Genesee, and then Friday night and Saturday would be the reunion. It would be a quick twelve days of fun without a lot of structure.

At the end of my cooking lessons, I drove to the Abbey for nine days of rest and relaxation. Bethlehem House is a silent house, so although there were twenty guests, there wasn't any noise as I checked my name off on the registration board and retrieved the door key that Father Jerome had left for me in the mail slot.

It always felt so peaceful in the chapel, and today was no exception. I got there just in time for afternoon Vespers. It was five years ago when I heard the monks begin to chant from Psalm 62: "Only with God is my soul at rest, from Him comes my salvation."

From that day on, that Bible verse had been imprinted in my memory. Five years ago I was thinking, "*My life is such a chaotic mess: my marriage is breaking apart, I'm still having surgeries for breast cancer, and I know that I'm not fulfilling God's will in my life. I keep chasing after things that only bring me more heartbreak. Please, God, speak to me and tell me what to do.*" It was the first time in my adult life that I had ever admitted to anyone, even God that I wasn't in control and needed help.

I was amazed that the first Psalm for Vespers today was again Psalm 62. I thought to myself, *why should I be surprised? The monks have continued their same routine for centuries. God is consistent throughout the ages, but brings "the dots" closer together so that we humans can connect them. We often keep pushing Him away, wanting to figure out everything on our own, but He is always there with a simple lesson: "Just rest and relax in My arms."*

By breakfast the next morning, I'd gotten used to "not talking" again. It was very different from my trip five years ago, when I had been disturbed by the silence. I'd realized then that I would try to impress people with my banter. I've learned that God knows me, and everything about me. It is through God that I feel loved. I can be nameless to others, but God knows every hair on my head.

I awoke on Monday morning to a bright crisp day with the birds hovering over the pond, and a mother skunk escorting her three babies across the field. Mornings are my favorite time to enjoy a cup of coffee on the back deck after celebrating Mass in the coolness of the dawn. I brought my prayer card with me, where I'd listed the twenty-eight people I was praying for. Some were on the list for discernment or vocation, others had physical issues, and some had emotional or spiritual needs. Other names reminded me to thank God for answered prayers. My prayer list starts my morning dialogue with God that continues throughout each day.

My thoughts turned to the visit I'd make later in the week to the Catholic cemetery in Perry, New York, where my parents, brother and grandmother were buried. There's one remaining plot there, but I had decided to be cremated and already made arrangements to have my ashes interred in the Columbarium at St. George's in Nashville. My burial service had been finalized, and Reverend Spruill had been gracious enough to include one of my favorite Catholic hymns, *The Servant Song*, by Richard Gillard.

I'd written a blog about planning the service and quoted Reverend Reuben Job: "Those who are at peace with God and seek to live in harmony with Him, die at peace with God and in harmony with Him, too. They are the persons who have realized that they have never lived outside of God's loving presence, even though they may have often forgotten that they were in God's presence.... Therefore, the very young and very old, held in the strong arms of God, find life good and fulfilling. Contentment, peace, joy, and hope blossom and bear the fruit of confidence, assurance, trust, and service to the world, and that is a life fully lived." I'd included the words to the Catholic hymn in my blog post and read it again on my iPad in the garden of the Abbey:

The Servant Song

Will you let me be your servant,
Let me be as Christ to you,
Pray that I might have the grace
To let you be my servant, too.

We are pilgrims on a journey,
We are brothers on the road,

We are here to help each other
Walk the mile and bear the load.

I will hold the Christ-light for you,
In the night time of your fear,
I will hold my hand out to you
Speak the peace you long to hear.

I will weep when you are weeping,
When you laugh, I'll laugh with you,
I will share your joy and sorrow
Till we've seen this journey through.

When we sing to God in heaven,
We shall find such harmony,
Born of all we've known together
Of Christ's love and agony

Two lines echoed in my head for the rest of the day: "I will share your joy and sorrow," and, "'till we've seen this journey through." They are the promises that God has made to us that He will never take away.

ళు ళు ళు

I spent all day Tuesday taking photographs at Letchworth State Park, and the new six-mile-long greenway close to the Abbey. Tuesday was definitely an outdoor day, and I had hundreds of great photographs to show for my travels. Returning around 2 p.m., I spent the rest of the afternoon resting on a bench near the monastery pond, emptying my mind of the world, and focusing on resting in God.

My favorite service is always the last one of the evening, Compline. We thank God for the day and ask for His protection throughout the night. I always feel like a little girl being tucked into bed. When the candles are extinguished at the end of the service it reminds me that all our lives will eventually come to an end. We must focus on living each day to the fullest, not regretting the past, or looking too far forward to the future. Living in the present day brings us immense freedom and rest.

℘ ℘ ℘

I woke up early to another crisp day on Wednesday and walked the half-mile to the chapel for morning service. The slight chill slowly lifted as the sun rose brightly on the horizon. I leisurely enjoyed my morning coffee on the back deck of the house, and knew by mid-morning that today was the perfect day for a visit to the cemetery.

℘ ℘ ℘

"Hi, Mom. I'm back for another reunion. It seems like forever since I've seen you and so much has happened."

"I know darling, we've been watching what has been going on in your life. Although we can see you, we don't always know what you are feeling."

"I hardly know where to start. I feel like I've lived a lifetime in the past five years. My life before 2006 is gone, and I've become a totally new person since then. Let me start from the end of our last visit."

Yes," Mom said, "Start where you left off five years ago. You had just had implant surgery for breast cancer and had played golf a time or two, but not very well. If I recall, you'd felt like you needed to go on an international mission trip and were considering going to South Africa. And of course, I remember that you're biggest concern was your marriage; you and Curtis were both struggling. What happened after you got back to Nashville?"

"Great memory, Mom! You are 100% correct about where my head was five years ago. I can say with confidence that I've totally changed, in a good way. After I saw you, I prayed the rest of the week before I went back to Nashville and I was pretty convinced that I was called to go to South Africa. Curtis wasn't convinced at all; said he didn't want to go but that he wouldn't stop me. Then after I signed up, he kept throwing up barriers, like there would be a bombing in the Johannesburg airport, or I would get sick all that way from home, or I'd run off and join the Episcopal Church."

"Well, Curtis was correct about that. You did join St. George's," Mom said.

"Yes. But there are some steps in between that God needed to take me through. I went to South Africa and met Archbishop Desmond Tutu. The acceptance and forgiveness I experience there are unlike anything I'd ever known. You tried to love me as best you could, but I never felt like I was quite living up to your expectations."

"I can see now how you felt. I loved you so much and didn't want to lose you. Your Dad loved you too, but he didn't know how to show you. We've heard you talk with your friends about people being a "STRICT FATHER", and we recognize that that was how we were. We only wanted the best for you, but it came off as harsh and demanding. It was the era, Agatha. The 1950s were a big transition in relationships, with women going back to work during and after the war. None of us handled the transition very well, men or women."

"It means the world to me to hear you say that, Mom. I used to think that it was just me not being good enough, but looking back, it was no one's fault. It all became clear when I was in South Africa. I realized that the people I'd traveled with from St. George's were different too; they all treated me like NURTURING PARENTS. I'd never experienced so many worldly successful people who give all the credit to God—I mean ALL the credit! They were incredible and embraced me as one of their own. To them, everyone they meet is a child of God. I'd never experienced that demonstration of love in any of the churches I'd ever been to. Maybe I was going to the wrong churches or going for the wrong reasons, but it was astounding for me to meet these people."

"Agatha, God has forgiven you for divorcing Curtis. You know that don't you?"

"Yes, Mom. But it's taken me a long time to get over feeling guilty for all the things I've done in my life. But I'm there now. I know I'm forgiven. Mom, there's some other things that I need to say. I'm sorry that I judged you. I had no right to ask why you never divorced Dad, or why you had all those abortions. I couldn't possibly have known the burdens that you had in your life. I've learned that it is God's job to judge people, not mine. But it is so hard. When I feel insecure, I slip into judging others so that I can feel better about myself. Will you accept my apology and forgive me?"

"Of course, my child," Mom said.

"I've finally gotten to the point where I believe that God loves me as I am and I don't have to prove I'm better than anyone else. It's taken a long time, as pride and judging others were two of my favorite sins. Of course, my favorite sin was lust. I was always trying to win Dad's approval, and never quite could. Because of my insecurities and fears of not being loved, I chose to use the gift of sex that God has given women to trap men into relationships, even marriages. The stupidest part is that I was always chasing the wrong guys. Some were churchgoers, but they didn't really know God or live their life caring for others. They would talk a good game, but they wouldn't live up to it. They were quick to judge, and slow to love."

"So tell me about this new guy that you met at the church conference. How are you acting differently?"

"Wow, you do know everything that's going on, don't you? But first I owe you another apology. When I was in college, I lied to you when you asked if I was having an affair. I'd rationalized that since I wasn't married, it wasn't an affair. It was just twisting words around. I'm sorry that I lied."

"It sounds like God has been convicting you, but in a good way. Repentance isn't just about promising not to do something again because we will always fail. Instead, repentance is recognizing how lost we are and that we need Christ. Life is impossible without Him."

"Yes, Mom, I've learned so much in the past five years. I have an incredible church family. They even attended the graduation ceremony when I completed my Ph.D. last summer! And I have a wonderful group of eleven women called LIFE from my church who have supported me through everything. I think I've mentioned the PORCH CLUB, too. We get together every six months and can talk about anything.

"It's good to have such supportive friends who lead faith-filled lives. They hold me accountable too when I'm getting off base again. I'm content knowing God, and understanding that He loves me. I know that His mercy, grace, and forgiveness are what I need in my life: I'm still a sinner and fight temptations every day. But I just keep reminding myself to put God first and then let the other relationships flow from my first love. That is the only way relationships can be truly holy, when God is always more important than everything and everyone else.

"I'm willing to live my life married or single, however God feels that it will most honor Him. That is a total change from my previous life, when having a husband and children were the most important thing to me, and obviously the most important thing to Satan. He used that against me repeatedly, but I've surrounded myself with good Christians who love me and care for me; their cloak of protection cannot be broken."

"Agatha, your Father and I were always proud of you, we just didn't know how to show you. And we are very proud of you now. You have your priorities right to put God first in all things."

Mom paused, but then continued, "I still want to hear about this guy that you met at the conference."

"He's from North Carolina and is in Cape Town now, doing missionary work. He knows God and I feel honored whenever we talk. I don't know if it will be a long-term relationship, but I'm excited to have him as a Christian friend. I'm leaving everything up to God, Mom. It's the first time I've known the real freedom that comes with an honest relationship."

"Agatha, it's time for us to go. Safe travels back to Nashville. May the rest of your life be blessed with the knowledge of God's goodness and mercy. Trust Him in everything. I love you."

"Thanks, Mom."

"Agatha, this is your Dad. I've been listening in on your chat with Mom. I love you too. I just didn't know how to love you when I was alive, but I've changed too. I've met good Christian men here who have supported me and their love has shown me God's love. I've come to trust in the Lord, and there is nothing else that can give you more freedom from the world. I'm so proud of you. Blessings to you, my dear, I love you."

"I love you, Mom and Dad. See you again soon."

I heard Mom wink as I walked away.

ço ço ço

The sun was setting over the lake as I drove out of the cemetery to go back to the Abbey for the night. It was a hot July sunset, with rays of red, yellow and orange welcoming in the coolness of the night. I replayed our conversation and warmed with delight, as I had never heard Mom sound so happy. We no longer had to earn Dad's love; he was freely giving it away.

ço ço ço

The moonlight danced on the heavy wooden doors of the chapel as I reached to open them for Compline. I settled into the second pew and was bathed in contentment as I heard the monks chant the soft, familiar opening notes of Psalm 62.

Instead of chasing after my Dad's love, I've learned to rest in my Father's.

ॐ ॐ ॐ

Therefore, I urge you, brothers and sisters, in view of God's mercy, to offer your bodies as a living sacrifice, holy and pleasing to God—this is your true and proper worship. Do not conform to the pattern of this world, but be transformed by the renewing of your mind. Then you will be able to test and approve what God's will is—his good, pleasing and perfect will.

– Roman 12:1-2

Note to My Readers

Chasing My Father is about my journey to find rest in a chaotic world. My new life started in Soweto, South Africa where I learned the real meaning of forgiveness and love. Returning home to Nashville, Tennessee, I finally found freedom and rest.

Your life can be different, too. *Chasing My Father* is your invitation to join me on this journey.

Everyone I have met has brought me one step closer, or one step further away, from God. All the lessons are valuable, and I've had untold opportunities to receive and give love. With my fellow conspirators, we have great expectations of the coming of the Holy Spirit as we see glimpses of God's Kingdom through the great power, wonderful light, contagious love, and holy fire that is all around us.

I have not sailed a straight course on my journey, but I've learned to put God first in my life. When he is my Commander, decisions become easier, and His whispers become crystal clear invitations to join Him in His work.

This book is dedicated to the countless people who have inspired me and held me up when I stumbled. It is their example and wisdom that has made me hungry to help others take those first tentative steps to a new life.

I pray that you will find healing in your relationships by putting God first, and allowing all other relationships to flow from your first love.

Blessings,
Agatha

や や や

www.ingramcontent.com/pod-product-compliance
Lightning Source LLC
Chambersburg PA
CBHW021614270326
41931CB00008B/687